Gardens and the Law

Gardens and the Law

Tony Blackburn
LLB, LLM, Solicitor

Published by
Tottel Publishing Ltd
Maxwelton House
41-43 Boltro Road
Haywards Heath
West Sussex
RH16 1BJ

ISBN: 978-1-84592-730-1

British Library Cataloguing-in-Publication Data.
A catalogue record for this book is available from the British Library.

Printed and bound in Great Britain by
Marston Book Services, Abingdon, Oxfordshire

Preface

In Britain, gardening is a major national hobby—indeed it is big business, as the ever increasing number of garden centres and annexes to DIY superstores testify. Television is giving more and more time to gardening programmes, and gardening magazines enjoy healthy circulation levels. It is perhaps strange that none of the many media gardeners and journalists who make a living out of advising the amateur garden owner have turned their hands to 'Gardens and the Law'.

Disputes with neighbours concerning tenants' rights, boundaries, trees, noise, nuisance as well as with garden centres as to non-growing seeds and plants, etc are on the increase. While I have been writing this book there have been press reports of garden owners being subject to injunctions in respect of barking dogs and crowing cocks, being fined for not cutting back their prize trees, being served notice to return well-established flower beds back to a rubbish tip, and having the council send in its workmen to cut down their carefully uncultivated nature reserve, to give only a few instances. A newspaper 'Hot Line' was recently said to have received hundreds of phone calls complaining of overshadowing leylandii. A considerable number of garden-related disputes end up in court, and as a result, professional legal advisers are becoming more and more involved.

In recent years domestic and European legislation to regulate the garden has grown apace. Readers may be surprised to learn of the wide legal powers given to national and local government officers which may affect domestic gardens. Statutes such as the Protection of the Environment Act 1994, the Noise Act 1996 and the Food Safety Act 1990 include provisions as to use of the garden, its waste, the sale of plants and seeds, and garden activities which may apply to many amateur, as well as professional, gardeners. In addition, recent changes in employment law may be relevant to those employing gardeners.

This book summarises current legal problems and provides answers to some of the questions which may arise in practice concerning the garden and its use. As such, I hope that it will be a useful tool for practitioners advising on garden-related problems. Where there is no clear answer to a legal issue I have tried to steer the garden

owner away from the trouble and expense of unnecessary court action towards compromise and peace to enjoy that most sacred of all possessions, the English garden.

It should be noted that this book is concerned with the law relating to gardens in England and Wales: in many of the areas covered, the law in Scotland and the Channel Islands may vary. The aim has been primarily to deal with issues that are likely to arise in connection with domestic rather than commercial gardens, although the latter may be mentioned. While I have referred in the main to 'the garden owner,' in many instances the text will equally apply to tenants of gardens—their specific problems are also dealt with where appropriate.

By the time this book goes to press the particular statutory provisions or amounts of social security payments, fines, etc may have changed and the reader should check the latest information.

I should like to thank all who have helped with this book. In particular, Dereck Penfold, whose ideas helped shape it, Andrew Penney and Max Rhymney (regarding treasure trove), and, above all, Renee Carpenter, who did all the typing (after the major prior task of interpreting my writing). I am most grateful to the Royal Horticultural Society for dealing with my enquiries, and to Mr Trigg of Camden Council's Environment Department for his input as to noise, and to others mentioned in the text. Finally, many thanks to those involved at Butterworths for their dedication and direction.

Tony Blackburn
August 1998

Contents

Table of statutes

References in the right hand column are to paragraph number. Those references in *italics* are to page number.

Table of statutory instruments

References in the right hand column are to paragraph number. Those references in *italics* are to page number.

Table of cases

S

Decisions of the European Court of Justice are listed below
numerically. These decisions are also included in the preceeding
alphabetical list.

1

Introduction

1.1 What is a 'garden'? The nearest thing to a general legal definition of 'a garden' is found in an 1896 case:

> 'A garden is a plot of ground on which fruit, vegetables or flowers are grown for food or pleasure'.[1]

For ownership, use, planning and tax legislation and other purposes a 'garden' will be covered under a certain category (usually 'land'), and it is necessary to check in each case to see if a particular provision applies to a garden.

1 Collins J in *Cooper v Pearse* [1896] 1 QB 562 quoted in *Stroud's Judicial Dictionary* (5th edn).

OWNERSHIP

1.2 As with all types of land in England and Wales a garden can be held either as or by:

(a) freehold;

(b) leasehold;

(c) easement;

(d) licence to use;

(e) tenancy.

Freehold[1]

1.3 Freehold is the absolute interest which the Land Registry will register in the name of the owner as 'Title Absolute', the State thus guaranteeing the title which will pass on to a successor.

1 Law of Property Act 1925, s 1 (37 *Halsbury's Statutes* (4th edn) Real Property).

Leasehold

1.4 Leasehold is for a term of years, eg for 21 years from a particular date or from a particular date until another date, or a tenancy from a date from year to year, month to month or week to week (etc) until the lease determines by expiry or by notice. There

may be a purchase price (a premium), there will usually be a rent payable by the tenant to the landlord and both tenant and landlord will enter into obligations (covenants) with each other, for example, as to paying outgoings, maintenance and insurance. The interest may pass on to a successor, if allowed under the terms of the lease, until the date of determination of the lease.

Easement

1.5   The right to use a garden may also be enjoyed as an easement, ie a right to enjoy a garden held with a freehold or leasehold estate.[1] For example, a right to use a common garden is often granted with a lease of a flat in a block of flats. Such a right will be freehold or leasehold, and will pass on to a third party with the freehold or leasehold. A right which is a legal easement must be distinguished from a right to use a garden which is given by licence only—the latter will not be able to be passed on and is likely to be determinable on short or even no notice.[2]

1   Law of Property Act 1925, s 1(2)(a).

2   *King v David Allen & Sons Billposting Ltd* [1916] 2 AC 54, HL; *IDC Group Ltd v Clarke* [1992] 1 EGLR 187.

Licence to use

1.6   A licence to use is an informally granted arrangement by word of mouth or in writing (eg by letter), which is personal to the person allowed to use the garden. It does not create any permanent interest capable of being passed on to a third party. Gardens held with council flats are usually in this category (although the council tenant may be a secure tenant with limited rights of security and if the right to use the garden is part of that tenancy the security may apply to the garden as well). Such a licence will determine on expiry or by notice as mentioned in the letter or agreement setting it up when vacant possession will be required. See further **1.9**ff.

Tenancy

1.7   Where the garden or the right to use the garden is comprised in a tenancy of property of which the tenant has statutory protection under the Rent Acts or, since 1989, the Housing Acts, or under a long term residential or business tenancy to which the Landlord and Tenant Act 1954 applies, or is part of an agricultural holding (such as a plant nursery) to which the 1954 Act or the Agricultural Holdings Acts 1948–1986 apply, then the tenant may be able to continue in possession subject to the particular legislation. The position is dealt with in more detail under in Chapters 17 and 18.

GARDENS ADJOINING OPEN LAND AND ISOLATED GARDENS

1.8   Gardens are usually enclosed by walls, fences or hedges. Where they adjoin open land and are not fenced there are the following consequences:

(a) The area of the garden may be unclear. It is important to mark it by physical features (eg boundary posts) and all documents dealing with the house and garden should refer to a plan.

(b) The owner may have the advantage of possibly being able to take over adjoining open land as part of his garden and may be able to claim title by adverse possession. However, he will also have the disadvantage of members of the public and animals trespassing on his land. This should be resisted.

(c) The adjoining open land may be common land.

See Chapter 2 for further details.

1.9   Gardens may also be enclosed but isolated, such as allotments and gardens in London squares and the Inns of Court. Where there is no contiguous house it is likely that the right to use the land as a garden will be enjoyed by licence only. For example, the use of many London square gardens is allowed by the owner, to persons living in the houses around the square by licence, subject to payment of maintenance costs and to keeping the rules for use of the garden which are scheduled in the letter giving the licence or put up on a notice in the square. The issue of keys to the gate is strictly controlled. The licence may not be capable of assignment and the owner of a house in a square with such rights should be careful not to offer them to a purchaser as he may not be able to pass them on and could be liable for misrepresentation. Examples of a licence to use a garden and specimen rules are set out in Appendix A.

1.10   When taking over an isolated garden such as an allotment or garden cut off from the house by a road, the new owner should have regard to:

(a) The need for a right of way, preferably with vehicles (as heavy work may have to be done at some time), to and from the house or the public highway to the garden.

(b) The planning requirements as to constructing an access from the public highway: see Chapter 11.

(c) The need for water. All gardens need water, but the water authorities have no public duty to supply a garden (as opposed to a dwelling) and there may not be a private supply. If there is

not a supply, any purchase or lease should be made conditional on a proper water supply being obtained. Where water is obtained from a well, borehole, river or private supply a licence under the Water Resources Act 1991 must be obtained, and where an existing licensed supply is being taken over notification must be given of any new owner or tenant to the Environment Agency.[1] For public water supply and hose pipe bans, see Chapter 22.

1   Water Resources Act 1991, ss 24, 49(3), as amended by the Environment Act 1995, s 120(1), Sch 22 para 128 (49 *Halsbury's Statutes* (4th edn) Water).

LEGALLY DOCUMENTED TITLE

1.11   As a garden is 'land' for the purposes of the Law Reform (Miscellaneous Provisions) Act 1989[1] any contract to buy or sell a freehold or leasehold interest in or to let a garden must be in writing contained in one document signed by the parties, or if 'exchange of contracts' is involved one part of the document must be signed by each party. However, an immediate letting of a garden for less than three years can be oral.[2]

1   Law Reform (Miscellaneous Provisions) Act 1989, s 2 (37 *Halsbury's Statutes* (4th edn) Real Property).
2   Law of Property Act 1925, s 54(2).

1.12   Because a garden is classified as 'land', the taking of legal title (freehold or leasehold) to a garden, whether subsequent to a contract for sale or letting etc or without a prior contract, must be by deed in order to pass a good title. A deed is a written document executed (ie signed and witnessed) by the parties intended to be signed as a deed.[1] The expression 'signed as a deed' before their signatures and that of a single witness adding his or her name and address is generally enough. A lease or tenancy (except an oral tenancy of less than three years: see **1.11**) and an assignment of a lease or tenancy (even an oral one of less than three years) must also be by deed.

1   Law of Property Act 1925, s 52 (37 *Halsbury's Statutes* (4th edn) Real Property).

1.13   Where the garden is conveyed, transferred or let with a house or building it usually passes by description, eg 'No 17 Acacia Avenue and the garden at the front and rear', or even if not expressly mentioned under the description of the building, eg 'the dwellinghouse known as ...' or 'the cottage'.[1] A garden will also pass within a supplementary part of the description, for example

land 'and appurtenances'[2] or 'land and premises'.[3] So also a garden is included 'within the curtilage' of a property.[4] It is, however, preferable,[5] and, where a garden is being transferred as part of land in a registered title, mandatory, to refer to the land comprising the garden accurately by reference to its boundaries and to a plan signed by the transferor and by or on behalf of the transferee.[6]

1 See *Re Willis* [1911] 2 Ch 563.

2 See *Bolton v Bolton* (1879) 11 Ch D 968.

3 See *Lethbridge v Lethbridge* (1862) 31 LJ Ch 737 (where the expression used was 'mansion house gardens and premises'), but 'premises' will not include a separate but adjoining meadow: see *Minton v Geiger* (1873) 28 LT 449.

4 See *Re St John's Church Bishop's Hatfield* [1967] P 113 (where it was held that a conveyance of a church included a garden and other void ground).

5 See the Land Registration Rules 1925/1093 Schedule, Form 20, note. See also the judicial comments in *Scarfe v Adams* [1981] 1 All ER 843, CA.

6 See Ruoff, *Land Registration Handbook* (1990) p 52.

1.14 If the land is in an area subject to compulsory registration (and this now applies throughout England and Wales), it will be liable to be registered at HM Land Registry upon first dealing. Freehold land or leasehold land held under a lease granted for at least 21 years will be registered with Title Absolute or Title Good Leasehold, indicating that the Land Registry has either been satisfied that the title (freehold or leasehold) has been investigated back to a good root of title (ie a document verifying the then ownership) at least 15 years old from which the current owner who is registered as 'registered proprietor' derives title, or in the case of Title Good Leasehold, that the leasehold title alone satisfies this test (the freehold not having been checked in this way).[1]

1 See the Land Registration Act 1925, ss 6, 11 and 20(3) (37 *Halsbury's Statutes* (4th edn) Real Property) and the Land Registration Rules 1925, SI 1925/ 1093, r 36.

1.15 Before registration, stamp duty (if payable) must be paid on the conveyance, transfer or lease at the current rate on the value of the price (consideration) or rent.[1] Land Registry fees for first registration or dealing must also be paid. There is a special category of Land Registry title, 'possessory' title, under which the Land Registry will recognise (but not guarantee) a limited title, for example such as to part of a garden where the owner is seeking to acquire a good legal title through encroachment: see **1.16ff**.

1 Stamp duty must be paid to the Inland Revenue and is currently charged at the rate of £1 per £100 over £60,000 and below £250,000, £2 per £100

£250,000–£500,000 and at £3 per £100 over £500,000 (subject to certificate). Stamp duty on rent varies with the length of the term.

TITLE WITHOUT LEGAL DOCUMENTATION

1.16 We have already seen that the right to use land as a garden can be legally valid without a document in the case of a lease of less than three years or licence. However, many persons cultivating land as a garden may wish to acquire a proper legal title. This can be done by exercising rights of ownership over the relevant land and applying to the Land Registry.

1.17 Under the Limitation Act 1980 the original owner of land cannot sue to recover his land where a person has been in possession of that land and produces evidence that he has excluded the original owner and all others for 12 years.[1] So a person may claim land used as a garden to which he has no 'official' legal title. This is often done where the claimant has cultivated open land immediately adjacent to his 'official' garden by encroaching on it, ie taking it over. To do this he must show that he has:

(a) the intention of excluding the original owner and all other persons from the land, eg by warning off trespassers, correspondence with the council etc;[2]

(b) taken physical action, usually by fencing it off or by planting it, to implement this intention;[3] and

(c) not done this by force or secretly or with the permission of the original owner.

This is called 'adverse possession', the serving of the 12-year period is 'prescription', and the rights acquired are 'prescriptive rights'.

1 Limitation Act 1980, s 15 (24 *Halsbury's Statutes* (4th edn) Limitation of Actions).

2 *Buckinghamshire County Council v Moran* [1990] Ch 623, CA (intention to wish to keep possession is enough; intention to acquire ownership need not be shown).

3 See *Treloar v Nute* [1976] 1 WLR 1295 (where land was fenced off and prepared for development); *Buckinghamshire County Council v Moran* (above) (where a padlock was put on the only access gate) and *Williams v Usherwood* (1983) 45 P & CR 235 (where land was fenced off, a driveway made up and cars parked); also see *Hounslow London Borough Council v Minchinton* (1997) 74 P & CR 221, CA (where building a summerhouse and use of fenced-off land as a compost heap was held to have been enough to prove title by adverse possession).

1.18 After the 12-year period[1] the person claiming adverse possession can make a statutory declaration (see Appendix A for an example) with a plan annexed showing the land and lodge this

at HM Land Registry claiming possessory title to the land and paying the relevant fee. The Land Registry may require an advertisement to be placed in a local paper inviting objections. Subject to this the Land Registry will register his interest as 'possessory title'. After 12 years the proprietor of the title can have it upgraded to Title Absolute giving a state guarantee. If the land claimed has been registered as common land (see **2.1ff**) then no claims can be admitted.

1   There are exceptions where the original owner is a tenant for life under a trust or subject to a Court of Protection Order).

1.19   The receipt of rents from a tenant for upwards of 12 years may also ground a valid claim.[1] If a tenant of a garden has ceased to pay rent to his landlord for 12 years without demand he can claim title by adverse possession in the above manner.

1   *R v Secretary of State for the Environment, ex p Davies* (1990) 61 P & CR 487, CA (where an offer of rent defeated a claim).

1.20   However, there is a difficulty for a council tenant claiming title by adverse possession to council land which he has used as a garden except if rent has not been demanded or acknowledged by him for upwards of 12 years. This is because in many cases he will be a licensee of the council and is deemed to be occupying any ancillary land 'by permission'.

1.21   From the opposite position, ie that of the garden owner against whom a neighbour or member of the public could be seeking to establish title by adverse possession or rights of way, it is important that immediate action should be taken to resist any such claim. A letter should be written by or on behalf of the owner to anyone seeking to park cars, fence off or plant on the former's land and to anyone taking a short cut across land which one considers as part of one's garden.

1.22   In the case of a neighbour, the matter of parking, planting, taking short cuts etc should be raised at the earliest opportunity, and if the neighbour's activities are unacceptable the garden owner should write a letter making it clear that the parking etc is only allowed by permission, and preferably making a charge for the privilege, as a permission which is paid for is better evidence of a legally binding intention than a gratuitous permission—the charge can be nominal eg £1 per annum. Failure to act could lead to the neighbour acquiring part of the garden by adverse possession after 12 years,[1] or a right of way over it after 20 years.

1   See *Merstham Manor Ltd v Coulsdon and Purley UDC* [1937] 2 KB 77.

1.23   Where members of the public are trespassing then a letter to the local authority to put on record that there is no intention to dedicate a public of right of way and the putting up of a notice to all comers should be enough to stop the period of 20 years required for such a right running against the owner.[1] A form of notice is set out in Appendix A.

1   See the Highways Act 1980, s 31(1) (20 *Halsbury's Statutes* (4th edn) Highways, Streets and Bridges).

1.24   An adjoining owner can establish title to a boundary wall by acts of user by maintaining it, raising its height, attaching guttering and security devices and cutting a hole for a night safe over 12 years.[1]

1   *Prudential Assurance v Waterloo Real Estate* [1998] EGCS 51.

2

Gardens in relation to neighbouring properties

GARDENS ABUTTING COMMON OR PUBLIC LAND

2.1 Where the garden is unenclosed and adjoins open land or seashore, care should be taken to check that no part of the garden is subject to public or commons rights. A proposing purchaser or tenant should always carry out a search in the Commons Register maintained by the local County or County Borough Council under the Commons Registration Act 1965.[1] This will establish whether or not any part of the garden is claimed as common land or is the subject of commons rights, eg of grazing sheep, cattle etc. Registration is conclusive evidence of the existence of common land or commons rights.

1 Commons Registration Act 1965, s 10 (6 *Halsbury's Statutes* (4th edn) Commons) and see *Hampshire County Council v Milburn* [1991] 1 AC 325, [1990] 2 All ER 257, HL.

2.2 If the garden is part of a common there may be a right of public access to it and there is a statutory restriction on building, fencing or other work enforceable by the local authority.[1] There is also a right for the public to enjoy right of access for air and recreation,[2] which can include access for horse riding.[3] This may be confirmed by deed. Although registration of a common or common land is now definitive, it may still be possible to challenge inclusion on the Register of a particular area or to object to a particular right (eg grazing) being exercised and there is an exception which may be relevant for gardens for 'land ancillary to a dwellinghouse so used at all times since 5 August 1945'.[4] This could be challenged up to 31 July 1992, and although the time limit is now expired there may be circumstances (eg where evidence was not available at the time) which might enable a garden owner to get part of a garden taken out of registration.

1 See the Commons Registration Act 1965, s 9 and the Law of Property Act 1925, s 194(2) (37 *Halsbury's Statutes* (4th edn) Real Property).
2 Law of Property Act 1925, s 193.

9

3　*R v Secretary of State for the Environment, ex p Billson* [1998] 2 All ER 587.

4　See the Common Land (Rectification of Registers) Act 1989, s 1 (6 *Halsbury's Statutes* (4th edn) Commons) and *Cresstock Investments Ltd v Commons Comr* [1993] 1 All ER 213 (where an uncultivated garden was removed from the register).

2.3　Note that adverse possession cannot be established against land registered as common land.[1] Nor can the area between the high and low tide marks on the sea shore, which belongs to the Crown, be the subject of a claim to adverse possession.[2]

1　*R v Norfolk County Council, ex p Perry* (1997) 74 P & CR 1.

2　*A-G for Southern Nigeria v John Holt (Liverpool) Ltd* [1915] AC 599.

GARDENS IN RELATION TO PRIVATE NEIGHBOURS

Boundaries, walls and fences

2.4　One of the commonest types of dispute concerning gardens to reach the courts concerns property rights between neighbouring private properties, especially as to walls, fences, hedges, overhanging branches, root encroachments and access to neighbouring gardens for trimming hedges and trees, repairs to buildings and drains and other conflicts 'over the garden fence'.

2.5　The best way of eliminating boundary disputes is by a clearly drafted conveyance/transfer or lease, with a plan on as large a scale as possible, which defines the garden's boundaries and deals with the ownership and maintenance of them. The description and plan should define the boundaries and any obligations concerned with them, ie who is to repair which boundary wall or fence, or maintain which hedge?

2.6　Where land is severed from a larger area of land, as in the sale of building plots or the sale of surplus land for a garden, it is important that an obligation is put on the buyer or seller to construct a wall, to put up a fence or grow a hedge dividing the new plot from the retained land.

2.7　Where the boundaries of a garden are unclear and where there is nothing in the title documents dealing with the ownership or maintenance of boundary fences or walls, then evidence such as repair or maintenance over a period, correspondence with neighbours etc can be deduced to ascertain who owns and maintains the fence or wall. A statutory declaration evidencing habitual maintenance for upwards of 20 years is usually accepted by the court as establishing the position, but it should be noted that the

voluntary assumption of maintaining fences does not result in a legal obligation to maintain the boundary passing on to successors in title.

2.8   No one may pull down a wall or fence belonging to a neighbour and anyone who does so may be liable, not only for the cost of reinstatement, but also for damages for inconvenience and distress.[1]

1   *Bernardt v Dhatariya* [1990] 10 CLY 1517.

2.9   Where the wall or fence belongs to the adjoining owner, the garden owner has no right to attach buildings (eg greenhouses), or to put up a trellis, or put nails etc into it,[1] and this regularly ignored point should be noted. It is also strictly a trespass for creepers, espalier fruit trees and the like to grow up such a wall. So a garden owner who wants to use his neighbour's wall should ask him for permission and a formal licence should be entered into to cover the legal position properly—an example is given in Appendix A. The right to grow a creeper etc against another's wall can be acquired by prescription (previous plants included) and after 20 years the owner cannot take legal action.

1   See *Simpson v Weber* (1925) 133 LT 46 (trellis) and *Hawkins v Wallis* (1763) 2 Wils 173 (nails).

2.10   It may be that the wall or fence is intended to be a party wall or fence (see **2.15ff**) where there are cross rights in favour of the adjoining owner for the support or maintenance of the wall or fence, in which case the documentation should say so.

2.11   Where, as in the case of innumerable existing boundaries, nothing has ever been done about defining ownership or the obligation to maintain, there is a tendency among surveyors and lawyers to assume that the wall or fence is a party wall, but a full investigation of the old deeds (and the deeds of neighbours where the properties were part of a contemporary development) should be checked before this is assumed.

2.12   A wall or fence dividing Owner A's garden from that of Owner B may:

(a) have been put on Owner A's land; or

(b) have been put up on Owner B's land; or

(c) have been put exactly on the median line.

It may be stated in the conveyance, transfer or lease that the wall or fence has to be put up by and/or then belongs to Owner A or Owner

B (even in case (c)). Fences, being narrower than walls, are more likely to be put up on one side of the boundary or the other. Wherever they are built and whoever is stated to own them, the documentation may provide that either Owner A or Owner B is to repair and maintain the wall or fence. There may be a plan with 'T' marks indicating the obligation to maintain (the boundary is shown as a line, with a 'T' drawn at a right angle to the boundary line on one side of the line: the owner on the side where the 'T' is has the obligation to maintain the wall or fence). Whatever is provided for will be the position, although ownership and the obligation to maintain are likely to go together.

2.13   Where nothing is said then in the case of fences with fence posts or struts on one side it is presumed that the owner on that side owns and is responsible for maintaining the fence. If the wall or fence is built exactly on the median line if there are separate parts of the wall or other circumstances or documentation stating that it is to be a party wall or fence or if the deeds do not say who owns or maintains it, then the wall or fence is likely to be a party wall or fence which means that certain statutes apply:

Law of Property Act 1925, s 38

2.14   By this provision a party wall or fence is deemed to be owned by the adjoining owners as tenants in common (ie joint owners), but each has an obligation to support the other part of the wall, giving redress in the event of collapse. There is no obligation to pay one half of the running costs of repairing and maintaining the wall.[1]

1   See *Sack v Jones* [1925] Ch 234.

Party Walls Act 1996

2.15   The Party Walls Act 1996[1] now applies the principles of the London Building Acts (Amendment) Act 1939 (which only applied to party walls in London) throughout England and Wales. If either owner wishes to demolish, reconstruct, build against or undermine any such wall (by altering the foundations or underpinning) he must serve notice with details of the works on the adjoining owner and pay the cost of a surveyor to record the pre-work state of the wall, to specify any protective work required and to supervise. In the event of a dispute between the building owner's surveyor and the adjoining owner's surveyor either can refer to a third surveyor to arbitrate by making an award ('a party wall award') stating what remedial work must be undertaken. This third surveyor can only deal with a dispute as to building works. He cannot

deal with legal questions such as ownership of the wall.[2] The surveyors can agree work to protect the party wall but should not prescribe ongoing obligations.[3] A building owner who carries out work without complying with the Act may be liable for damage caused to the adjoining property and loss of profit on sale.[4]

1   See the Party Walls Act 1996, s 1 (35 *Halsbury's Statutes* (4th edn) Public Health and Environmental Protection).

2   *Woodhouse v Consolidated Property Corpn* [1993] 1 EGLR 174.

3   *Marchant v Capital & Counties plc* [1983] 2 EGLR 15c, CA (party wall surveyors could prescribe work for protection of other part of a party wall but not a continuing obligation).

4   *Louis v Sadiq* (1996) 74 P & CR 325 (a case under the London Building Acts (Amendment) Act 1939).

2.16   This wide-reaching provision will apply to most walls between semi-detached and terraced properties. Although the side walls of buildings are more likely to be the subject of works falling within the Act, it also applies to party walls and 'party wall fences', as the Act calls them, between gardens. Thus any garden owner contemplating building a new wall or building even a temporary building against such a wall or fence should take the advice of a lawyer and a surveyor.

Access to Neighbouring Land Act 1992

2.17   The obligations as to party walls in the Law of Property Act 1925 are in the most basic terms only and can only be enforced in the event of a collapse of the wall. There are no rights for either adjoining owner to go on to the property of the other to carry out preventive work, unless such right is contained in the conveyance, transfer or lease of one or both of the properties. The Access to Neighbouring Land Act 1992 was passed to remedy this situation—a garden owner has the right, following service of notice as prescribed by the Act, to go into the next door garden to carry out 'basic preservation works'. This right is enforceable by court order if access is refused. This applies to work to the other side of a party wall but not to work to reinforce a wall to support a new building.

2.18   Among the 'basic preservation works' for which an order can be made are the following, particularly relevant to gardens:

'The clearance, repair or renewal of any drain, sewer, pipe or cable so comprised or situate;

The treatment, cutting back, felling, removal or replacement of any hedge, tree, shrub or other growing thing which is so comprised and which is, or is in danger of becoming, damaged, diseased, dangerous, insecurely rooted or dead;

Filling in, or clearance, of any ditch...'[1]

1   See the Access to Neighbouring Land Act 1992, s 1(4)(a) (37 *Halsbury's Statutes* (4th edn) Real Property). Note that the Act applies to party walls: *Dean v Walker* [1996] NPC 78, CA.

Trespassing walls

2.19   Where a wall or fence has been wrongly erected by Owner A on land belonging to Owner B, this is a legal trespass and Owner B can obtain an injunction against Owner A to remove the wall and can sue for damages. He also has the right of self help and can demolish the wall, but this right ceases when an injunction has been obtained or refused.[1] Similarly if the wall/fence has been built too high or not in accordance with an agreed specification, eg it was to be made of Cotswold stone, the other party to the agreement can take legal action.

1   *Burton v Winters* [1993] 3 All ER 847, [1993] 1 WLR 1077, CA (where a wall encroached on a garage and an injunction was refused, it was held that the right of self help dies with refusal of an injunction—the plaintiff was imprisoned for two years for demolishing the wall contrary to the court order).

The duty to fence

2.20   Unless there is a covenant to do this in the title documents there is no obligation on a garden owner to erect a fence between his and his neighbour's land, although, of course, 'good fences make good neighbours' and what is said in **2.5** about the need for clear and established boundaries should be noted. Where there is a covenant to maintain a fence, then although it is a positive covenant (which does not usually bind successors in title) the obligation may become an established easement to fence by prescription and this will be binding on any new owner. There is, however, an obligation to fence in the following cases:

(a)   There is no general obligation on a garden owner to fence his land even where the garden adjoins a public highway, but the garden owner must prevent the escape of animals on to the public highway (see (b)) and also must fence any source of danger on his land where it adjoins the highway. The Highway Authority also has power to enter and fence off the highway but not if this involves closing an established access.[1]

(b) Where animals are kept in the garden which may cause damage by straying on the highway (see (a)) or to neighbouring owners or their stock.[2]

(c) A garden which is part of a churchyard, or Church of England Vicarage, is subject to special rules. The Parochial Church Council and the incumbent, respectively, are responsible for maintaining fences.[3]

(d) A garden which is part of a farm or other agricultural holding may be the subject of an obligation to fence implied in tenancies of agricultural holdings by the Agriculture (Maintenance Repair and Insurance of Fixed Equipment) Regulations 1973.

(e) There is a duty on the owners of railways,[4] canals[5] and mines[6] to fence and if a garden adjoins any of these the undertaking may have a duty to keep up the dividing fence.

1   Highways Act 1980, ss 155 (straying animals on highway), 165 (fencing dangers) and 80 (power to fence but not access permitted by planning permission, or existing before 1 July 1948).

2   Animals Act 1971, ss 4 and 8: see Chapter 7.

3   Parochial Church Councils (Powers) Measure 1956, s 4 and the Repair of Benefice Buildings Measure 1972, ss 2–6.

4   Railways Clauses (Consolidation) Act 1845, s 68.

5   See eg Manchester Ship Canal Act 1885, s 70(4) and Canals Protection (London) Act 1898, s 1.

6   Mines and Quarries Act 1954, s 151 as amended by the Environment Act 1995, s 120(3) and Sch 24.

2.21   Planning permission is necessary for a fence more than one metre in height bounding a public highway (including public footpaths) and on other boundaries if more than two metres in height or if they obstruct the view of road users or cause them danger. With regard to planning restrictions on the height of fences see Chapter 11.

2.22   It has long been established that a garden owner may put up obstacles to deter trespassers on his wall or fence and a party wall owner may put these up on his side.[1] They may take the form of spikes or broken glass or barbed wire but where the wall with the obstacles borders the public highway note that:

(a) the local authority has powers to require barbed wire etc which might cause a danger to be removed;[2]

(b) the garden owner may be liable for nuisance or negligence for injury to passers-by or damage to their clothing.[3]

The putting up of an electric barrier or a fence against intruders may be regarded as excessive and an intruder who is electrocuted might be able to sue the garden owner and, indeed, the owner might be liable for a criminal offence.[4]

1   *Ilott v Wilkes* [1820] 3 B & Ald 304, 318; *Fenna v Clare & Co* [1895] 1 QB 199; *Elgin County Road Trustees v Innes* (1886) 14 R 48 Ct of Sess.

2   Highways Act 1980, s 164.

3   *Stewart v Wright* (1893) 9 TLR 480 (damage to clothing).

4   See Offences Against the Person Act 1861, s 31 ('setting traps' etc) but there is a defence if the device is set only at night and in order to protect a dwellinghouse. See also *Revill v Newbury* [1996] QB 967, CA (where a 76-year-old allotment owner was held liable to an intruder for shooting in self defence).

Hedges

2.23   The ownership of and responsibility to grow and trim a boundary hedge may be dealt with in the title documents or by reference to a plan (usually with the conventional 'T' marks on the boundary line towards the owner obliged to maintain) as in the case of walls and fences. If there is no express provision, here again other evidence may be used to ascertain who owns it. A statutory declaration by a person with knowledge that the owner on one side or the other has planted it or tended it for upwards of 20 years will be accepted by the courts. If the hedge has a ditch alongside it then the court will presume in the absence of other evidence that Owner A in digging the footings for the hedge will have dumped the earth back on his land and not on the land of Owner B and therefore the boundary is taken as the furthest line of the ditch beyond the hedge.[1] This presumption does not apply where the land is described by reference to an Ordnance Survey map showing the boundary in the middle of the hedge.[2]

1   See *Fisher v Winch* [1939] 1 KB 666.
2   *Alan Wibberley Building Ltd v Insley* [1998] 2 All ER 82.

2.24   Where Owner A has taken it upon himself to trim, repair and replant a hedge that does not mean that he has assumed legal responsibility for it.[1] It has never been decided whether there can be a 'party hedge'.[2] If there can be, then in such a case Owner A would have to keep up 'his part' of the hedge so that it does not cause Owner B's part to collapse.

1   *Jones v Price* [1965] 2 QB 618 (Welsh farmer had no obligation to maintain hedge even though predecessor had kept it up for over 50 years).

2   In *Jones v Price* the court discussed 'party hedges' but Diplock, LJ doubted that a 'party hedge' could exist.

2.25   But there is no obligation on either owner to keep the hedge below a reasonable height and a land owner can put up a hedge or trees on his own side of the boundary to whatever height he wants (unless it interferes with a right to light to windows in a neighbouring building or contravenes planning law, eg a condition in a planning permission for a new house). The recent adverse criticism of garden owners planting cypress leylandii (a dense, fast-growing conifer) to the detriment of the light to a neighbour's garden in the popular press has no legal basis (as we will see a right of light can only be enjoyed by a *building*). They may not be considered good neighbours, but they are legally within their rights.

2.26   Until recently the Town and Country Planning Acts did not deal with hedges but the Hedgerows Regulations 1997[1] now provide that it is a criminal offence to uproot a hedge without notice to the local authority. Most garden hedges are exempt as being 'within the curtilage of a dwellinghouse' but where the hedge extends beyond the immediate area of the house and is over 20 metres in length and is adjacent to agricultural or common land and has been there for 30 years or more then the rules will apply.

1   The Hedgerow Regulations 1997, SI 1997/1160.

2.27   Also, in a recent County Court case in Hull (Colin Seymour's case 2 January 1997), a member of the public obtained a court order stopping a hedge being removed as it was mentioned as a boundary in an old Enclosure Act and there was therefore an obligation on the local authority to maintain it.[1]

1   Enclosure Acts were local legislation common in the eighteenth and nineteenth centuries whereby Parliament allowed the division among local landowners of previously common land.

2.28   Garden owners who wish to cut down or alter their hedges are warned to check the legal position against the new general law and also the old local law as above.

Rivers, lakes and streams

2.29   Where a garden is bounded by a river or lake and the title documents do not make it clear whether the boundary is the bank

or in the middle of the water covered feature, the courts use a presumption that the boundary is the median line of the river or lake.[1] This can be rebutted by circumstances (eg a change in the course of the river plus prescriptive use of the accretion). No such presumption applies where the garden abuts a canal. Garden owners are warned that as owners of land abutting a river they may have statutory obligations to the river authority to maintain the banks, and not to take water from the river without licence.

1   *Micklethwait v Newlay Bridge Co* (1886) 33 Ch D 133.

3

Rights that cross the boundary

3.1 All garden owners have neighbours and even if the boundaries and ownership and the obligations to maintain walls and fences are clearly dealt with, there may be other legal rights or duties sometimes apparent such as overhanging eaves or trees, or sometimes invisible, such as restrictive covenants which affect the garden owner, just as there may be similar rights benefiting his garden over that of his neighbours. The most frequently found are easements. These are legal property rights enjoyed by one property ('the dominant tenement') against another ('the servient tenement'). These may be:

(a) rights of way; or

(b) other rights.

RIGHTS OF WAY

3.2 An adjoining property (and indeed a property not contiguous but some distance away) may have a right to cross (or 'pass and repass' as old documents put it) the garden, and the garden owner may have similar rights over the next door or other properties. He may have a shared right over a common driveway or over a back passage at the rear of the garden. The right of way can be on foot or with vehicles or animals.

Express rights

3.3 A right of way is usually granted or reserved in a conveyance, transfer or lease. If a new right of way is being created it should be made clear who it is for, what is its nature eg on foot or with vehicles, and its course by reference to a plan eg 'between points A and B shown on the plan', 'along the track shown coloured brown on the plan'.

3.4 Unless expressly provided in the conveyance, transfer or lease granting or reserving the right of way, there is no obligation on either the owner of the right or the land owner over which it passes to maintain the surface of the right of way, fence it off or provide gates.

3.5   An easement such as a right of way is 'land' for the purposes of the Law of Property Act rules mentioned earlier (see **1.11**), and therefore must be granted or reserved by deed. However, any written agreement may entitle a party to claim an equitable easement so an arrangement for a shared driveway will be held by the courts to be legally binding between neighbours. Such an equitable right will also be legally binding on successors in title to the property over which it is enjoyed if it is registered as a Land Charge at the Land Charges Registry or, if the land is registered, protected by notice or caution at HM Land Registry. In the case of registered land it may be binding on a successor in title if the claimant is exercising the right and it is therefore 'an overriding interest'.[1]

1   *Thatcher v Douglas* [1996] NPC 206 (where a successor in title to a joint owner and builder of a shared driveway was held bound by the right of way—the other party had an 'overriding interest': see Land Registration Act 1925, s 70(1)(g)).

Implied rights

3.6   Even if the right is not mentioned in the conveyance, transfer or lease it may nevertheless be valid under the following rules:

(a) Law of Property Act 1925, s 62

If the right was enjoyed with the property at the time it was comprised in the relevant legal transaction then this section provides that the new owner is to take the benefit of it with the property.[1] This can mean that rights not intended to be easements, such as parking rights enjoyed by lessees of flats, can pass as legal easements.[2]

(b) *Wheeldon v Burrows*[3]

Under this case any right which is 'continuous and apparent' may pass on to a new owner as an easement. This may apply particularly in the case of gardens where gates or tracks may indicate a right of way.

A purchaser of a property with a large garden should therefore look out for signs of such rights and raise enquiries about them before he commits himself to take it. The usual form of solicitors' pre-contract enquiries should elicit replies revealing whether or not any such rights are existent. Indeed, there may be a duty on the seller to make enquiries of third parties (eg neighbours or the local authority) to find out and tell the prospective buyer.[4]

1   See the Law of Property Act 1925, s 1(2)(a) (37 *Halsbury's Statutes* (4th edn) Real Property).

2   *Handel v Stephens Close Ltd* [1994] 1 EGLR 70.
3   *Wheeldon v Burrows* (1879) 12 ChD 31.
4   *William Sindall plc v Cambridgeshire County Council* [1994] 3 All ER 168, CA.

Prescriptive rights

3.7 Under similar rules to those relating to title by adverse possession (see **1.16ff**) long uninterrupted use of a right of way may entitle the person exercising it to claim a legal easement. He must prove:

(a) such use for upwards of 20 years;[1] and/or

(b) that the legal presumption whereby long use is assumed to have been enjoyed under a 'lost' grant of easement dating back for a long period applies ('lost modern grant').

As in the case of adverse possession the owner of the land potentially affected by a claim must take steps to prevent continuous use by closing off the route, putting in a locking gate, etc.

1   Prescription Act 1832, s 2.

Public right of way

3.8 Public rights of way can be:

(a) footpaths—used by members of the public on foot (but also with dogs etc);

(b) bridle ways—used by members of the public leading horses or on horseback; or

(c) drove roads, by ways, highways, roads, streets etc—used by the public driving animals and riding bicycles, motor bicycles or with vehicles.

So a public footpath or bridle way cannot legally be used by motor cyclists, four-wheel drive vehicles etc.

3.9 Existing public rights of way on foot or otherwise should be revealed by a search with the local authority. The public footpaths map showing these is meant to be definitive, and if such a path is shown crossing a garden the owner must accept public use and cannot obstruct it, although he can fence it and put in gates or stiles (subject to planning consent). However, the public may acquire a new prescriptive public right of way if a track is used without interruption for upwards of 20 years.

Here again, action should be taken to stop such use by notice and closure. Closure for one day a year is enough. Photographs of the locked gate or other obstruction should be taken, and a note of the date made, in case it is necessary at a later stage to make a statutory declaration resisting a claim.

MAINTAINING, DIVERTING AND STOPPING UP RIGHTS OF WAY

Private rights of way

3.10 Where there is a private right of way across a garden and there is an obligation on the garden owner to maintain the surface of it (eg by deed),[1] then he must keep it in a state usable in the worst kind of weather (eg put down straw over flooded sections in winter).[2] Where a private right of way becomes impassable by reason of an obstruction (including major ground repairs but not snow and ice) the user is entitled to deviate on to neighbouring land of the garden owner.[3]

1   There is no implied obligation on either the owner of the dominant tenement or of the servient tenement to maintain a right of way in the absence of an express or prescriptive obligation.

2   *Bullard v Harrison* (1815) 4 M & S 387; *Taylor v Whitehead* (1781) 2 Doug KB 745.

3   *Cluttenham v Anglian Water Authority* (1986) Times, 14 August, CA.

Public footpaths and bridle ways

3.11 Where a public footpath or bridle way crosses a garden, the Highway Authority has powers to remove obstructions and must give consent to the putting in of gates or stiles.[1]

1   Highways Act 1980, ss 146 and 147.

3.12 There is no obligation to provide a hard surface (except where the highway has become publicly adopted and is to be made up as a dedicated highway).

3.13 Land owners are not allowed to disturb the surface of or plough up a public right of way[1] and the local authority must remove obstructions and keep a public right of way in repair.[2]

1   Highways Act 1980, ss 131A and 134.

2   Highways Act 1980, ss 56, 130 and 143, but failure to untangle vegetation from fencing is not a breach of this duty: *Westley v Hertfordshire County Council* (1998) Times, 5 March.

3.14 Where a garden owner wishes to see a public right of way diverted (eg to allow development) or stopped up there is a procedure under the Highways Act 1980, ss 118 and 119 whereby, upon application to the local authority and after advertisement with 28 days for objection (followed by a local public enquiry by the Secretary of State if there is sufficient objection), the Secretary of State can confirm stopping up or diversion to a new route of a public footpath or other right of way. This is frequently done, and the owner has to bear the local authority's costs.[1]

1   Rights of Way Act 1990, s 134; Highways Act 1980, ss 118 and 119.

EXCESSIVE USE

3.15 Where the right of way is on foot only then it must not be used with vehicles. The nature and extent of user depend upon the circumstances at the date of grant of the right. Where a right of way with vehicles to a field which was originally used occasionally for caravans and camping was swamped when the field was turned into a 200 caravan park, the court held that the servient owner was entitled to an injunction to restrain the excessive user which interfered with the use of his property (it was used for farming but the position would be the same if the right of way had been over a garden).[1]

1   *Jelbert v Davis* [1968] 4 All ER 1182.

THE GARDEN PASSAGE

3.16 In South London and in the North of England in particular, the rear gardens or yards of a row of houses are often served by a passageway running along the back connecting with the public highway at the end of the row. Sometimes this is a back lane wide enough for vehicles, served by garages put up at the back of the house plots, or it may be a very narrow foot way used for rubbish collection etc only.

3.17 Each owner may own the particular length and width or half the width of the passage at the rear of his land subject to the right of way of the others over it, as he will enjoy similar rights over their parts of the passage way. Such an owner may be able to put up a gate where he owns his part of the passageway but if there is a legal right of way this must not be locked against the other users. It is unlikely that a passage of this nature will be a public right of way. Only the owners will have a private right of way in common with

the other owners along its length, although the local authority may, with implied permission, use it for collection of refuse.

3.18　A purchaser of a property with such an access should:

(a) check by the usual pre-contract search and enquiries of the local authority whether or not this passage is a public right of way and/or publicly maintained (which is unlikely); and

(b) if it is not, raise enquiries of the seller/landlord—who owns the site of the passage, what rights are enjoyed over it by the property and who is responsible for maintaining the walls/fences/gates on it and for maintaining the path itself?

3.19　The legal rights may arise under the title deeds or lease or it may be (as is frequently the case) that there is no established legal position. In the latter case a purchaser should get the seller or landlord to make a statutory declaration as to use for upwards of 20 years and as to the maintenance obligations (if any) and try and get his rights recorded. Such informal rights do not have to be registered at the Land Registry which regards them as 'overriding interests'.

3.20　Where the title to such a right of way, having been vested in the individual house/garden owners, returns to one ownership, the right will be extinguished and will not revive on a later grant to an individual owner.[1] The right may also be lost through abandonment which may be implied (eg through not using a rear gate for upwards of 20 years) or express (by the owner signing a deed releasing it).

1　*Simmons v Dobson* [1991] 4 All ER 25; *Payne v Inward* (1996) 74 P & CR 42.

3.21　Where the right of way was granted under a lease, landlords of a back lane were held liable for failing to keep it clear of parked cars.[1]

1　*Hilton v James Smith & Sons (Norwood) Ltd* (1979) 251 Estates Gazette 1063.

3.22　Where a passageway is a public way and, indeed, in some cases where it has accepted responsibility for scavenging it by long use, the local authority has a duty to clear litter[1] (including dog faeces)[2] from the passageway and may also be able to remove private property such as abandoned shopping trolleys.[3]

1　Environmental Protection Act 1990, s 86.
2　Litter (Animal Droppings) Order 1991, SI 1991/961.

3   Environmental Protection Act 1990, s 99 and Sch 4 (but this only applies to the public highway).

OTHER RIGHTS

Eavesdrop and intruding buildings

3.23 A roof from an adjoining property may be allowed to overhang or part of a building to intrude into part of the garden by a legal easement. This may arise by express documentation or by prescription (see Chpater 1). The intrusion into air space over land by neighbours' trees is considered natural user and is dealt with in detail below. Note that an adjoining owner does not have any right to enter another's garden to effect repairs (except if expressly mentioned in the deeds or nowadays under the Access to Neighbouring Land Act 1992: see Chapter 2).

Drainage and service rights

3.24 Drainage and service rights are frequently provided for over gardens. The right is usually granted or reserved in a form such as:

> 'the right for [the grantee] and his successors in title the owners and occupiers of the land edged red on the attached plan to lay and maintain pipes wires cables services and service conducting media over and across (the garden) in the position shown by a black dotted line on the plan and the right of running of water sewage gas and electricity through the same together with the right to enter (the garden) to dig up the same and to inspect repair maintain and renew the said pipes etc [the grantee] causing as little damage as possible and making good the soil and/or damage caused.'

3.25 Rights to put up and maintain wires and cables over a garden are also frequently found. Often these are created by licence only so do not bind a successor in title and the terms of the relevant document should be carefully considered when a property is being purchased. Water, gas and electricity authorities have compulsory powers to acquire easements over gardens, and other land, subject to payment of compensation.[1] Where such rights exist the garden owner is not to interfere with the pipes etc and can be sued for damages if he digs them up even by accident.[2]

1   See Chapter 23.
2   *Robins v Tupman* [1993] 15 EG 145, CA.

3.26 The rights may be defined so as to apply, for example, not only to the pipes put in at the time of the transaction but also to pipes to be put in in the future. However, for such a right to have future application, there must be reference to a period for which the right will exist, the 'perpetuity period'. The perpetuity period is often defined by reference to a life or lives of members of the royal family, but can be any period up to 80 years.[1] If there is no reference to a valid perpetuity period a right to put in future pipes will be void and the garden owner can resist any proposal to do so.[2]

1   Perpetuities and Accumulations Act 1964, s 1.
2   *London and Blenheim Estates Ltd v Ladbroke Retail Parks Ltd* [1993] 4 All ER 157.

Septic tanks and cesspools

3.27 Similarly, a land owner may reserve the right to put in, repair, maintain and replace a septic tank or cesspool under the garden. Rights should include the right to allow entry by the local authority to empty and clean the tank. Even without this express right the local authority has rights to do this under the Public Health Act 1936.[1]

1   See Public Health Act 1936, ss 39, 48, 50 and 287.

Rivers and streams

3.28 A garden owner whose land is alongside a river or stream may take water for usual domestic garden purposes but not for irrigation or large scale commercial horticulture.[1] A licence under the Water Resources Act 1991 is required. An upper owner must not dam or substantially interfere with a river or stream flowing through or alongside a downstream garden.[2]

1   *McCartney v Londonderry and Lough Swilly Rly Co* [1904] AC 301.
2   *Robins v Gwyrfai RDC* [1899] 2 Ch 608.

Right to light

3.29 Contrary to popular opinion, there is no right to light benefiting a garden. Nor is there 'a right to view' over a neighbour's garden. No such right exists in English law.[1] There may be a restrictive covenant prohibiting the erection of any building etc on the garden (see Chapter 12) but this is not a 'right to light'. The right to light, which is a right to receive sun light for reasonable enjoyment for dwelling or commercial purposes, can only be enjoyed by windows or skylights in a building. So a right to light may be

enjoyed by neighbours' windows over a garden and if the right is valid (ie granted by title documents or acquired by prescription (see above but special rules as to 20 or 40 year use apply))[2] then the garden owner cannot build or allow trees to grow obstructing those windows and may be restrained by injunction and sued for damages if he does. A greenhouse also enjoys a specially enhanced right for light (and solar heat) which can be the subject of injunction proceedings if diminished.[3]

1   *Re Ellenborough Park, Re Davies, Powell and Maddison* [1956] Ch 131, [1955] 3 All ER 667, CA. As to a restrictive covenant which may protect a right of view over garden, see Chapter 12.

2   See Prescription Act 1832, s 3.

3   *Allen v Greenway* [1980] Ch 119.

Support

3.30   There is a right of support for land or a wall from a neighbour's land or wall (see **2.15**ff). For land, it is rarely granted in a title document and prescription does not have to be proved (obviously the land has been there for over 20 years!). So if a garden owner causes a land slip through excavation or tipping he can be made subject to an injunction[1] and he may be sued for damages by an adjoining owner downhill of him[2] in nuisance and negligence and under the case law in *Rylands v Fletcher* (1868) LR 3 HL 33 (a nineteenth century case providing for redress where land owners cause a danger to arise on their land). This easement may be enforced by injunction, but the garden owner will only have a right of redress where there is damage. The court will not allow anticipated costs for remedial work to be recovered.[3]

1   *Redland Bricks Ltd v Morris* [1970] AC 652 (injunction against a brick company which caused a landslip to a market garden).

2   *Holbeck Hall Hotel Ltd   v Scarborough Borough Council* (1997) Times, 2 October (an owner of land uphill of his neighbour may have a duty to prevent earth movement).

3   *Midland Bank plc v Bardgrove Property Services Ltd* (1992) 65 P & CR 153, CA.

The right to television reception

3.31   In the recent House of Lords case of *Hunter v Canary Wharf*[1] it was decided there was no right to sue for interference of television reception by buildings (at least not for licensees such as council tenants). However, there may be a right to sue for interruption by electrical interference.[2] Its only relevance to gardens is that a garden owner should be careful about the use of unsuppressed electrical

equipment such as mowers and hedge cutters which might lead to neighbouring land owners taking legal action. There is a statutory duty requiring electrical equipment to be safe. Nowadays this may also extend to radio-electrical interference.[3]

1   *Hunter v Canary Wharf plc* [1997] 2AC 655.

2   *Bridlington Relay Ltd v Yorkshire Electricity Board* [1965] Ch 436.

3   Electrical Equipment (Safety) Regulations 1994, SI 1994/3260; Electromagnetic Compatibility (Amendment) Regulations 1994, SI 1994/3080.

The right to park

Planning

3.32   Often part of a garden and indeed sometimes all of it (particularly a front garden) may be used for parking vehicles. The first point to be considered is whether planning permission is necessary for the access to the highway, or for the type of vehicle[1] or nature of use.[2] The creation of hardstanding for parking is permitted under planning law provided that the vehicles parking are doing so for a purpose incidental to the use and enjoyment of a dwellinghouse as such.[3] Parking of vehicles is not a change in residential use of the house, and the parking of a car or caravan, including cars or caravans of persons other than the house owner, does not require planning consent. But where a part of a garden is given over to parking a number of caravans, or strangers are given a right to park for reward, there may be a change of use for which permission is required. If the garden owner is to allow use of the garden for parking, the arrangements should be properly dealt with by a form of licence, an example of which is included in Appendix A.

1   Provision of a hard surface is permitted by the Town and Country Planning General Development Order 1998, 1988/1813, Sch 2, Pt 1, Class F.

2   See (1975) JPL 104, (1976) JPL 586 and (1978) JPL 489.

3   Town and Country Planning General Development Order 1988, 1988/1813, Sch 2, Pt 1, Class F.

Commercial parking

3.33   The receipt of parking fees may have tax consequences, for example, commercial use of the land may take it out of the capital gains tax exemption for private residences and the payments may be subject to VAT. As to security and occupier's liability it is important that parking should be at the car owner's risk—such a provision excluding liability is included in the suggested form of licence but it will be subject to the courts not holding that the provision is invalid under the Unfair Contract Terms Act 1977.

Unauthorised parking

3.34   Where a garden has an open access to a road or is unenclosed, car owners may trespass by parking their vehicles in the garden without authority. A recent case has established that a garden owner in such circumstances may clamp the wheels of vehicles wrongfully parked and will not be guilty of any criminal offence nor for the tort of interference with property provided that a contract is established with the car owner through display of a notice and by the car owner acting in compliance with the notice.[1] While the police and local authorities have statutory powers to clamp on the public highway, garden owners are not in the same position so must ensure that:

(a) sufficient notice is given to the vehicle owner that a vehicle parked without authority will be clamped and released on payment of a fee;

(b) the release fee is reasonable;

(c) the vehicle will be released without delay upon a tendering of the fee; and

(d) the vehicle owner is able to communicate his offer to pay the fee.

In *Arthur v Anker* the notice was displayed on a noticeboard. A form of notice is included in Appendix A. The vehicle owner who sees the notice has assented to clamping and cannot complain about the otherwise tortious acts of applying the clamp to the wheel and detaining the car. Furthermore, the owner has committed neither a criminal offence connected with the car, nor blackmail, in England and Wales.[2]

1   *Arthur v Anker* [1997] QB 564, CA.

2   In Scotland private vehicle clamping has been held to be the criminal offence of theft through appropriation: *Black v Carmichael* (1992) SCCR 709.

Cars: garden access to the road

3.35   The provision of a means of vehicular access to a trunk or classified road requires planning permission. Under the Town and Country Planning Act 1990, s 336(1) 'engineering operations' which require permission include 'the formation or laying out of means of access to highways'. A 'trunk road' is one maintained by the Department of Transport. A 'classified road' is a public highway adopted and maintained by the local authority.

3.36   By the General Development Order ('GDO'), Pt II, Class B the formation, laying out and construction of a means of access to a highway which is not a trunk road or classified road do not require permission. This means that to use one's garden as a car-parking space or to build a garage and to get a car in and out from the highway it will be necessary to apply for planning permission to put in a kerb access, but only if the road is trunk or classified, ie a public road. If the garden in question fronts a private road permission is not required, nor is permission needed to remove a front hedge, fence or wall, where these are outside planning law. Gates, gate posts, walls and fences are also permitted by the GDO, Pt II, Class A, provided they do not exceed one metre in height above ground level fronting the highway (or two metres on other boundaries). The latter exception does not apply in conservation (etc) areas or to listed buildings.

3.37   As a condition of planning permission the local authority may require the area 45° to the access to be kept as open land (a 'sight splay') so that traffic is able to see cars coming out of the access way. If a sight splay requirement is not adhered to, an enforcement order may be served on the property owner requiring fences, posts, shrubs etc to be removed. It is a criminal offence not to comply with any notice: Town and Country Planning Act 1990, ss 310 and 311. If the highway authority does the remedial work it can recover the cost from the householder: s 305.

3.38   By the Highways Act 1980, s 184 the highway authority has powers applying to an occupier of premises adjoining or having access to the highway who habitually takes his mechanically propelled vehicle across a kerbed footway and may serve notice on him followed by executing such works (eg putting in a kerb access) or imposing such conditions as they think fit.

4

Trees

OWNERSHIP OF TREES

4.1 The trees or shrubs growing in a garden belong to the owner of the title of the land in which they are enrooted even though the branches and extraneous roots may extend over or under the land of an adjoining owner. Where a tree grows exactly on the boundary line it will belong to the owner of that boundary. There is no such thing as a 'party tree'. The branches and fruit of a tree, even if they encroach over a neighbour's land, belong to the owner of the tree. In a case where apple trees grew over the boundary and the adjoining owner picked and sold the fruit he was held guilty of the tort of conversion and liable to account for the proceeds to the apple trees' owner.[1] This also applies to fruit falling of its own accord or windfalls.[2] As well as being a wrongful act in civil law, taking fruit (even windfalls) may be a crime. The Theft Act 1968 excepts from the criminal offence of theft 'wild flowers, fruit and foliage from any plant' but only where this is not for sale or commercial gain, so taking and selling another's fruit will be a crime.[3]

1 *Mills v Brooker* [1919] 1 KB 555.
2 'It is equally his (the tree owner's) property after it has been detached from the tree whether it has fallen from being ripe or been blown off by wind or has been severed by the hand of man': Lush J in *Mills v Brooker*.
3 Theft Act 1968, s 5(1).

4.2 The leaves falling from the trees also belong to the tree owner but falling leaves are considered to be a natural occurrence. One cannot require the adjoining owner to come in and sweep up leaves or collect fruit dropped from his trees. Neither it is likely that a court would grant damages or an injunction for falling leaves or fruit despite the technical infringement. In such matters the land owner would be well advised to keep a sense of proportion and 'keep powder and shot dry' for other, worse intrusions. If leaves block a gutter and cause an overflow which results in damage, however, the neighbour could be sued in damages.[1]

1 *Fusco v Georgiou* (9 February 1994, unreported) Ilford County Court (damage from damp and mould from blocked gutter recoverable).

4.3   When cutting a hedge, if Owner A has to go on to the other side of the hedge or lean over without a right to do so he needs the permission of adjoining Owner B, which he should obtain. The clippings from the hedge, if his hedge, will belong to Owner A. It is likely that Owner B will make it a condition of his licence to allow access to the far side of the hedge that the clippings are collected up by Owner A and taken back onto Owner A's land.

4.4   In summary, if Owner A's fruit trees overhang and the fruit can only be picked from Owner B's side then:

(a) Owner A is not entitled to come into Owner B's garden to pick the fruit without B's permission; but

(b) Owner B must obtain A's permission to pick what is A's fruit from A's tree; and

(c) fallen fruit or windfalls will still belong to A and B should ask A's permission before collecting them but, provided B does not sell them, he is committing no crime and although the fruit is A's property under civil law, it is unlikely that it will be economic for him to take legal action for such a minor matter.

It is a simple matter in such a situation to ask first, which will put the asker in the right.

4.5   As dealt with in detail in Chapter 2 (see **2.17ff**), an order can be obtained from the court under the Access to Neighbouring Land Act 1992 for access to a neighbour's property to cut back, fell etc diseased, dangerous or dead trees.

INTRUDING BRANCHES AND ROOTS

4.6   There is a Latin maxim that an English land owner owns not only the ground upon which he stands but 'usque ad coelum, et ad inferos': literally 'up to the sky and down to the uttermost parts of the earth'. This position is qualified, as aircraft can fly over his land and there can be mining beneath it, but the basic position remains today as in the twelfth century when English Common Law began.

4.7   So intrusion by overhanging branches into a land owner's air space and by creeping roots into his subsoil is treated as follows:

(a) The intrusion is a trespass (infringement of property rights) and can not only be the subject of legal action in the courts (see below) but can be resisted by lopping the branches and cutting the roots where they have crossed the boundary line provided that:

(i) the land owner does not go onto his neighbour's property (that would be an infringement of the latter's property rights);[1] and

(ii) the branches lopped and the fruit on them (and also in theory roots cut, although this never seems to have been in issue) should be returned to the neighbour whose legal property they are: see **4.1ff.**[2]

This can be done without any notice to the neighbour (although out of courtesy and also in anticipation of any court case which may follow it would be wise to give warning and document this). As with many garden disputes, the legal position has been fought all the way up the courts and was eventually decided by the House of Lords (the highest legal authority).[3]

(b) No legal right can be acquired in respect of intruding branches or roots by prescription, and upwards of 20 years' uninterrupted intrusion by the branches or roots will *not* entitle the neighbour whose trees are doing the encroaching to a legal easement, nor will 12 years' user give immunity under the Limitation Acts from legal proceedings if the intrusion causes damage.[4] The law treats the intrusion by the branches or roots as natural user of land until one owner or the other asserts his legal position. So what began as a privilege (ie something enjoyed by one person and suffered by another without a duty) may, after such assertion, be enforced by full legal action.

1   *Earl Lonsdale v Nelson* (1823) 2 B & C 302 (cut branches belong to owner of tree).

2   See *Mills v Brooker* above.

3   *Lemon v Webb* [1895] AC 1 (owner of land with overhanging branches can lop trees provided he does not go on neighbour's land).

4   In *Lemmon v Webb* (above) the overhanging branches had been there for over 20 years; in *Davey v Harrow Corpn* [1958] 1 QB 60, CA, the roots had been there for over 80 years. See also the 'highways' cases of *Chapman v Barking and Dagenham London Borough Council* [1997] 2 EGLR 141 (horse chestnuts planted in the 1930s); *Russell v Barnet London Borough* (1984) 83 LGR 152 (trees planted before adoption of road in the early 1900s).

Damage by intruding branches and roots

4.8   To the extent that they cross the boundary line whether in the air, along the ground or under it, intruding branches and roots are infringing the property rights of the adjoining owner,[1] and many disputes arise between neighbours and between the garden owner and the local authority about damage caused by such infringements. The adjoining land owner has the following legal remedies.

1   *Davey v Harrow Corpn* [1958] 1 QB 60, CA (encroaching roots actionable).

Damages

4.9 He can sue for damages to recover the loss suffered to his land for:

(a) Trespass (the actual intrusion over the boundary).

(b) Nuisance (the detrimental effect to the use and enjoyment of his land)—if the interference with his property rights is continuous and substantial and results in damage).

(c) Negligence (if the land/tree owner has failed to keep a duty of care which he owes to others affected by his acts or omissions such as his neighbour or users of the public highway, by allowing overhanging branches to become dangerous).

For the court to find in the plaintiff's favour damages must be proved for nuisance and negligence. To sue for trespass it is not necessary to prove physical or economic loss, but without such loss a case for damages would not be worth bringing.

4.10 Intruding branches are unlikely to cause any great financial loss to property rights, but it is possible, and can lead to damages being payable, as when a neighbour's fruit trees were blighted by excessive foliage and droppings from overhanging branches[1]. On the other hand, intruding roots growing under the foundations of a building often lead to substantial damage, either directly (by causing the foundations to crack[2] and become unsafe) or indirectly (by soaking up moisture in the soil causing subsidence[3]). The damages will be:

(a) the cost of repairs; and

(b) the diminution in the value of the house, eg loss on sale;[4] and

(c) any other expenses directly arising from the wrongful act.[5]

The legal costs of bringing the matter to court are also likely to be awarded (but there will always be an element of 'solicitor and own client' costs to be paid by the plaintiff). In some cases the court will reduce the damages, for example if part of the damage is caused by the plaintiff's own trees.[6]

---

1 *Smith v Giddy* [1904] 2 KB 448 (overhanging branches interfered with growth of Kentish fruit farmer's trees).

2 *Davey v Harrow Corpn* [1958] 1 QB 60, CA (encroaching roots actionable).

3 *Butler v Standard Telephones and Cables Ltd* [1940] 1 KB 399 and *McCombe v Read* [1955] 2 QB 429 (black poplar absorbed moisture in dry soil).

4 *Bunclarke v Hertfordshire County Council* (1977) 234 Estates Gazette 381 and 455 (damages for tree roots affecting a block of flats included a sum for the

diminution in value of the flats, as the block now had a bad reputation and flats were achieving lower prices than before the root damage was discovered).

5 *Ward v Cannock Chase District Council* [1986] Ch 546 (negligence case: plaintiff who had to vacate was entitled to damages to cover the cost of alternative accommodation and removals).

6 *Greenwood v Portwood* [1985] CLY 2500 (subsidence to plaintiff's house: half caused by defendant's beech tree, half by plaintiff's own hedge: 50% reduction in damages).

Injunction

4.11 The court can grant an injunction requiring the infringing owner to do some act, eg to cut back the roots or branches or the tree itself, or to refrain from doing some act, eg not to plant over the boundary of a garden, and in each case to make good any damage. The court has a discretion but will be likely to grant an injunction where the 'balance of convenience' in a situation favours the plaintiff, eg he is suffering more loss than the value of the enjoyment of the defendant's act of trespass, nuisance etc.[1] So where trees on land of a private or public land owner adversely affect a neighbour the courts may grant an injunction to lop or fell regardless of the age or alleged benefit of the tree.[2] As part of their 'discretion' some courts appear now to have a further requirement that the root damage is reasonably foreseeable.[3]

1 *American Cyanamid Co v Ethicon Ltd* [1975] AC 396.

2 *Elliot v Islington London Borough of Islington* [1991] 1 EGLR 167 (ancient chestnut pressing on wall) and *Butcher v Perkins* [1992] CLYB 3223 (willow tree on clay soil).

3 *Greenwood v Portwood* [1985] CLY 2500, following *Leakey v National Trust for Places of Historic Interest or Natural Beauty* [1980] QB 483.

Self help

4.12 The owner may take action himself in cutting off any intruding branches and severing roots at the boundary line. This is so even if the latter action destroys the tree, but he cannot poison the roots. The lopped branches and any fruit and leaves from the tree belong, as already noted, to the owner of the land on which the tree grows and the right of return should be acknowledged. Where a neighbour's branch seems to threaten one's own property, for example by overhanging a greenhouse, it may be that the neighbour is being negligent in allowing continued growth and he should be asked in writing to cut back the branch. If the request is refused, then the garden owner should exercise his right of self help by cutting back the branch himself. It would be a good idea to get a tree specialist to advise and to do the work. This should be preceded by a letter telling the neighbour of the proposed action: see Appendix A.

The local authority also has a right to enter a garden adjoining a highway to abate a nuisance[1] by eg grubbing up a hedge or pulling down an obstructing fence.[2] See Chapter 5.

1   Highways Act 1980, s 136.
2   *Reynolds v Presteign UDC* [1896] 1 QB 604.

Insurance

4.13 Damages and legal costs paid by the garden owner to third parties for intruding trees should be covered by a normally-worded householder's insurance policy. Where the tree on his land damages his own house directly (eg by falling branches) or, if specifically covered, subsidence and heave, again he may be able to recover under his own insurance policy. Although the damage by roots is gradual, it nevertheless can be an 'accident' in the terms of the relevant policy wording.[1]

1   *Mills v Smith* [1964] 1 QB 30.

Redress against professional advisers

4.14 A garden owner whose property is damaged by intruding roots etc may also be able to sue the surveyor or architect who advised him prior to purchase or development for negligence if he failed to notice the potential danger.[1] So too a solicitor might in some cases be liable for professional negligence. In this connection it should be noted that the usual search and enquiries of the local authority prior to purchase will only cover the property itself *not* adjoining property (unless the area searched against is expressly extended to cover it) so a tree preservation order indicating mature trees near to a boundary may not be revealed. If these trees had intruding roots, would a failure to enquire about them be negligence? The answer is probably 'no'.[2]

1   See *Matto v Rodney Broom Associates* [1994] 2 EGLR 163 (a surveyor who did not notice sandy soil required underpinning, and should have stated the risk was held liable for £18,000 damages).
2   It is normal professional practice to search only against the land being purchased unless there are special circumstances.

4.15 If the local authority had failed to record protected trees (a) within the property or (b) in the above case, next door, would they have been negligent? Answer (a) probably 'yes' (b) probably 'no'.[1]

1   See Local Land Charges Act 1975, s 5(1) (duty to register) and s 10 (compensation), and Town and Country Planning Act 1990, s 69 (TPOs are registrable in Part 3 of the Local Land Charges Register).

TREE PRESERVATION ORDERS AND TREES IN CONSERVATION AREAS

4.16 Another factor which the garden owner must bear in mind concerning trees is the legislation as to the preservation of established trees under theTown and Country PlanningAct 1990.[1] The local authority has power to make a Tree Preservation Order ('TPO') for the preservation of a tree or group of trees or woodlands to prohibit felling, topping, lopping or uprooting, wilful damage or wilful destruction of listed trees without consent and for the planting of trees, and trees in a Conservation Area established by the local authority are also subject to a similar restriction.

1 Town and Country PlanningAct 1990, s 198(3);Town and Country Planning (Tree Preservation Orders) Regulations 1969, SI 1969/17, as amended by SIs 1975/148, 1981/14 and 1988/963.

What trees do TPOs apply to?

4.17 A TPO can be made in respect of any kind of tree, free standing or in a hedgerow provided that they are of a kind which attains 6m or more in maturity on a single stem or divide above the ground where the trunk has a diameter of greater than 1.5m. Fruit trees cultivated for fruit are not covered, and nor are shrubs (eg rhododendrons) or hedges covered. Trees of less than 750mm in diameter 1.5m above ground, or less than 100mm, if obstructing growth of another tree, are excepted in conservation areas.

4.18 When the tree is dead or dying or dangerous or if such action (felling etc) is necessary in order to comply with any obligations imposed by or under an Act of Parliament or so far as may be necessary for the prevention or abatement of a nuisance then the Order does not apply. A 'nuisance' for this purpose means the infringement of the rights of some third party, not merely a potential danger within the property.[1]

1 *Re the Vicarage Nassington Peterborough* [1992] JPL 389.

What is 'destruction' of a tree?

4.19 Lord Widgery in *Barnet London Borough Council v Eastern Electricity Board* [1973] 1 WLR 430 at 434 gave some very useful guidance as to what 'destroy' means for the purposes of the TPO legislation:

'We think it right to start consideration of the problem with one of the dictionary definitions of destroy to which we have already

referred, namely, "to render useless". Before a tree can be said to be destroyed we feel that it must have been rendered useless—but rendered useless as what? This last inquiry raises immediately the question of the purpose for which the use of the tree may or may not continue to exist. Consequently in our judgment one must bear in mind in this case that the underlying purpose of the relevant legislation is the preservation of trees and woodlands as amenities, as living creatures providing pleasure, protection and shade; it is their use as such that is sought to be preserved, and a tree the subject of a tree preservation order is destroyed in the present context when as a result of that which is done to it, it ceases to have any use as amenity, as something worth preserving. For example, if a person intentionally inflicts on a tree so radical an injury that in all the circumstances any reasonably competent forester would in consequence decide that it ought to be felled, then in our opinion that person wilfully destroys the tree within the meaning of that word in the relevant legislation and order.'

When and how do the planning authorities enforce a TPO against you?

4.20   It is a criminal offence to cut down, uproot or wilfully destroy any preserved tree to which a TPO applies or a tree within the specified size category in a conservation area (see **4.17**).[1] A fine not exceeding Scale 4 (currently £20,000) can be levied on conviction by a magistrates' court.[2] The local authority responsible for enforcement can also obtain an injunction against the wrongful owner, and its costs. Replanting can also be required.[3]

1   Town and Country Planning Act ('TCPA') 1990, s 198(1). TCPA 1990, s 192(6) and Town and Country Planning Act (Tree Preservation Order) Regulations1969, SI 1969/17 as amended by SIs 1975/148, 1981/14, 1988/963.
2   TCPA 1990, s 210.
3   TCPA 1990, s 197.

4.21   Where it is proposed to make a TPO the local authority must serve a notice on the land owner on whose land the tree(s) is/are and advertise the proposed Order. Objections must be made in writing within 28 days, and objections must be taken into account. A local enquiry can be convened at which objectors can be represented and have a right to state their case. The Order may then be confirmed. Persons aggrieved by the making of the Order may appeal to the High Court on a point of law.[1]

1   TCPA 1990, ss 284 and 288.

4.22   Once an Order is in force or in a Conservation Area, application for consent for the required work must be made in writing to the local authority. Except in cases of emergency, five days' notice is required for work on TPO trees, and six weeks' for work on trees in a Conservation Area.[1] Where leave to fell etc is refused or conditions are imposed compensation may be payable, but not if the local authority certifies that the refusal or condition was imposed in the interest of good forestry or if the tree is part of a group having outstanding or special amenity value. Compensation may be payable where replanting is required[2] but not if a Forestry Authority grant would not be available.[3]

1   TCPA 1990, s 211.
2   *Buckle v Holderness Borough Council* [1996] 39 EG 179 (Lands Tribunal) (£15,346 compensation reduced to £13,000 to allow for the cost of remedial works the plaintiff would have done anyway).
3   TCPA 1990, s 203.

How to get the local authority to take action against a neighbour

4.23   Before a local authority will take action against a neighbour who, for example, is preparing to cut down a tree, there must be a TPO or Conservation Area covering the tree: apart from that 'the price of [the] liberty [of the tree] is eternal vigilance'. As soon as the tree cutters arrive the person wishing to prevent the action should apply immediately to the Environment Department of the local authority and require them to take out an injunction against the anticipated felling of the tree. Should this fail, it is not open to the adjoining owner to take out an injunction, but the dilatoriness of the authority could be a subject of a complaint to the Local Government Ombudsman, who could require the council to compensate the person adversely affected by the cutting of the tree. TPOs affect statutory undertakers such as the gas, water and electricity authorities so if a protected tree is damaged by them they will be liable to a fine and to replant.[1]

1   *Barnet London Borough Council v Eastern Electricity Board* [1973] 1 WLR 430.

5

Gardens abutting the public highway

LOCAL AUTHORITY POWERS

5.1 There are a number of local authority powers which affect the garden owner. Briefly, these are as follows:

(a) Highways Act 1980, s 79

The Highway Authority (ie local authority) can require trees and other obstructions to be removed to create a sight line on corners. Where an adjoining land owner has created the obstacle the Highway Authority itself is not liable to third parties.[1]

(b) Highways Act 1980, ss 137, 152 and 153

The Highway Authority can take proceedings against an owner of property abutting the highway to remove an obstruction or so that there is no projection or gate opening outwards on to it.

(c) Highways Act 1980, s 141

The trees are not to be planted by a land owner within 15 feet of the centre of a made up carriageway of a publicly adopted road.

(d) Highways Act 1980, s 136

Trees or hedges are not to interfere with light or air to the public highway and the council may order such trees or hedges to be lopped (note: not topped[2]).

(e) Highways Act 1980, s 154(1)

Where branches of trees overhang or roots undermine a highway the Highway Authority can lop trees or fell dead, dying or insecurely rooted trees if they are likely to cause a danger by falling on the highway. The lauthority has right of entry to the garden to lop, fell etc themselves and can recover the costs of doing this from the owner. A garden owner cannot stop the local authority cutting down trees bordering the highway in exercise of its powers.[3]

---

1 *Stovin v Wise (Norfolk County Council, third party)* [1996] AC 923, HL.

2   *Unwin v Hanson* [1891] 2 QB 115, CA ('lopping' means cutting off branches laterally: it does not include 'topping', ie the cutting off of the top of a tree).

3   *Stilwell v New Windsor Corpn* [1932] 2 Ch 155.

LIABILITY TO HIGHWAY USERS IN NEGLIGENCE

5.2   The garden owner may be directly liable to highway users in vehicles or passers by on foot in negligence, for example, if they are injured by a falling lamp[1] or wall[2] or through allowing a tree to become dangerous so that a branch falls on a road user,[3] but he must have known of the bad state of the tree and failed to fell it or take other required action.[4]

1   *Tarry v Ashton* (1876) 1 QBD 314.

2   *Mint v Good* [1951] 1 KB 517.

3   *Noble v Harrison* [1926] 2 KB 332.

4   *Cunliffe v Bankes* [1945] 1 All ER 588; *Caminer v Northern and London Investment Trust Ltd* [1951] AC 88 (falling tree).

5.3   A pipe left across a road causing injury has been held to be negligence[1] but where a garden hose was unwound across the road to another part of the owner's garden it was held that he was not negligent when a pedestrian fell over it as he had attempted to warn everyone who might be affected.[2]

1   *Farrell v John Mowlem & Co Ltd* [1954] 1 Lloyd's Rep 437.

2   *Trevett v Lee* [1955] 1 All ER 406.

5.4   Again, liability to third parties is usually covered by a household insurance policy and if not the garden owner should see that it is.

LOCAL AUTHORITY'S LIABILITY AND HIGHWAY VERGES

5.5   The local authority may itself be liable to highway users for negligence in failing to take notice of and to fell or cut back a diseased or dangerous tree[1] and also may be liable to a garden owner for damages for branches or roots intruding from the public highway.[2]

1   *Paterson v Humberside County Council* (1945) Times, 19 April; *Chapman v Barking and Dagenham London Borough Council* [1997] 48 EG 154.

2   *Hurst v Hampshire County Council* (1997) 30 LSGaz R 30, CA.

5.6   As to whether the verge bounding the public highway is a part of it or of the garden it will be necessary to refer to the title deeds of the land concerned and any relevant plan, eg a plan on a deed of dedication of the land as the highway.[1] Whoever the verge belongs

to, the owner will be liable for nuisance and negligence for damage from trees or other activities there. The Highway Authority may license an adjoining owner to plant, eg trees, on the verge.[2] Liability in negligence for the trees will apply whether the trees were planted by the authority or not and whether they are self sown or not but the damage must be reasonably foreseeable and if the tree appears to be disease free there may be a valid defence. Also, the disproportionate expense to council tax payers of a general tree inspection may be relevant in the defence.[3]

1   *Russell v Barnet London Borough Council* (1984) 83 LGR 152.
2   Highways Act 1980, s 142.
3   *Salloway v Hampshire County Council* [1981] 9 LGR 449.

5.7   The garden owner should keep an eye on his own trees and the trees in the highway near his garden and write to the local authority reporting if he suspects that any of the latter is diseased or dangerous or likely to be dangerous to his own property or to the highway users.

5.8   In some cases, particularly in the country, the verge may be common land (see Chapter 2) or left over land (waste) which formerly belonged to a Lord of the Manor (before 1925 land could be held under what was called customary or manorial tenure, but not nowadays) and if so the former Lord of the Manor may have continuing rights. He may require money to extinguish them before the verge land is planted, or acquired for road widening etc.[1] The former manorial rights are, however, unlikely to be enough to make the 'Lord' liable for negligence through dangerous trees etc.

1   See 'Property Owners are taken to the outer limit' article by R Crathorne in *Property Week* (1998) 13 March.

5.9   For the law as to construction of vehicular access, gates, fences etc adjoining the highway see Chapter 11. Other occasions where a garden owner whose garden abuts the public highway may be legally liable, eg animals, slippery paths, etc, are dealt with separately below.

6

The use of the garden (1): problems which may arise

PROBLEMS WHICH MAY ARISE

Earth and water movement or escape

6.1 Where damage is caused by movement or escape of earth or water to adjoining land owners or to third parties the garden owner may be liable under *Rylands v Fletcher*[1]—a branch of the law of negligence which imposes strict liability on a land owner who collects or allows a dangerous thing on his property and who will be liable for all damage as a result of its escape. So a garden owner will be liable if by excavation or tipping he causes the earth in his garden to slip and damage a downhill owner's property.[2] Under the usual negligence rules, however, it appears that he will not be liable if he does not know of the danger and could not have reasonably taken steps to prevent it.[3] So water damage from a dammed pond which escapes will be his responsibility. Where osier beds were filled in, causing flooding by water 'squeezed out' it was held that the owner could be liable for nuisance, but the 'reasonably foreseeable' test had not been satisfied.[4]

1   *Rylands v Fletcher* (1868) LR 3 HL 330.
2   *Holbeck Hall Hotel Ltd v Scarborough Borough Council* (1997) Times, 15 October.
3   *Leakey v National Trust for Places of Historic Interest or Natural Beauty* [1980] QB 485.
4   *Home Brewery Co v William Davis (Leicester) Ltd* [1987] 1 QB 339.

NUISANCE

6.2 Activities in the garden or in a neighbour's garden may infringe the law of nuisance and be actionable under one or more of the following heads:

(a)   private nuisance;

(b)   public nuisance;

(c)   statutory nuisance.

6.3   For private and public nuisance the nature of the locality may be relevant. As noted in a nineteeenth century case,'what would be a nuisance in Berkeley Square would not necessarily be so in Bermondsey'[1] and a particular type of noise in a neighbourhood, eg a car revving in a mews of garages, may not be a nuisance.

1   Thesiger LJ in *Sturges v Bridgman* (1879) 11 Ch D 852 at 856.

Private nuisance

6.4   Private nuisance is continuous activity generating noise, smells, smoke etc which constitutes 'interference for a substantial length of time by an owner or occupier of property to the use and enjoyment of neighbouring property'.[1] It is actionable in the civil courts by the owner or occupier affected who has suffered damage, and his legal remedy will be damages and an injunction restraining the activity complained of.

1   Talbot J in *Cunard v Antifyre Ltd* [1933] 1 KB 551 at 557.

6.5   The activity must be unreasonable:

> 'If user is reasonable the defendant will not be liable for consequent harm to his neighbour's enjoyment of his land but if the user is unreasonable the defendant will be liable even though he may have used reasonable skill and care in avoiding it'.[1]

Self help in abating the nuisance can sometimes be exercised after notice to the perpetrator.[2]

1   Lord Goff in *Cambridge Water Co Ltd v Eastern Counties Leather plc* [1994] 2 AC 264 at p 297.
2   *Jones v Williams* (1843) 11 M & W 176 (plaintiff allowed to enter and remove manure heap provided notice given first).

Public nuisance

6.6   If the activity is so substantial that it is likely to affect not just a neighbour but the public generally then it will be a public nuisance and be actionable by members of the public. The Attorney General upon complaint will commence the action in the civil courts for compensation and an injunction. The local authority also has a right to take legal action.[1]

1   Local Government Act 1972, s 222.

6.7   Exemplary damages are not usually granted for a public nuisance.[1]

1   *AB v South West Water Services Ltd* and *Gibbons v South West Water Services Ltd* [1993] QB 507, CA.

Statutory nuisance

6.8   As well as falling within public or private nuisance,[1] an activity may also be contrary to the provisions of specific legislation, eg the Control of Pollution Act 1974, the Environmental Protection Act 1990 and the Noise Act 1996, and, if so, the local authority will take criminal proceedings in the magistrates' court for an abatement order, fine and costs. Statutory nuisance is dealt with in more depth at **6.29ff.**

1   *Lloyds Bank plc v Guardian Assurance plc* (1986) 35 BLR 34, CA.

TYPES OF ACTIVITY CONSTITUTING NUISANCE

6.9   It is perhaps more useful to consider each activity in turn and see how the law of nuisance applies than to deal with the particular classification into which it fits.

Noise

6.10   The habitual generation of noise (eg from a record player) from a garden may be both a private and a public nuisance, as well as a statutory nuisance. If the noise comes from building operations or on a neighbour's land, the person suffering should check that planning permission and byelaw consent (if required) have been obtained for the works. Even if they have, excessive noise outside normal working hours, may be the subject of an injunction restraining the use of particular tools (eg a pile driver[1]) or outside particular hours.[2] Damages will usually be ordered only where the noise is excessive.[3]

1   *Andraeae v Selfridge & Co Ltd* [1938] Ch 1; *Hoare & Co v MacAlpine* [1923] 1 Ch 167 (pile driver).

2   *Boyton v Helena Rubenstein* (1960) 176 Estates Gazette 443 (noise restricted to 9 am to 6 pm).

3   *Andraeae v Selfridge* (see above).

6.11   An act which would not normally be a nuisance may be made so by malicious intent of the perpetrator.[1] The owner of the property from which the noise comes may be liable even if he/it had no knowledge of the noise, for example where the owner is a private landlord or local authority and is not resident in the property. The Environmental Protection Act 1990 and the Noise Act 1996 provide for both local authority and private individuals to initiate

proceedings for breach of either Act following service of an 'abatement notice' and 21 days for appeal. Proceedings are in the magistrates' court and conviction can lead to a Scale 5 fine (presently £500) for domestic property plus £500 per day after a court order for abatement.

1   *Hollywood Silver Fox Farm Ltd v Emmett* [1936] 2 KB 468.

6.12   Examples of cases where noise has been held to be a public or private nuisance include:

(a) an electricity generating station;[1]

(b) the noise of model aeroplanes;[2]

(c) children playing from dawn to dusk;[3]

(d) 'go kart' racing;[4] and

(e) the noise from a problem family.[5]

The noise in the garden of:

(a) tractors;

(b) a motor mower;

(c) mechanical hedge clippers; and

(d) a chain saw;

could all be private and possibly public and statutory nuisances (see **6.29**ff).

1   *Colwell v St Pancras Borough Council* [1904] 1 Ch 707.

2   *Hall v Beckenham Corpn* [1949] 1 KB 716.

3   *Dunton v Dover District Council* (1977) 76 LGR 87.

4   *Tetley v Chitty* [1986] 1 All ER 663.

5   *Smith v Scott* [1973] Ch 314.

Parties

6.13   Parties with noisy music will probably not be a private nuisance if they are held only occasionally but may infringe the Environmental Protection Act 1990 provisions: see **6.29**ff. The defence of 'reasonable excuse' to non-compliance with an order under the Act was held to be not available in the case of a birthday party with loud reggae music, air horns and whistles.[1] An individual seeking to invoke the Act need not give an abatement notice first.[2]

1   *Wellingborough District Council v Gordon* (1990) 155 JP 494.

2   *R v Newham Justices, ex p Hunt* [1976] 1 All ER 839; *Sandwell Metropolitan Borough Council v Bujok* [1990] 3 All ER 385.

6.14 Where a garden owner lets or licenses his land for a party he may be liable for statutory nuisance. It is no excuse that he was away at the time of the party if he should reasonably have foreseen that the nuisance complained of would be likely at the type of party licensed.[1]

1   *R v Peter Shorrock* [1994] QB 279, CA. Other cases of public or statutory nuisance caused by noisy parties are *R v Ruffell* (1992) 13 Cr App Rep (S) 204 and *R v Taylor* (1991) 13 Cr App Rep (S) 466, CA.

Barking dogs and crowing cocks

6.15 The continual barking of dogs[1] or crowing of cocks[2] within a garden has been held to be a private and public nuisance, and may also be a statutory nuisance.

1   *Galer v Morissey* [1955] 1 All ER 380 and *Clemons v Steward* (1969) 113 Sol Jo 427.

2   *Hunt v WH Cook* (1922) 66 Sol Jo 557 and *Leemon v Montagu* [1936] 2 All ER 1677. The reader may also recall the North Devon case of Corky the cockerel widely reported in the national press in 1996.

6.16 With regard to dogs kept in professional kennels it may be noted that a planning authority was upheld by the courts in imposing a condition upon such premises following an enforcement notice restricting it to six dogs, the barking of the 41 kept there at the time having been complained of as a nuisance.[1]

1   *Wallington v Secretary of State for Wales and Montgomeryshire District Council* [1990] JPL 112.

6.17 With regard to barking dogs and crowing cockerels the garden owner with potential offenders should exercise self criticism and animal psychiatry. Why is the dog barking? Is it being left alone for long periods? Has it got water? Is it hungry? Is it kept in part of the garden where it can be provoked or petted by passers-by? May the dog be ill? Are the kennels or chicken coops too near a neighbour's boundary and could they be made sound-proof or re-positioned?[1]

1   See 'Constant barking can be avoided' National Dog Wardens Association and Association of Pet Behaviour Counsellors 92 EP 381 (Department of the Environment pamphlet).

Motor mowers

6.18 There are European Union regulations prohibiting the supply of motor mowers of high noise levels. The noise level differs depending upon the width and size of the mower, but basically those that generate a noise of over 96-105 decibels at 4-10 metres

(both measurements deepnding on width) cannot legally be sold in the EU.[1]

1   Lawnmowers (Harmonisation of Noise Emission Standards) Regulations 1992, SI 1992/168; EU Council Directive 84/538 EEC 17.9.84.

What is excessive noise?

6.19   Two judicial pronouncements in traffic cases are helpful in giving a rough guide to what constitutes excessive noise. Veale J in *Hasley v Esso Petroleum Co Ltd* [1961] 2 All ER 145 at 156A–B:

> 'Scientific evidence is helpful in that it may tend to confirm or disprove the evidence of the witnesses. The scale of decibels from nought to 120 can be divided into colloquial descriptions of noise by the use of words: faint, moderate, loud, and so on. Between 40 and 60 decibels the noise is moderate, between 60 and 80 it is loud, between 80 and 100 it is very loud and from 100 to 120 it is deafening.'

Buckley, J in *Gillingham Borough Council v Medway (Chatham) Docks Co Ltd* [1992] 3 All ER 923 at 971 summarised an expert's evidence as to the decibel level of domestic activities with approval as follows:

> 'Mr Ratcliffe produced a chart depicting the level of common sounds measured in decibels, the dB(A) scale. This was agreed. It is interesting to note that a quiet bedroom is about 35 on the scale, at 55 communication starts to become difficult, a car travelling at a steady 60 kph at 7 metres distance is just over 70, a heavy diesel lorry at 40 kph at 7 metres is 85, a pneumatic drill at 7 metres is 95 and 120 is the threshold of pain. Dr Walker put a normal television programme with music at about 60. Many lorries' peaks were recorded on Dr Walker's graphs at about 80. However, he explained without challenge that the true peaks were in excess of this measurement but were recorded at 80 because of the restrictions of the equipment used to compile the graph. His maximum reading by alternative direct measurement was over 100 dB(A). He also made the point that lorries, particularly in low gear, generate low frequency sound which, even inside a house with double glazing, would be 60 dB(A) or more. A busy general office is 60 dB(A) according to Mr Ratcliffe's chart.'

This case related to lorry noise but garden activities in excess of the level of approximately 85 decibels at 7 metres (ie approximately over the garden fence) would, it is thought, be unacceptable and be considered a nuisance of all kinds by the courts.

6.20 Nevertheless, it must be said that there is no set definition in decibels or other measurement as to what is an excessive noise. The pitch and type of noise or vibration may be as relevant as the volume. Moderately loud rap music and low buzzing can be just as annoying. Unexpected sounds such as a loud bang or screech, occurring often, although irregularly, may also be offensive even though they are not continuous. Local authorities have no set standard as to garden noise. A motor mower may be offensive at 90 decibels at 5m but not at 10. The distance of the mower or hedge clipper, obstacles (such as thick hedges) and wind direction may all be relevant. A rough table of typical sound levels is set out below with examples of noise at each level.

Table: Sound levels in decibels

120	Discotheque
100	Pnematic drill at 5m
90	Heavy goods vehicle from pavement
	Powered lawnmower at operator's ear
70	Vacuum cleaner at 3m
	Telephone ringing at 2m
50	Boiling kettle at 0.5m
40	Refrigerator humming at 2m
0	Threshold of hearing

6.21 Garden noise (other than noisy parties) is not a very frequent local authority complaint, at any rate in London Boroughs. Of all garden nuisance causes, noise is probably the most susceptible to mediation. The person affected should try and talk to the garden owner and to his neighbours (it may be that the perpetrator would accept advice from an older neighbour but not from someone newly moved in next door). Mediation is preferable to and cheaper than court action (mediation services are available from Mediation UK telephone number 0117 924 1234).

The Noise Act 1996

6.22 This Act, which came into force on 23 July 1997, puts a duty on local authorities to investigate a noise nuisance issuing from and to 'a dwelling' at night. Warning notices can be served and if the noise continues over a prescribed limit a criminal offence is committed. A private individual cannot bring an action under the Noise Act.[1] It is not clear whether a garden can be part of a dwelling for the purposes of the Act, but it is submitted that if the garden is held with a residential house it would be and that the Act applies.

---

1   *Issa v Hackney London Borough Council* [1997] 1 All ER 999.

6.23   At night when the garden owner's neighbours are sleeping the toleration level should be much less than what is acceptable during the day. The World Health Organisation's recommended level above which disturbance of sleep becomes apparent is 35 decibels, but the Court of Appeal has recently held that factory noise above this level was not a statutory nuisance.[1] The Noise Act 1996 contains provisions for a new night time noise offence which local authorities can adopt with effect from spring 1997. The Act introduces an objective standard against which noise at night from domestic premises may be assessed. There is also an additional 'on the spot' £100 fixed penalty available. Few local authorities have adopted this new code as yet; many feel it is too like setting up a 'noise police'. Two months' notice must be given in the local press before the new regime is introduced into an area.

1   *Murdoch v Glacier Metal Co Ltd* [1998] 07 LS Gaz R 31, CA.

Games in the garden

6.24   Garden owners and their children and guests often play games in the garden, while an owner of large grounds or an estate may licence it for horse trials, motor or motor cycle racing. It is not proposed to go into the legal ramifications of such large events, but see Chapter 7 on occupiers' liability.

6.25   Golf practice, cricket or archery may result in balls or arrows being hit or shot out of the garden. The garden owner will be liable to neighbours for broken windows and for injury to persons using the public highway under the usual laws of nuisance and negligence. Thus, the owner of a cricket ground was held not liable because he had taken reasonable precautions (by putting up a seven foot high wooden fence around the ground plus another seven feet of wire above that) to avoid injury to a passer-by 100 yards from the ground. (Only six 'sixes' had been hit in over eight years.)[1] But a l andowner was held liable to a passer-by hit by a golf ball from an unfenced course.[2]

1   *Bolton v Stone* [1951] AC 850, cf *Miller v Jackson* [1977] QB 966 (injunction against cricket not given).
2   *Castle v St Augustine's Links Ltd* (1922) 38 TLR 615.

6.26   Where the ball passes into the land of a neighbour then it will be trespass to go and collect it. The neighbour has no property in the ball and should return it on request but if he refuses to do so it would be unlikely that the court would force him to do so by

injunction. The property in abandoned or lost golf balls appears to vest in the owner of the land on which they are found, at any rate to enable him to sue trespassers who go on to his land to take the balls.[1]

1   *Hibbert v McKiernon* [1948] 2 KB 142.

6.27   Where dangerous activities such as stock car racing[1] or less dangerously horse jumping[2] are to happen within his grounds a land owner should try to exclude liability for damage and injury through a provision in the ticket or notice but it will be subject to the Unfair Contract Terms Act 1977: see **7.10ff**.

1   *White v Blackmore* [1972] 2 QB 651, CA ('jalopy' racing organisers were liable to competitor not exempted by exclusion clause).
2   *Pidington v Hastings* (1932) Times, 12 March (where a polo pony ran off the field, an injured spectator could not claim).

6.28   Games, if frequent and noisy, eg paintball war games, could lead to an action for nuisance or statutory nuisance. Participators in a game are usually taken as having consented to the risk of injury and will not be able to sue the garden owner.[1] Where children are the games players, it is important that an adult is in charge of the game at all times: see **7.15ff**.

1   *Potter v Carlisle & Cliftonville Golf Club* [1939] NI 114.

STATUTORY NUISANCE

The Environmental Protection Act 1990

6.29   The Environmental Protection Act 1990 has the following provisions which may be relevant.

(a) Section 79(1): a 'nuisance order' or an 'abatement order' may be obtained from a magistrates' court.

(b) Section 81(5): an injunction may be obtained against the owner of premises or perpetrator of offending activities.

(c) Section 81(3): the local authority can enter premises to stop the nuisance.

(d) Section 81(4): the local authority can charge the owner or person responsible with the costs of abatement.

(e) Section 82: an individual who is aggrieved by a nuisance can take the initiative in applying to the magistrates' court for a nuisance order which will be granted where there is 'no reasonable excuse'. By s 82(6) a warning notice must be given to the owner/person responsible. If the warning notice is not

complied with within the given period the local authority or complainant may take proceedings in the magistrates'court: see **6.35**.

6.30   The items covered set out in s 79(1) which in all cases must be prejudicial to health or a nuisance are:

(a) the state of the premises themselves;

(b) smoke emitted from premises (but not from a chimney);

(c) fumes or gases emitted from premises;

(d) any dust, steam, smell or other effluvia arising on industrial, trade or business premises only (so not from a garden);

(e) any accumulation or deposit, eg refuse, damp and mould;

(f) any animal kept in such a place or manner as to be prejudicial to health or a nuisance ('animals' includes 'birds': see **7.30ff**);

(g) noise emitted from premises;

(h) noise that is prejudicial to health or a nuisance and is emitted from or caused by a vehicle, machinery or equipment in a street;

(i) any other matter declared by any enactment to be a statutory nuisance;

Note that:

'Dust' does not include dust emitted from a chimney as an ingredient of smoke.

'Fumes' means any airborne solid matter smaller than dust.

'Gas' includes vapour and moisture precipitated from vapour.

'Noise' includes vibration.

'Premises' includes land and so would include a garden.

'Private dwelling' means any building, or part of a building, used or intended to be used, as a dwelling and would include a garden held with a dwelling.

6.31   It is the duty of every local authority to cause its area to be inspected from time to time to detect any statutory nuisances which ought to be dealt with and, where a complaint of a statutory nuisance is made to it by a person living within its area, to take such steps as are reasonably practicable to investigate the complaint. The local authority has a duty to serve an abatement notice in respect of any statutory nuisances found.[1]

---

1   *R v Carrick District Council, ex p Shelley* [1996] Env LR 273.

6.32 The above covers things used in a garden such as noisy tractors, motor mowers, hedge clippers, model aircraft, musical instruments, CDs, record players etc as well as barking dogs and crowing cocks. By s 81(3) 'equipment' which includes musical instruments, CD players, record players, can be seized without prior warning.

Noise and Statutory Nuisance Act 1993

6.33 Audible intruder (ie burglar) alarms which are left to ring are specifically covered by the Noise and Statutory Nuisance Act 1993, s 9 and are subject to criminal offence control procedures similar to those in the Environmental Protection Act 1990. There is a code applying to such alarms whereby the names of two keyholders must be notified and the names are retained at the police station. There are also codes concerning model aircraft noise, loudspeaker (eg ice cream) vans, and contractors' noise.

Other Acts

6.34 There are similar general powers in the Housing Act 1985 and in the Public Health Act 1936 as to nuisances, such as houses being unfit for habitation and overflowing and insanitary drains. Details are not set out here but the relevant Act should be referred to in appropriate circumstances.

Conviction and sentencing

6.35 Contravention of any of the above legislation will lead to a conviction by the magistrates' court with a fine on Scale 4 (up to £20,000). The fine can be repeated for each day that the offence continues. By the powers in the Powers of Criminal Courts Act 1976, s 35 the magistrates' court can order compensation for an individual complainant. Compensation orders will be made even in simple, straightforward cases and the magistrates are bound to make an order for costs to a successful complainant.[1]

1   *Davenport v Walsall Metropolitan Borough Council* [1996] Env LR 33.

Byelaws

6.36 Many local authorities have their own byelaws prohibiting nuisance such as noise, smells etc. In *Kruse v Johnston* [1898] 2 QB 91 a challenge to such a byelaw by judicial review failed. A garden owner should check with his local council as to any particular activity which may be caught. As stated, a fine would be imposed by the local magistrates' court on conviction for breach of a byelaw.

European Union law

6.37   Some acts of environmental pollution may be so grave as to be in contravention of the European Convention on Human Rights. So, in the case of *Lopez Ostra v Spain* (1995) 20 EHRR 277 the European Court of Human Rights held that Spain should compensate a home owner for unlicensed fumes and smells from a waste treatment plant.

Noise abatement zones

6.38   Under the Control of Pollution Act 1974, ss 63–67 and European Union legislation it is proposed that noise abatement zones should be established prohibiting noise above a certain level subject to criminal sanction. None has yet been established but if and when it does happen, their establishment will no doubt be announced in the press.

BONFIRES AND BARBECUES

6.39   The burning of leaves and garden refuse, particularly in the autumn, seems to be a natural use of the garden but if there are circumstances such as the small size of the garden or proximity to a neighbour's buildings, parked cars etc the land owner lighting the fire could be held to have reasonably foreseen the damage alleged to be caused by escaping sparks. Smoke from bonfires and from garden barbecues can adversely affect the amenity of a neighbour and there may be a liability for negligence, and if the smoke and cooking smells are frequent, nuisance.

6.40   By the Fires Prevention (Metropolis) Act 1774 (which applies throughout England and Wales despite its name), s 86 no action is to be maintained against any person 'on whose estate any fire shall accidentally begin' but this only applies to chance fires and not bonfires.[1] Under the Highways Act 1980, s 161A it is an offence to light a fire on land so smoke interferes with or injures or endangers a user of a highway. This applies to bonfires of leaves and dense smoke from barbecues as much as to stubble burning[2] which it was intended to cover. A garden owner on whose land an intruder starts a fire will be liable if he is negligent in not excluding such person.[3]

1   *Filliter v Phippard* (1847) 11 QB 347.
2   For stubble burning see also Environmental Protection Act 1990, s 152 and regulations under it.
3   *Smith v Littlewoods Organisation Ltd* [1987] AC 241, [1987] 1 All ER 710, HL.

Smells

6.41 With regard to smells, the test of locality referred to above may be relevant. Where a neighbour of a pig farm complained it might have been a factor in excusing nuisance that the area was an agricultural area, but this was held not to be decisive. Nor was it an excuse that planning permission had been granted for the pig farm.[1]

1   *Wheeler v JJ Saunders Ltd* [1996] Ch 19.

6.42 However, the issuing of smells such as from pig slurry,[1] chicken excreta and by-products[2] etc from a garden and cat excreta[3] will be both a private and statutory nuisance.

1   *Bone v Seale* [1975] 1 WLR 797 and *Milner v Spencer* (1976) 239 EG 573.
2   *Shoreham -by-Sea Council v Dolphin Canadian Proteins Ltd* (1972) 71 LGR 761.
3   *R v Walden-Jones, ex p Coton* [1963] Crim LR 839 (cats in bungalow; smell of excreta contrary to Public Health Act 1936, s 92(1)(b)).

6.43 The most likely offensive smell will be from a manure or compost heap and the garden owner should endeavour to contain this in a suitable receptacle and spread the contents as often as possible.

Occupiers with common title

6.44 There used to be a rule that where the plaintiff occupied the same property as the defendant under a common lease or they were landlord and tenant in a nuisance case no action could be brought,[1] but this seems now to be obsolete. In any event, it has no applicability to statutory nuisance, so a local authority can validly serve a noise abatement notice on its housing association tenant.[2]

1   *National Coal Board v Neath Borough Council* [1976] 2 All ER 478. See also *Toff v McDowell* (1993) 63 P & CR 535 (but the Crown, the landlord, was held not negligent also).
2   *Network Housing Association v Westminster City Council* (1994) 93 LGR 280. See also *Carr v Hackney London Borough Council* (1995) 93 LGR 606 (council obliged to tenants for statutory nuisance of damp and mould but not liable as the tenant failed to use the heaters provided).

NUISANCE DIARY

6.45 To prepare for a successful claim for nuisance a daily (and indeed nightly if the nuisance persists at night) diary should be kept with details of the incidents, a tape recording of any relevant noise and photographs taken with time and date of any relevant

visual evidence, eg fireworks, strobe lights etc. These can be referred to in an affidavit if private proceedings are taken, or passed to the Environmental Protection department of the local authority for action (in which case a receipt should be obtained).

1   For guidance on completion of nuisance diaries, see Appendix A.

INSECTS, PESTS, PLANT DISEASE, DAMP AND MOULD

6.46   The garden owner may be liable under the above categories of nuisance for negligence and even *Rylands v Fletcher* if he allows his garden to become a refuse tip or breeding ground for pests or plant disease which spreads to adjoining owners' property causing damage. For the statutory liability see **6.30** on the Environmental Protection Act 1990, s 79(1) items (a) 'premises' and (e) 'accumulation of deposits etc'. There are also specific statutory controls over pests, eg rats,[1] mice and rabbits[2] and insect and plant pests (eg Colorado beetle),[3] with criminal sanctions on garden owners who contravene. A manure heap on which flies breed,[4] or leaving loose grain encouraging rats may be acts of nuisance or negligence, but not if the pests move from the garden to the adjoining land where they cause damage naturally.[5]

1   Prevention of Damage by Pests Act 1949 (rats, mice, insects and mites).
2   Pests Act 1954 s 1 (rabbits).
3   Agriculture Act 1947, s 98 and orders made under it, and Plant Health Act 1967.
4   *Bland v Yates* (1914) 58 Sol Jo 612 (manure heap bred flies).
5   *Stearn v Prentice Bros Ltd* [1919] 1 KB 394 (but land owner not liable for rats as they were held to have moved on naturally).

Pesticides

6.47   The spraying of pesticides on the garden which by being projected or naturally spreading destroys an adjoining owner's plants will also be actionable as a nuisance. Certain pesticides are prohibited by statute and using them is a criminal offence.[1] Damage caused by their use by an adjoining garden owner may ground a claim for compensation. Pesticide containers must be labelled to indicate what they contain so a garden owner has notice of whether or not he is using a dangerous pesticide which might adversely affect his neighbour's garden.[2] Where a farmer continued to use pesticide which he had been warned was harmful to bees he was held liable for negligence and had to pay damages to local bee keepers.[3]

1   See Chapter 9.

2   Agriculture Act 1947 and Food and Environment Protection Act 1985, 16 and the Control of Pesticides Regulations 1986, SI 1986/1510 and EEC Directive 78/631 and Farm and Garden Chemicals Act 1967, s 1 (labelling of pesticides etc).[55]

3   *Tutton v AD Walter* [1986] 1 QB 61.

Weeds

6.48   With regard to the spreading of weeds, the famous case of *Giles v Walker*[1] decided that a land owner was under no liability to a neighbour for the natural spreading by wind of thistles, but nowadays the position is regulated by the Weeds Act 1959 which applies to gardens and it is a criminal offence to allow weeds to spread after notice.

1   *Giles v Walker* (1890) 24 QBD 66.

Damp

6.49   The spreading of damp or mould to another's property can also be a nuisance[1] although most of the cases relate to damp and mould spreading to and from buildings rather than gardens.

1   *Habinteg Housing Association v James* (1995) 27 HLR 299, CA (damage and mould: council liable).

BUILDING WORK

6.50   Noisy building work or excavation in the garden will be a nuisance, just as building work on a house or commercial building construction site will be, and the noise of heavy machinery such as pile drivers can be restrained by injunction and limited to daytime working hours, eg 8.30 am to 6.30 pm.[1] An adjoining owner who is suffering should first check that building control and (if necessary) planning permission have been given for the construction work, as if not the local authority may take action to stop it.[2]

1   *Andraeae v Selfridge & Co Ltd* [1938] Ch 1; *Matania v National Provincial Bank Ltd* and *Elevenist Syndicate Ltd* [1936] 2 All ER 633; *Lloyds Bank plc v Guardian Assurance* (1986) 35 BLR 34, CA (a case under the Control of Pollution Act 1974).

2   Building Regulations 1991, SI 1991/2768 (and later amendments). Building Act 1984, s 36.

6.51   Excavations in the garden near the boundary with a public highway or public footpath may be negligent if not properly fenced so that passers-by can fall in and suffer injury[1] (but not if the garden owner could not have done anything about the risk, eg a gap in railings about which he did not know).[2]

1   *Phipps v Rochester Corpn* [1955] 1 QB 450.

2   *Barker v Herbert* [1911] 2 KB 633 (child fell through railings: owner did not know of gap).

6.52   If the garden owner has taken reasonable steps in engaging an independent specialist contractor then it will be the contractor who is liable to the injured party and not the garden owner.[1]

1   *Salsbury v Woodland* [1970] 1 QB 324 (garden owner not liable for damage to car through a tree felling by his incompetent contractor); *Rowe v Herman and Others* (1997) 1 WLR 1390, CA (land owner not liable for contractors leaving hazard on highway after completion of work).

6.53   As to the garden owner's redress against an independent contractor or garden expert who incompetently installs eg a swimming pool or pond or does planting, pesticide spraying etc negligently, see Chapter 10.

WHAT ONE MAY AND MAY NOT DO IN ONE'S GARDEN

6.54   It has already been mentioned that it is illegal to grow cannabis and the dangers of infringing the law of nuisance and the legal position regarding games in the garden have also been covered. There are generally no other restrictions on the conduct or activities of the garden owner and his family in the garden. It would, however, be prudent not to sunbathe in the nude and to refrain from sexual acts or from the display of obscene advertisements there because these may:

(a) be contrary to local byelaws resulting in prosecution in the magistrates' courts and a fine; or

(b) amount to indecency—

   (i) Under the Indecent Displays (Control) Act 1981 (mainly for strip clubs and sex shops) the display of any such matter so as to be visible from a public place is a criminal offence.

   (ii) Under the Vagrancy Act 1824, s 4 lewdly and obscenely exposing one's person is a criminal offence.

The Criminal Justice Act 1982, s 70 applies a fine or probation order rather than imprisonment for the penalty.

6.55   Someone who incites persons to come into the garden for sex may be guilty of the criminal offences of:

(a) keeping a brothel; or

(b) permitting premises to be used for prostitution (Sexual Offences Act 1956, ss 33–35) and if a man, soliciting men (s 32).

In the North of England it was unheard of to sunbathe in one's garden (even partially clothed) well into the 1950s. What would the neighbours have said?

7

The use of the garden (2): by the family and others

USE BY THE FAMILY

7.1 The Royal Society for the Prevention of Accidents' latest report estimates that there are 350,000 garden accidents every year from being poisoned by plants, garden forks piercing feet, being maimed or electrocuted by grass cutters (25,000 accidents) hedge trimmers etc down to such matters as cricked backs and eyes injured by branches. So 'it's a jungle out there' (whether literally or not). The garden is a very dangerous place and the greatest care must be taken, particularly where children and old people are concerned. A garden owner should ensure that his household insurance policy includes garden accidents, that there is no particular liability limit and also that it covers death and injury to all family members as well as third parties. In our increasingly litigious age a family member, including one's children or resident elderly parents, may be advised to sue a garden owner for negligence and under the Occupiers' Liability Act 1957(see **7.4ff**), and what is said about use by non-family members below may apply in the case of injury to (or even, although one hopes that it will never happen, the death of) family members in one's garden.

USE BY OTHERS

Planning considerations

7.2 If the proposed use by others is to be of a different planning use to the current use of the garden and is to be permanent, then it may well require planning permission for change of use,[1] apart from any works which may require planning permission and byelaw consent (like engineering works or alterations). A temporary or incidental use within the garden or of the house with which the garden is held does not require permission, for example temporary parking of a caravan[2] where the caravan is not an independent dwelling unit with its own electricity etc. The development of a

garden, for example as a building plot, a caravan park, for a market garden or for use as a car park or regular use for car boot sales would require planning permission.[3] The first consideration where there is a proposed long term use by others is to check whether planning permission is necessary: see Chapter 11.

1   See the Town and Country Planning Act 1990, s 55(1), (3) (46 *Halsbury's Statutes* (4th edn) Town and Country Planning).

2   See [1975] JPL 55.

3   *Peake v Secretary of State for Wales* (1971) 22 P & CR 889.

Private use

7.3   Often persons other than the members of the garden owner's family may come into the garden, eg guests, the postman or milkman, delivering van men, the char, the gardener and innumerable others, who may visit by invitation, express or implied, or as part of their employment. The garden owner may also extend his hospitality by letting or licensing his garden for a fete, wedding or car boot sale, or allow visitors in under the National Gardens Scheme for charity, which might properly be called 'public' rather than 'private' use. The legal position of the garden owner in relation to these persons must be considered in detail.

The garden owner's liability to visitors

7.4   Under the Occupiers' Liability Act 1957 a garden owner has a duty of care to ensure that any visitor is reasonably safe for the purpose that he or she is invited or permitted to be in the gardens. Any garden owner inviting:

(a) his own guests who will be there gratuitously; or

(b) the public or a group of strangers (eg a local horticultural society, women's institute, political party or under the National Gardens Scheme) who may pay, if not the owner directly, then by making a payment to the organisation concerned,

is under this common duty to ensure the garden is reasonably safe for such persons.

7.5   Whether the fact of payment increases his duty or not is no longer meant to be important, but a judge might take it into account as increasing the garden owner's responsibility. Certainly invitation to the garden widens the duty of care. Therefore, the garden owner must ensure that the garden is made free of hazards such as slippery

paths, unfenced ponds and dangerous garden machinery. Any letter, agreement or other form of invitation fixing up the arrangements with the proposed visitors should make it clear that the garden owner does not accept any liability for any accident, injury or damage and that the visitors are there at their own risk and ask for an acknowledgement of this. A draft licence for access is included in Appendix A. Where the hazards are natural such as cliffs, waterfalls etc he must endeavour to warn his guests.[1]

1   But see *Cotton v Derbyshire Dales District Council* (1994) Times, 20 June (where it was held that the local council was not negligent in not putting up a notice at a beauty spot where cliffs created an obvious danger) and *Staples v West Dorset District Council* (1995) 93 LGR 536 (council did not have to put notice warning users of The Cobb (a harbour wall) that it might be slippery or dangerous from seaweed).

7.6   Where there is a swimming pool this is a hazard,[1] particularly for young children, and the garden owner would be well advised to attempt to protect his interest by putting up a warning notice. A warning notice must be direct about the risk, eg it is better to put up a notice saying 'No diving' than one saying '2.6 metres' (of water).

1   *Davies v Tenby Corpn* [1974] 2 Lloyd's Rep 469; *O'Shea v Royal Borough of Kingston upon Thames* [1995] PIQR P208, CA.

7.7   'Occupiers' under the Act have been held liable for dangers such as slippery paths,[1] lack of hand rails on steep steps and dog leads,[2] and the garden owner should be aware of the risks which he must eliminate.

1   *Bradford Metropolitan Borough Council v Murphy* [1992] PIQR P68 (slippery path with no hand rail).

2   *Carroll v Garford* (1968) 112 Sol Jo 948 (a pub case: customer tripped over dog lead).

7.8   Where the weather has brought frost or snow the garden owner must take action, eg sanding or salting steps and paths within his premises to make them reasonably safe.[1] Where a house adjoins a street, it used to be the convention, at least in the North East of England, that the house owner cleared the path in front of his house. With the duty to clear snow from public highways now put on the local authority,[2] this custom is no longer observed and, indeed, the poor house owner might expose himself to a claim for negligence if he left a slippery patch resulting in injury. The old service motto

'Never volunteer' now applies. He should still clear snow off his roof as soon as possible, however, as he might be liable to passers-by if it fell on the public highway, and the longer it is left a danger the more likely he is to be liable.[3]

1   *Wood v Morland & Co Ltd* (1971) 115 Sol Jo 569 (hotel guest slipped on snow—not liable as reasonable precautions taken).

2   Highways Act 1980, s 150.

3   *Slater v Worthington's Cash Stores 1930 Ltd* [1941] 1 KB 488 (where five day old snow fell off shop roof, owner held liable to injured passer-by).

7.9   The common duty of care under the Occupiers Liability Act 1957 only applies to invited visitors. With regard to uninvited visitors such as delivering postmen, canvassers etc the Occupiers Liability Act 1984 applies a lesser standard of care, only to warn of dangers. Again, this can be done by notice: see Appendix A for an example of a notice.

7.10   It should be noted that the exclusion in the initial letter confirming the arrangements, notices and other written attempts at exclusion of liability of the garden owner under the 1957 and 1984 Acts and for negligence generally which operate by including a term in an express or implied contract between the garden owner and the visitor are now to be considered by the courts in the context of the Unfair Contract Terms Act 1977.

7.11   If the garden owner is a 'business occupier' the Unfair Contract Terms Act 1977 provides that in so far as they relate to death or bodily injury such notices and disclaimers are ineffective, although they may operate to exclude other types of liability, eg damage to clothing, provided that they are reasonable. Is the garden owner who opens his garden to the public a 'business occupier'? In most cases 'no', but some owners of landed estates may be exceptions. As to market gardeners and farmers, the Occupiers Liability Act 1984 provides that a land owner who carries on business may allow persons on his land for educational and recreational purposes without it being a business liability.

7.12   Under the Disability Discrimination Act 1995 the garden owner who invites the public generally has a duty to disabled visitors, and ramps, wide gates and accesses etc may have to be installed and physical features removed or altered so that the 'service' of the garden can be provided for them without discrimination, on penalty of civil proceedings.[1]

1   Disability Discrimination Act 1995, ss 19, 21 and 25.

7.13   Where the garden owner deals with consumers in a business relationship the Supply of Goods and Services Act 1982 (as to which see Chapter 9) may also apply to visiting members of the public.

7.14   A garden owner allowing visitors in under the National Parks and Access to the Countryside Act 1949 (note that this is *not* the same as the National Gardens Scheme) is allowed to exclude liability under the 1957 Act, and so only the 1984 Act will apply.

Children

7.15   Where the visitor is a child the duty of care is higher. The Occupiers Liability Act 1957, s 2(3) provides that when assessing the common duty of care, an occupier must be prepared for children to be less careful than adults.

7.16   A child who is not an invited visitor, ie a trespasser, will be liable to proceedings by the owner as if of full age but of course the courts are unlikely to grant damages etc against a child. However, the parent of a trespassing child may be held liable in negligence where he or she has failed to exercise control over the child after warning. Where a child is invited, eg to a children's firework party, it should be made clear that the parent accompanying him or her is to be in charge of the child. A specimen invitation is included in Appendix A. Where the garden owner has something in the garden that is attractive to children, 'an allurement', as the court cases[1] call it, then the garden owner is more likely to be held negligent and liable for injury to the child. So a land owner was held liable where he left an unfenced climbable tree near an electricity cable.[2] So too where the land owner failed to fence a grass slope with broken bottles at the bottom he was liable for injury to a four year old.[3] A pond is not an allurement but it is thought that a swimming pool would be. What is said above about warning notices for swimming pools would not, of course, be relevant to children below reading age and a garden swimming pool should never be allowed to be used by young children without adult supervision. An attractive looking poisonous plant may be an allurement for young children and the land owner was held liable where a child died from eating its berries.[4]

1   *Phipps v Rochester Corpn* [1955] 1 QB 450.
2   *Buckland v Guildford Gas Light and Coke Co* [1949] 1 KB 410.
3   *Williams v Cardiff Corpn* [1950] 1 All ER 250, CA.
4   *Hastie v Edinburgh Magistrates* 1907 SC 1102.

7.17 It will therefore be seen that a children's party with games in the garden such as a 'bouncy castle' is a risky operation and a children's firework party even more so. Indeed, with fireworks it is assumed that non-negligent management of the fireworks will not result in anyone being injured, and injury of a guest[1] (and in particular a child) has the effect of reversing the onus of proof, which is usually on the plaintiff, so that the host must excuse the act causing the injury.

1   *Whitby v CT Brock & Co* (1888) 4 TLR 241, CA; *Glasgow Corpn v Taylor* [1922] 1 AC 44.

7.18 A garden owner should not give a young children's firework party in his garden without:

(a) making it clear in the invitation that parents are invited and are to be responsible for their child; and

(b) having checked that his insurance policy covers damage and injury by fireworks to third parties.

Also preferably, although this may seem officious, the invitation or notice on the door should try and exclude liability (see the example given in Appendix A) but this will be construed subject to the Unfair Contract Terms Act as mentioned in **7.10**.

7.19 If reasonable precautions, for example cordoning off the area where the fireworks are let off and putting young children in the charge of adults, are taken then liability in the event of injury or damage to property may be avoided.[1]

1   *Horsenail v Kennedy* (1988) Times, 30 April (where a 'jumping jack' escaped into house causing fire it was held that all reasonable precautions had been taken: not negligent).

7.20 The Explosives Act 1875[1] and the Highways Act 1980[2] prohibits the setting off of fireworks in a public place or within 50 feet of a public highway (including footpaths), respectively.

1   Explosives Act 1875, s 80.
2   Highways Act 1980, s 161(2) inserted by the Highways (Amendment) Act 1986, s 1(2).

7.21 The letting off of fireworks will be a private nuisance even though the display only lasts 20 minutes.[1]

1   *Crown Rover Cruises Ltd v Kimbolton Fireworks Ltd and London Fire and Civil Defence Authority* [1996] 2 Lloyd's Rep R 533 (fireworks in barge a legal nuisance).

Letting or licensing others to use the garden

7.22   A garden owner may wish to allow a neighbour or unconnected person or company to use his garden for a particular function for a particular period, eg fete, wedding, car boot sale.   As has already been mentioned the first consideration is to check whether planning permission is necessary. If the property is leasehold, landlord's consent may be required and must be sought and obtained well before the event. If consent is not required, then the terms of the arrangement should be agreed and clearly documented. This may seem superfluous where members of the family or neighbours are involved but there have been numerous troublesome and expensive law suits which have happened just because someone thought 'just this once ...' he could rely on a 'gentleman's agreement'. In one case known to the writer the 'gentleman' concerned went off on his honeymoon leaving his host with the washing up and drinks bill for the wedding reception and the lavatories to clean up and was never seen again.

7.23   Included in Appendix A is a form of letter adaptable for most types of function. It is in everyone's best interests that a letter of this type should be written and acknowledged well before the occasion. The nearer the event, the more likely it is to be overlooked.

Lease or licence?

7.24   For the reasons which will be apparent from Chapter 1 only a licence (*not* a lease capable of passing on to successors) should be entered into, even if the event for which the garden is to be used is to be a regular one, eg car boot sale every last Sunday in the month.

Insurance

7.25   It is vital that the activity licensed should be covered by insurance and the draft letter provides for either:

(a) the garden owner to take out extra insurance and the licensee to pay the additional premium; or

(b) the licensee to take out insurance and pay for it and to produce to the garden owner a copy of the policy.

The former is preferable in that the garden owner will be in control of claims and will receive the policy money in the event of a claim.

7.26   If the garden is held under the terms of a lease or is subject to a mortgage whereby the landlord or mortgagee insures or which prescribes the detail of the insurance, eg that it is to be in the joint

names of the mortgagee and mortgagor, or of the landlord and the tenant only, special application should be made to the landlord or mortgagee so that any additional insurance is not in breach of covenant.

Income, capital gains and value added tax

7.27 The garden owner should be reminded that by taking money for licensing his garden for use in accordance with the terms of the draft letter in Appendix A he may be letting himself in for adverse tax consequences which he has not taken into account. If the garden owner is considered to be carrying on a trade or business any profit will be taxed for income tax purposes under Sch D of the Income and Corporation Taxes Act 1988. Alternatively, income from regular licensing of use of the garden may be a receipt 'by virtue of ownership of a right or interest held in land' and be taxable under Sch A.

7.28 A single capital payment would not be taxable as income tax under either Sch D or Sch A but may give rise to a capital gain. In most cases the garden will be part of the garden owner's 'only or main residence' and so should be exempt (see Chapter 20) but commercial use may deprive him of this exemption.

7.29 Also, if the payment is in respect of 'the grant of an interest or right over land', although residential land is exempt there may be circumstances where value added tax is payable on the amount payable under the licence. For this reason, a clause stating that any payment is deemed to be net of value added tax and that the licensee must pay the amount of this should be included in any agreement or letter.

ANIMALS IN THE GARDEN

7.30 The position as to animals being a legal nuisance (eg barking dogs and smelly pigs) has already been dealt with in Chapter 6, but in view of the large number of disputes which come to court involving domestic animals it is pertinent to consider the legal position regarding:

(a) keeping animals in the garden;

(b) escape of animals from the garden;

(c) injury to visitors (and animals) by animals in or from the garden;

(d) wild animals and birds which visit the garden.

Keeping animals in the garden

7.31 If the animals are to be kept for breeding or commercial sale then planning permission for this use may be required. Conditions

attached to such a permission would be as to the provision of suitable stables, kennels etc and the arrangements as to keeping down smells, noise and the like.

7.32   The keeping of certain wild animals, which includes reptiles such as crocodiles and insects such as tarantulas, is covered by the Dangerous Wild Animals Act 1976 and their keepers must be registered with the local authority who will grant or refuse a licence to keep them prescribing things such as the cage or other place where they are to be kept, restraint, arrangements for feeding, and failure to comply is a criminal offence.

7.33   Other wild animals may be kept in a garden, but at the owner's risk, under the other legislation dealt with below.

Escape of animals from the garden

7.34   As we have noted, there is a duty to fence a garden so as to prevent animals straying on the highway or on to the land of others. Where escaping 'livestock' do damage then the garden owner who has failed to fence or who has otherwise been negligent in keeping them will be liable for damages and may be obliged by injunction to put up fences or restrain them.[1] So a land owner who allowed diseased sheep to escape was liable to neighbouring owners whose flocks were affected.[2]

1   Animals Act 1971, ss 2, 4 and 8(2) (straying on highway). See also Chapter 5.
2   *Theyer v Purnell (or Parnell)* [1918] 2 KB 333.

7.35   It should be noted that although there is no definition of 'animals' in the Act, straying 'livestock' for which there may be liability includes cattle, horses, sheep, asses, mules, hinnies, pigs, goats and deer (not wild deer) and while in captivity, pheasants, partridges, peacocks etc. The normal rules of negligence apply so a land owner was held not liable for pheasants which trespassed on an adjoining owner's land as he could not be held, by preserving a large number of pheasants for shooting, to have reasonably intended to cause damage to an adjoining owner's land.[1]

1   *Farrer v Nelson* (1885) 15 QBD 258.

7.36   The obligation to fence, again, is subject to the normal rules of negligence as to reasonableness so where a fence is strong enough in normal circumstances liability will be avoided.[1]

1   *Cooper v Railway Executive Southern Region* [1953] 1 All ER 477.

7.37 Where animals stray on to common land, this is excused under the Act (while the animals are on common land but not if they go outside it) where the owner of the animals has a commoner's right to graze.

7.38 There are statutory controls of movement over animals with rabies, foot and mouth disease and BSE[1] etc.

1 Animal Health Act 1981 and orders made under it.

7.39 Animals which stray can be detained by the land owner until the cost of damage by them is paid.[1] Cats are naturally nomadic and there is no liability for straying cats.[2] Nor can they be detained under s 7.

1 Animals Act 1971, s 7.
2 *Buckle v Holmes* [1926] 2 KB 125, CA (cat owner held not liable for cat eating next door's pigeons).

Injury to visitors and animals by animals in or from the garden

7.40 The Animals Act and other legislation lay down certain rules as to liability in negligence for an injury or damage by:

(a) wild animals;

(b) other animals; and

(c) dogs.

7.41 The Animals Act 1971 places liability on 'the keeper' of the animal. This can be the garden owner or another person having charge of the animal, eg the owner of the animal, if he or she is not the garden owner.

7.42 For both escape of animals and damage or injury caused by them the owner of a garden with such animals in it would be well advised to put up a notice attempting to restrict his liability: see Appendix A.

Wild animals

7.43 If animals are of a 'dangerous species'—see the definition in the Act (which includes lions, monkeys, and elephants)—then the keeper is strictly liable for all damage traced to the animal. As to native British wild animals and birds, which are generally not of a 'dangerous species' (except possibly wild cats), see **7.50ff**.

Other animals (including dogs)

7.44   The keeper will only be strictly liable as above in the case of ordinary domestic animals such as horses and dogs:

(a) if the damage was of a kind that the animal was likely to cause or if caused was likely to be severe;

(b) this likelihood may be due to abnormal characteristics found in that animal or found at particular times or circumstances (eg bitches with puppies); and

(c) the keeper or person having charge of the animal (even if that person was under the age of 16) knew this.

This is the origin of the old saw, 'every dog has one bite'. Until the savage characteristic is known then the keeper is not liable for damage by the animal. Cats are not in this category of animals so cats can have more than one bite or scratch (but the owner may be liable for negligence under the general law).

Dogs

7.45   Dogs, although they are man's best friend, have especially restrictive legislation applying to them (or rather to their owners).

(a) The keeper of a dog is strictly liable if the dog kills or injures livestock (regardless of the rules in **7.44** (b) above) except:

    (i) if the damage is due to the person suffering it (eg provoking the dog);

    (ii) if the dog belongs to the garden owner or was authorised by him to be there on the garden owner's land (so the livestock were trespassing);

    (iii) where the injured party was contributorily negligent (eg again, by provoking the dog).

    It will be seen that (ii) is particularly likely to apply in gardens.

(b) By the Guard Dogs Act 1975 guard dogs must not be allowed to roam not under control on commercial premises but they can in a garden to protect a dwellinghouse.

(c) By the Dogs (Protection of Livestock) Act 1953 the owner of a dog attacking livestock is guilty of a criminal offence.

(d) By the Dangerous Dogs Act 1871 dangerous dogs must be kept under control and muzzled, and by the 'Baker' Dangerous Dogs Acts of 1989 and 1991 certain breeds such as pit bull terriers can only be kept or sold subject to strict police control and are not allowed in a public place (such a dog in a private car is in a public place)[1] and can be seized and destroyed but a dog on a garden path within a private garden

is not in a public place and cannot be the subject of prosecution.[2]

(e) By the Dogs Act 1906 the police can seize a dog and destroy it (having given seven days' notice to the owner whose name is on the collar) and the local authority can now round up and destroy stray dogs under the Highways Act 1980, s 189.

(f) By the Animals Act 1971, s 9 a dog worrying livestock on agricultural land (the definition of which also includes market gardens, allotments, nursery grounds and orchards but does not include domestic gardens) can be killed provided the killer:

   (i) is acting to protecting livestock; and

   (ii) is entitled to act (eg is the land owner or a gamekeeper); and

   (iii) tells the police within 48 hours.

If a garden comes within one of the above categories the garden owner could shoot a dog for attacking his cat or chickens in his garden, but would be well advised not to do so. Rather, he should try to restrain it (eg by a net or noose, failing which, a rake or hoe) rather than shooting it, as apart from the query over the definition of 'garden', other questions (eg has the owner a licence for firearms?) may arise. One cannot shoot a cat or animal other than a dog for worrying livestock and rely on this provision for defence. This is a digression from 'Gardens and the Law', but as many disputes concerning animals begin and end in a garden, it may be of some relevance.

1   *Bates* v *DPP* (1993) 157 JP 1004 (pit bull dog in car parked in street).
2   *Fellowes* v *DPP* (1993) 157 JP 936 (dog on garden path).

Bulls

7.46   A bull may not be kept in a field through which a public footpath passes unless it is with cows and heifers (except certain breeds of cattle) or under 30 months old.[1] This is separate from the land owner's civil liability to any one injured by the bull under normal occupancy liability/negligence law as above.

1   Wildlife and Countryside Act 1981, s 59.

Hunting

7.47   Hounds (and the hunters or their horses) can only come into or cross a garden with the owner's consent.[1] Tenants should be aware that their landlord may have reserved a right for hunting over the garden. Hounds straying into the garden are the same as

any other dog under the above rules. The Master of Foxhounds is their 'keeper' and could be sued but apparently will only be liable if negligent in failing to exercise a general control over the whole pack.[2]

1   *Paul v Summerhayes* (1878) 4 QBD 9, CA.
2   *League against Cruel Sports Ltd v Scott* [1986] QB 240.

7.48   Although in an old case the keeping of an anti-dog trap in a garden[1] was held to be lawful and in another killing a trespassing dog by poisoned meat was in order,[2] these actions would not be allowed today as against the Cruelty to Animals legislation. See also **7.50ff**.

1   *Deane v Clayton* (1817) 7 Taunt 489.
2   *Daniel v Janes* (1877) 2 CPD 351.

7.49   With regard to the escape of animals from places other than the garden or in transit, the usual rules of negligence apply. So if the 'Tamworth Two' pigs which escaped from the abattoir in 1997 (headline news in *The Sun*!) had damaged property or injured anyone the abattoir owner or transport company which allowed the escape might have been liable under the duty of care owed to the public to keep the animals safely. There are also special EU rules for the transport of animals and so the private purchaser of eg a Vietnamese pot bellied pig may have to engage and pay expensively for specialist transport to take the pig home to the garden.[1]

1   Animal Health Act 1981, ss 8 and 37; Transit of Animals (General) Order 1973, SI 1973/1377 and SI 1988/815; Movement of Animals (Restrictions) Order 1990, SI 1990/760, SI 1991/1155, SI 1991/1251.

Wild animals and birds which visit the garden

7.50   The garden owner has no right of property in a wild animal or bird which comes into his garden. If he tames it then he will have a limited ownership in it determinable when it leaves his land to roam free again. Where wild animals or birds are born or hatch on his land then he has a right in them until they leave his land, at least, to the extent that he may sue poachers for trespass. So too he may kill and hunt and capture wild animals which stray into his garden, subject to the law as stated below. Bees belong to the owner of the land on which they hive. If they swarm and go to another hive then the original hive owner loses property in them and has no redress. For the liability of a landowner for killing bees by pesticide see **6.47**.[1]

1   *Rowley v Murphy* [1964] 2 QB 43; *Karry v Pattinson* [1939] 1 KB 471.

7.51 The Bees Act 1980 relates to bee keepers and applies criminal sanctions to the spread of plant diseases by bees.

7.52 We are lucky in Britain to have a delightful variety of native animals and birds. However, many garden owners may find foxes, moles, pigeons, jays etc a nuisance in the non-legal sense which may interfere with their planting, growing and keeping of domestic animals. A brief summary of the law of what may and may not be done to deter them and how the garden owner may co-operate in protecting them is set out below.

Wild birds

7.53 Under the Wildlife and Countryside Act 1981 it is a criminal offence to kill or injure any wild bird as defined by the Act, or to destroy the nest or take eggs of any such bird. It is also an offence to have a live or dead wild bird or its eggs in one's possession or control. Certain rare species must not be intentionally disturbed on the nest. There are further restrictions on advertising and selling live birds and eggs with further exceptions for cage birds, eg linnets.[1]

1   Game Act 1831.

Wild animals

7.54 Similarly, parallel criminal offences are prescribed in respect of killing, injuring or having possession of certain wild animals and insects such as martins, otters, rare moths etc.

Game and pests

7.55 Another part of the 1981 Act and the Game Acts[1] make it lawful to shoot game birds such as pheasants, grouse, ptarmigan within particular dates ('the season') each year. There is a further exemption for 'authorised persons', which will include the garden owner and his gardener, to shoot or destroy the nests of certain birds which are regarded as pests such as crows, pigeons etc. There are other exceptions for both wild animals and birds under the Agriculture Act 1947 where the killing etc is to prevent animal or plant disease or is the result of an otherwise lawful operation and could not reasonably have been avoided (eg removing a hedgerow and accidentally destroying a protected bird's nest) and for 'mercy killing' a wounded bird not likely to recover.

1   Game Act 1831; Ground Game Act 1881.

British wild animals

7.56   In addition to the Wildlife and Countryside Act 1981 there is specific legislation protecting the following:

Bats   These are dealt with in s 10 and Sch 5 of the Act. Garden owners must not disturb any building or place with roosting bats, however, this does not apply within a dwellinghouse. As to outbuildings in the garden, English Nature (formerly the Countryside Council) should be notified and will advise, and consulting them will be a defence if the owner is summonsed by the Magistrates Court.

7.57   Badgers   The Badgers Acts 1973 and 1991 make it a criminal offence to wilfully kill, injure or take any badger or attempt to do so. Digging for a badger is also prohibited, but there are exceptions for fox hunters allow them to temporarily block the entrances to setts.[1]

1   See *Lovett v Bussey* (1998) 162 JP 423 (but only with loose, not compacted, soil).

7.58   Deer   By the Deer Acts of 1963 and 1991 it is a criminal offence to take or wilfully kill deer of the four British species except during a prescribed season. This applies to deer which stray into a garden but there is an exception so that 'an authorised person', eg a garden owner may take or kill a deer (although not at night) if it is on cultivated land, ie in his garden and is causing damage to crops, vegetables, timber etc if the action is necessary to prevent more serious damage.

7.59   Traps and poisons   Setting dangerous traps for humans is a criminal offence.[1] Neither birds nor animals are allowed to be killed or taken by self locking snares which are 'of such a nature and are so placed as to be calculated to cause bodily injury to any wild animal coming into contact with them'. Other methods, ie instant snares and poison etc are also prohibited for certain species[2]. Deliberate ill treatment of any animal or bird is a criminal offence.[3]

1   Offences against the Person Act 1861, s 31.

2   Animals (Cruel Poisons) Act 1962 and Regulations 1963/1278; Small Ground Vermin Traps Order 1958, SI 1958/24; Spring Traps Approval Order 1975, SI 1975/1647.

3   Protection of Animals Act 1911.

8

Employing a gardener

8.1 Next to the 'char' (and possibly nowadays the au pair), the gardener is probably the most numerous of domestic employees in the UK. Part-time gardeners are the norm and no garden owner should engage a local old age pensioner or his neighbour's green-fingered young son or daughter on a paying basis without considering UK employment law, most of which applies as much to the gardener doing 12 hours per week as to the managing director of ICI.

ADVERTISING FOR AND INTERVIEWING A GARDENER

8.2 Advertising in a local newspaper or by card in a newsagent's shop can be a successful way of obtaining a gardener. The classified advertising department of the local newspaper will quote rates which are binding if accepted, and similarly an advertiser is bound to pay the shopkeeper per number of weekly or monthly periods of display. There is no entitlement to a refund if no suitable applicant presents him or herself.

8.3 The wording in advertisements must not discriminate against potential applicants on grounds of colour, national origin, sex or sexual orientation (eg married or not) and to do so is a criminal offence. Nor can a garden owner employer discriminate on these grounds in or after interviewing the prospective gardener, in making his choice of applicant. If suspected of doing so, the employer could be reported by an unsuccessful candidate for the criminal offence and he could also sue for compensation.[1]

1   Race Relations Act 1976, s 29; Sex Discrimination Act 1975, s 38.

References

8.4 Before engaging a gardener written references from a previous employer or other person with personal knowledge of the potential employee should be requested by the prospective employer. Similarly, a garden owner may be asked for a written reference by a gardener he has previously employed. There is, however, no obligation on the garden owner employer to give a reference.

8.5 Such references should usually qualified by words such as: 'This reference is given in confidence and without personal responsibility'. References given for an ex-gardener most certainly should be qualified in this way. This means that if the employee proves to be dishonest, a shirker or otherwise not in accordance with what has been written then the person giving the reference cannot be sued for breach of contract or negligence. Where references are not qualified it may be possible (but rare) for the employer to be able to sue the reference giver for damages,[1] for example, if the gardener was a known thief and absconded with the family silver on his first day.

1   *Spring v Guardian Assurance plc* [1994] ICR 596.

8.6 A former employee may also be able to sue the employer for the civil wrong of libel or slander should a reference defame the gardener, but only if it is done maliciously, as otherwise the 'old employer–new potential employer' relationship is subject to legal privilege which gives immunity.

Spent convictions

8.7 The Rehabilitation of Offenders Act 1974 provides that once a conviction has become 'spent' (eg prison sentence served) failure to disclose a conviction is not a ground for excluding any person from employment. An offender who conceals his conviction cannot be sacked once it is discovered by the employer, but he cannot sue the (prospective) employer for not giving him or renewing the job.

CONTRACT OF EMPLOYMENT

8.8 All employees have a contract of employment, even if it is only an oral one, but it is better for the garden owner and gardener that the contract is in writing. If someone is employed for more than one month, the employer must write to them within two months of the start of the employment stating the main terms.[1]

1   Employment Protection (Consolidation) Act 1978, s 3 as amended by the Trade Union Reform and Employment Rights Act 1993, Sch 4 and the Employment Rights Act 1996.

8.9 These are the basic details which must be stated:

(a) the employee's name and job title;

(b) the date on which the employment started;

(c) rates of pay, working hours and details of holiday entitlement;

(d) period of notice for determining the employment;

(e) place of work;

(f) disciplinary procedure (what the employer must do prior to sacking the employee, written warnings etc).

Any change in these terms has to be notified to the employee within one month.[1] These requirements need not be complied with if the period of employment is less than eight hours weekly. It is nevertheless suggested that even a gardener working less than eight hours a week should have a letter of employment: a specimen letter is set out in Appendix A.

1   Employment Protection (Consolidation) Act 1978, s 4(1).

Employer's liability insurance

8.10   The garden owner employer must have insurance against accident covering death or injury of the employee even if he or she is the only employee (but not if it is a close relative). Insurance arrangements must be in place before the gardener starts work (it may be possible to arrange a package with occupiers' liability insurance). A certificate of insurance should strictly be displayed at the place of work (the garden shed?) and can be inspected by the local authority.[1]

1   Employers' Liability (Compulsory Insurance) Act 1969.

Health and safety issues

8.11   A gardener is just as entitled as any other industrial employee to the benefit of the duty owed by his employer in negligence under the civil law (eg for injury through dangers on the premises) and by statute to a safe system of work, safe equipment and reasonably competent fellow employees. These statutory rights, which are embodied in the Health and Safety at Work etc Act 1974 and orders made under it, are contained in detailed EC and UK delegated legislation with effect from 1 January 1993.

Management of Health and Safety Regulations 1992

8.12   These regulations (SI 1992/2051) impose a general statutory duty to provide a safe system of work, safe equipment and safe fellow employees. There is no separate civil liability (see reg 15) but there is such a liability under the following more detailed regulations.

Workplace (Health, Safety and Welfare) Regulations 1992

8.13   The employer must train and instruct his gardener as to the use of, eg motor mowers, hedge clippers etc and provide toilet and washing facilities.

Provision and Use of Work Equipment Regulations 1992

8.14   These regulations are concerned with provision of safe equipment and material and protection from injury. Expressly scheduled are garden tools etc which will need to be checked and maintained with proper protective features, eg tractors, power handsaws and lawnmowers. There will therefore be a duty on the employer, eg to provide a guard to a chain saw and protective gloves for handling irritant plants. There is also a general duty to provide information, instruction, training and supervision over the gardener for all such equipment.

Personal Protective Equipment at Work Regulations 1992

8.15   There is a duty to provide protective equipment, eg respiratory mask for spraying, lawn mowing etc, ear protectors and goggles for chainsaw operators and 'hard hats' for tree fellers. Wellington boots must be provided for working in a wet environment and warm clothing in excessively low temperatures.

Manual Handling Operations Regulations 1992

8.16   There is a duty to provide machinery and to stop employees lifting heavy loads, eg in tree felling, moving paving stones etc.

Sanctions for breach

8.17   Most of the above give rise to a criminal offence if the employer is in breach. The local authority enforces the law and can send inspectors who have rights of entry into the employer's garden at all times. In most cases there is also a separate civil liability to the employee, ie the injured gardener. The duties under **8.12** and **8.13** apply to temporary employees as well as to permanent ones.

8.18   The garden owner employer will also be liable under the Employers' Liability (Defective Equipment) Act 1969 for injury through defective equipment, as well as under the regulations which provide for civil liability.

8.19   The garden owner employer may also be separately liable to the gardener employee at common law:

(a) under a breach of the implied terms in the contract of employment; and/or

(b) for negligence.

For example, an employer will be liable to his gardener in damages for the result of any failure in his duty to warn the gardener of

hazards (eg exposed cables, land slips) or defective equipment (eg loose headed hoes) which might cause him injury. *Knowles v Liverpool City Council* [1973] IRLR 6, CA provides an example of civil liability for breach of regulations—the Corporation was held liable to a gardener who slipped on a flagstone which was held to be 'material' and thus 'equipment' under the legislation, which was unsafe. Damages were awarded against the Corporation.

8.20 If the garden owner is engaged in agricultural or horticultural business, eg market garden or nursery, the following Acts and Regulations impose further duties on him:

(a) Agriculture (Avoidance of Accidents to Children) Regulations 1958, SI 1958/366;

(b) Agriculture (Circular Saw) Regulations 1959, SI 1959/427;

(c) Agriculture (Safety, Health and Welfare Provisions) Act 1956;

(d) Agriculture (Ladders) Regulations 1957, SI 1957/1389;

(e) Agriculture (Safeguarding of Workplaces) Regulations 1959, SI 1959/428; and

(f) Agriculture (Poisonous Substances) Act 1952 (Repeals and Modification) Regulations 1975, SI 1975/45.

These regulations apply to seed nurseries, hospital grounds and gardens around offices, factories etc.

Ladders

8.21 Garden owners should particularly note the standards for ladders: they must be of good construction, of sound material and properly maintained.

Electrical hedge cutters, mowers and fences etc

8.22 Under the Electrical Equipment (Safety) Regulations 1994, SI 1994/3260, electrical equipment such as hedge clippers, lawn mowers, trimmers, electric fences etc must be safe and constructed in accordance with good electrical engineering practice so as not to endanger persons, domestic animals and property, and it is a criminal offence to be in breach. All such equipment must be earthed and have cut out devices.

Lawn mowers

8.23 In addition to the employee safety and electrical safety duties above, lawn mowers are subject to detailed control as to noise under EU regulations which apply a criminal sanction against breach: see

6.18. There is a prohibition against selling, displaying for sale or storing any mower which does not comply.

General warning

8.24 The garden owner must therefore check the garden itself for hazards (eg wires and cables), and all garden tools and equipment provided. He should keep a log book about servicing mowers, chainsaws etc and provide his staff with the latest user guides.

8.25 He should also take out an employers' liability insurance policy (this can be done in conjunction with a general occupiers' and third party liability cover) which should indemnify him against damages, for any breach of the above Health and Safety regulations, breach of contract and negligence and legal costs arising in this regard, and keep this up to date. Unfortunately, it is not possible to insure against the cost of fines for breach of the legislation.

PAY

8.26 By the Equal Pay Act 1970 (as amended) men and women must get the same rate of pay. At the moment there is no minimum wage but the new Labour government and European Union are about to change this, so the position may have altered since this book went to press.

Tax and national insurance

8.27 The employer is responsible for deducting tax and national insurance payments from the gardener's pay, and for accounting to the authorities for these deductions and the employer's own national insurance contribution. The employer must also provide the gardener with a pay slip showing these deductions, as well as a running total from 6 April to the following 5 April (the tax year). However, the above does not apply to persons earning less than £64 per week, which will include many part-time gardeners. If the gardener is self-employed, it is understood that only he is liable for (reduced) national insurance payments.

Statutory sick pay

8.28 Any employed gardener is entitled to receive statutory sick pay from his employer under the Social Security and Housing Benefits Act 1982. At present, the employer will be able to recover the amount paid from the Department of Social Security

(assuming that tax and national insurance have been fully paid up), however this right to recover is shortly to be stopped. When the employee has been off sick for three days after presentation of a doctor's certificate or other prescribed notification, the Act provides for:

(a) up to a maximum (currently) of £55.70 per week;

(b) up to 28 weeks' pay maximum;

(c) payment in four-day units (the first three days of any month being disregarded).

Statutory maternity pay

8.29 A female gardener is entitled to statutory maternity pay by the Social Security Contributions and Benefits Act 1992, Pt XII. She is entitled to receive up to 18 weeks' pay if she:

(a) has worked at least 26 weeks by the end of the fourteenth week before her expected week of confinement;

(b) is not being paid less than currently £64 per week;

(c) is not being confined 11 weeks before her expected date of confinement; and

(d) gives the appropriate notice to her employer.

Only six weeks at 90% pay with a maximum of £55.70 a week is recoverable.

MATERNITY LEAVE

8.30 However short a time a female gardener is employed she will also be entitled to a minimum of 14 weeks' maternity leave. If she has worked for the employer for six months she can claim 18 weeks' maternity leave (up to forty weeks' unpaid leave can be claimed depending on length of employment). When she returns to work she is entitled to be employed on the same terms and conditions as before she went off to have the baby.

YOUNG GARDENERS

8.31 There are special provisions both as to hours of work and health and safety for young persons employed in a garden. As to the hours of work EEC Directive 94/33 provides (shortly to become UK law) that persons aged 15 to 18 must only work 14 hours in 24

and must have a break every 4½ hours in 30 hours. Those under 15 are only allowed to work two hours in a school day for 12 hours a week and seven hours a day, 35 hours a week in school holidays and must have at least 2½ weeks off work in that school holiday. As to health and safety, they must have special instruction and are not to be exposed to harmful, physical, biological or chemical conditions or agents.

DETERMINING THE EMPLOYMENT OF A GARDENER

8.32 One of the items which must be specified in the contract of employment or note of it required by the Employment Protection (Consolidation) Act is a 'disciplinary procedure'. This is because although an anti-social act such as theft or assault on the employer, drunkenness, swearing[1] (but not a single occasion of swearing),[2] or a serious breach of safety or security will enable an employer to sack the employee forthwith, in most cases the courts will hold that a breach must be specified in writing and required to be remedied before the final step is taken. In the draft letter in Appendix A it is contemplated that one written warning at least will be given before the gardener is given notice. A form of notice to determine the employment is also given in Appendix A.

1   *Pepper v Webb* [1969] 2 All ER 216 (generally insolent and inefficient gardener could be sacked for swearing).

2   *Wilson v Racher* [1974] 1 ICR 429 (gardener using obscene language on solitary occasion could not be given notice).

Notice

8.33 A statutory minimum period of notice must be given if the gardener has been employed for four weeks or more. The minimum notice periods are:

(a) less than two years employed—one week's notice;

(b) 2–12 years' employment—one week's notice for each year;

(c) 12 years or more—12 weeks' notice.[1]

1   Employment Protection (Consolidation) Act 1978, s 49.

Unfair dismissal

8.34 If the gardener is dismissed without the minimum notice for anything other than major misconduct (see **8.32**) then he may have a claim for breach of contract for unfair dismissal. Such a claim would be heard by the local Employment Tribunal

(formerly known as the Industrial Tribunal). Damages (which are separate from the statutory damages for redundancy) will be the amount of wages for the period during which a lawful notice would have been worked (less any moneys which have or could have been earned elsewhere). A deduction in respect of income tax and national insurance should be made from damages for loss of earnings.[1]

1   *British Transport Commission v Gourley* [1956] AC 185 (but not applicable over £30,000).

8.35 An employee is entitled to be provided with a written statement as to the reasons for dismissal within 14 days of request. Any claim for payment arising from a contract of employment or unfair dismissal may be challenged in an Employment Tribunal,[1] but not claims for 'tied cottages', as to which see **8.48ff**. The Employment Tribunal can order reinstatement of the employee or compensation. Claims to it must usually be made within three months of notice.[2]

1   Employment Protection (Consolidation) Act 1978, s 53.
2   Employment Rights Act 1996.

Redundancy payments

8.36 These are rare in the case of gardeners as most redundancy payments arise from the cessation of a particular business (eg by takeover), but where the gardener is laid off or put on short time (because eg he is one of two and only one is now required) he may be able to claim a statutory redundancy payment under the Employment Protection (Consolidation) Act 1978, ss 81–88. The employee must:

(a) have been employed for at least two years;

(b) not be of retiring age (usually 60 for women and 65 for men);

(c) work 'normal' working hours as provided in the Act.

The entitlement is for each year of employment:

(a) at age 41 up to 65—1½ weeks' pay;

(b) over 22 but under 45—one week's pay;

(c) over 18 to 22—half a week's pay.

The maximum payment under the Act is for 20 years' work or £210 per week. Claims are considered by the Employment Tribunal (see **8.34**) but must be referred within six months.

8.37   Employment Tribunals have no power to order payment of an unsuccessful party's costs except where the proceedings are frivolous, vexatious, abusive or disruptive, and so the employer and sacked gardener will each have to pick up their own legal bills.

INSOLVENCY OF GARDEN OWNER

8.38   Where the garden owner goes bankrupt or is a company which goes into liquidation a gardener's wages would be included in the four months' salaries up to £800 plus holiday pay[1] which have has priority over other debts and can be paid from the National Insurance Fund. If an administrative receiver is appointed or the company goes into receivership,[2] the receiver has a period of 14 days during which he has to adopt the contract of employment or not and, if not, then the gardener would have no claim.[3]

1   Employment Protection (Consolidation) Act 1978, Pt VII.
2   Insolvency Act 1986, s 44(1), Sch 6.
3   Insolvency Act 1994 applying after 15 March 1994, ss 19(5) and 44(2).

8.39   Where there is a transfer of a company's general business, the Transfer of Undertakings (Protection of Employment) Regulations 1981 may apply to bring about a transfer of the gardener's employment to the new owner.

DEATH OF EMPLOYER OR GARDENER

8.40   Even if it is not stated in the employment contract, the death of the garden owner or of the gardener will determine the contract. If the gardener is re-employed by the garden owner's personal representatives or widow(er), any period of employment will be counted towards the minimum periods for maternity and redundancy payments above.

FRUSTRATION

8.41   The garden owner moving house or selling off the garden or the gardener being called up for military service or prolonged illness will be considered to be frustration—an intervening act by which a personal contract of this nature is put to an end—and the employment will end without outstanding liabilities (except back pay, tax etc up to date). The sending to prison of either party may also put an end to the employment.

8.42 If the garden owner sells his house and garden, then he should give proper written notice determining the contract to expire on or before the date of completion of the sale. It may be that sale of his house is a frustrating event, but it is likely that the courts would regard it as self induced and hold the employer liable to the gardener for damages for breach of contract etc if the circumstances justify this. The new owner can then make a fresh contract of employment with the gardener or not as he wishes. A claim for redundancy should not arise if the matter is dealt with in this way.

OTHER THAN FULL-TIME GARDENERS

Casual labour

8.43 Employing a jobbing gardener or workman to assist temporarily to carry out tasks in the garden should be simpler than under the above rules but, sadly, this is not necessarily so, and the above employment legislation (and proposed minimum wage legislation) is likely to apply.

Jobbing gardener

8.44 A gardener who works for a number of garden owners may be self employed, rather than an employee (as can a gardener who works for only one person, if he so chooses). In such case the individual garden owners will not be liable to pay national insurance or to deduct PAYE income tax from pay.

Part-time and casual gardeners

8.45 Where the gardener earns less than (currently) £64 per week there is no need to make any national insurance contribution. A person can work up to 16 hours a week (or 24 hours a week to include a partner's, eg wife or husband's hours) and can earn £5 a week (£10 a week with partner) without losing his or her right to jobseeker's allowance (formerly 'unemployment benefit'). An old age pensioner can work for pay of up to (currently) £12 per week in occasional employment without moneys being deducted from his or her pension. The statutory 'unfair dismissal' law does not apply to workers working less than 16 hours per week.

MANAGEMENT AGREEMENTS

8.46 Arrangements are often made by the National Trust and owners of private estates to license a management company to

maintain part of the gardens of a large house and allow access to the public. A short form is given in Appendix A. The arrangements for maintenance and collection of payment from visitors are included in the agreement, but attention is drawn to possible adverse tax consequences to the garden owner and the management company, both of whom may be liable for VAT and income tax. Such agreements should not be used without detailed advice being taken as to the need for planning permission, occupiers' liability and as to the tax consequences before the agreements are signed.

GARDENERS WORKING FOR NOTHING

8.47   The employment law detailed above does not apply where a person voluntarily does work in the garden for, eg a neighbour, but note what is said above about the garden owner's liability to warn of dangers etc. under the Occupiers' Liability Act 1984. From the gardener's point of view, note also the recent case of *Taylor v Dickens* [1998] 1 FLR 806 where a person worked as gardener in expectation that the garden owner would leave him the house in her will. It was held that there was no written agreement or estoppel not in writing which entitled the gardener to any interest and the house owner's will leaving the property elsewhere was perfectly valid. The moral of the story behind the case is self evident.

SERVICE OCCUPANCIES AND 'TIED COTTAGES'

8.48   Sometimes the gardener (and spouse) may be given living accommodation as part of the job. It is important to consider whether:

(a) the gardener (and spouse) is (are) being let a house for a term at a separate rent, in which case he is (or they are) a tenant(s). The landlord should grant him (or them) an Assured Shorthold Tenancy under the Housing Acts 1988 and 1996 with a minimal security of tenure; or

(b) the gardener (and spouse) is (are) to occupy the property as part of the terms of the contract of employment and no separate rent figure is mentioned. In this case he/they hold under a service occupancy.

8.49   If the gardener has exclusive possession of the house and there is a notional rent attributable and there are other features of a tenancy (eg liability for council tax, repairs etc) then he (and any

spouse) may be a tenant and the Housing Acts will apply. If the garden owner is carrying on the business of agriculture his employee (or the widow or widower) may be entitled to an Assured Agricultural Occupancy under the Housing Act 1988, s 24, in which case vacant possession can only be obtained after six months' notice on specified grounds (including use by another agricultural worker when local authority re-housing can be provided).

8.50 If the owner is not carrying on the business of agriculture it may be that the tenancy has become protected or is or will become an assured tenancy under the Rent or the Housing Acts. If so, there are specific grounds for getting out a service tenant, but only after court proceedings in which the ground relied on must be pleaded.

8.51 It is much better from the garden owner's point of view if the occupation by the gardener (and spouse) is by way of licence under the contract of employment only, in which case notice of dismissal will also determine the right to occupy the house and no further notice will be required.[1]

1   *Norris v Checksfield* [1991] 4 All ER 327.

8.52 If the occupants refuse to leave county court proceedings will have to be taken to evict them. At least one month's notice must be given to any lawful residential occupier and his or her rights can only be determined by a court order.[1]

1   Protection from Eviction Act 1977, s 3 (court order) and s 7 (notice).

9

Buying things for the garden

9.1 With regard to all purchases of seeds, bulbs, plants, pesticides, plant foods, fertilisers, equipment and other goods for use in the garden, the garden owner has the protection of the general law of contract, ie he can sue the seller, and, in some cases, the producer/manufacturer of such items for breach of condition, warranty and misrepresentation. In the case of a breach of condition he can reject what he has purchased and get his money back. In cases where he is dealing with a business supplier he may have further remedies as a consumer and be protected by the criminal law in respect of goods of a false trade description or which fail to conform to statutory standards.

GENERAL

9.2 In respect of all such goods, the garden owner must have a contract with the seller under which he can sue (and as mentioned above he may also have redress by statute or in negligence against the producer or supplier). The contract for sale or hiring, eg of garden machinery:

(a) may be written or oral; but

(b) will have a buyer and a seller; and

(c) must be for the sale and purchase of goods for a price or hire for a hire payment ('the consideration').

So where the garden owner enters into informal arrangements (eg exchange with a neighbour or loan of hedge clippers) where there is no consideration, these are likely to be free of any legal consequences and, if, for example, he is electrocuted his widow cannot sue the neighbour unless he has been negligent in not warning of a defect. Assuming that the basic element of a contract for the sale or hire of goods exists then the garden owner as a buyer will have the following rights:

9.3 In all contracts there are terms of the contract which may be:

(a) conditions; or

(b) warranties.

Conditions are terms which are so fundamental that the buyer can rescind (ie withdraw from) the contract and require return of the price. He may also sue for damages for any loss he has incurred. If the broken term is not fundamental and the contract is substantially performed (eg by delivery of 60% of seeds by a due date), then the breach may be of a warranty and the buyer must accept performance but he may have a claim in damages for a part refund of the price.

9.4 Conditions and warranties can be expressly stated in the contract (eg delivery by a particular date, time being of the essence, or a requirement as to the type and number of seeds, plants etc or a lawn mower of suitable size to mow a large lawn), and if so the contract should say what is to happen if there is a breach and state the facts such as time for delivery, quality of items, etc grounding the right to rescind or amount to be deducted from the price as the case may be. Many contracts will state certain warranties or 'guarantees' (eg no failure of working parts within three years) and these are legally binding. These terms and 'guarantees' may be in small print on the back of an order form.

SALE OF GOODS ACT 1979

Implied terms

9.5 Even if the parties do not provide them the Sale of Goods Act 1979 provides implied terms for contracts for the sale of goods. In some cases these will apply even though the contract purports to exclude them. Also, and this is widely misunderstood by many laymen, the implied warranties will *apply in addition to* any express warranty (usually called 'a guarantee') in the written contract. Implied terms in a contract for sale of goods are as follows:

Section 12

9.6 A condition as to the seller's title—so if he does not own the item purported to be sold, for example if it is subject to a hire purchase agreement, or it infringes a trademark, the buyer can sue. As in the following cases, this can be treated as a warranty in that the buyer may choose to accept the item and sue for damages.

Section 13

9.7 A condition that the goods will correspond with the description under which they are bought (eg 'sunflower seeds' must not be aster seeds, a six metre trellis must not be three metres high). Here again,

the goods can usually be rejected unless the buyer elects to accept them.

Section 13(2)

9.8   Sales by sample often happen, for example, in sales of seeds or bulbs. In a sale by sample, s 13(2) provides that the goods supplied must correspond with the sample and also with the description. Section 15 also states that the bulk must correspond with the sample, that the buyer will be able to inspect, and that the bulk will be free of defects not appearing from the sample. So in the sale of 'foreign refined rape oil warranted only equal to sample' which was not rape oil (as the sample) but instead was hemp oil, it was held that the buyer could reject the supply and sue for damages.[1]

1   *Nichol v Godts* (1854) 10 Exch 191.

Section 14(1)

9.9   Where the seller sells goods in the course of business there is a condition that the goods are of satisfactory quality except:

(a) as regards defects specifically drawn to the buyer's attention before sale; or

(b) if the buyer examines the goods, as regards defects that examination should have revealed.

Note that this relates only to sales 'in course of business', so will apply in a sale of plants, equipment etc by a shop or garden centre but *not* from another garden owner.

9.10   'Satisfactory quality' means capable of resale *even if* the resale could be for another purpose, so in *Henry Kendall & Sons (a firm) v William Lillico & Sons Ltd* [1969] 2 AC 31 ground nut extract bought for cattle and poultry food, which was poisonous to poultry, could be resold for cattle food and could not be rejected (although the buyer could get damages for breach of warranty as he had wanted it for poultry). (Although *Kendall* was on the former 'merchantable quality' term, the case remains relevant.)

Section 14(3)

9.11   Where the seller sells goods in course of a business and the buyer makes it known to the seller (or the seller's credit broker where, eg, the price is payable by instalments) that there is a particular purpose for which the goods are bought, then there is an implied condition that the goods are reasonably fit for that purpose (except in certain circumstances, eg the buyer did not rely on or it was unreasonable for him to have relied on the seller's skill and judgment).

9.12   So, for example, if a customer asks at a garden centre for a plant suitable for a shady patch or for an outdoor plant and an unsuitable indoor plant is sold then the implied condition will have been breached and the customer can repudiate the sale and take the plant back and get a refund.

Consumer Sales: Unfair Contract Terms Act 1977

9.13   In the case of consumer sales, ie where the seller deals in the course of business with a 'lay' customer for private use and consumption then the Unfair Contract Terms Act 1977 applies. The Act provides that a term of the contract attempting to exclude any of the seller's conditions and warranties as above is ineffectual except insofar as such condition is reasonable.

9.14   The Act also applies to sales between non-consumers in which certain factors (eg economic bargaining position of the parties, custom of trade etc) are taken into account.

What is reasonable?

9.15   The conditions may include limits on time for complaint, limitation of damages etc. Examples are:

RW Green Ltd v Cade Bros Farms Ltd:[1] a time limit missed for making a complaint about seed potatoes was held to be unreasonable but a clause limiting damages to repayment of the price was held reasonable.

George Mitchell (Chesterhall) Ltd v Finney Lock Seeds Ltd:[1] where 30lbs of late Dutch cabbage seed had been specified but white cabbage seed was supplied, the House of Lords held that a clause negotiated by a trade association for the seed trade limiting damages (claimed at £61,000 plus interest) to the price of new seeds (£201) was reasonable in view of the acceptability to parties in the seed trade and the availability of indemnity insurance.

1   *RW Green Ltd v Cade Bros Farms Ltd* [1978] 1 Lloyd's Rep 602.

2   *George Mitchell (Chesterhall) Ltd v Finney Lock Seeds Ltd* [1983] 2 AC 803.

Consumer Protection Act 1987

9.16   The Consumer Protection Act 1987 may apply. This makes the producer/manufacturer of any goods (excluding game and agricultural produce unless it has undergone an industrial process (see Chapter 13)) liable to the consumer who suffers loss or injury from any product for damages. It covers the position, for example,

where a defective garden tool has caused injury, or fertiliser has caused a skin infection. In such case, both the garden shop selling the product and the manufacturer may be sued.

Trade Description Act 1968, s 1 and Fair Trading Act 1973

9.17   The Trade Description Act 1968, s 1 and Fair Trading Act 1973 may entitle a garden owner to report a seller or supplier to the local authority for criminal prosecution in the magistrates' court and a fine and to sue for damages or give other rights as follows.

9.18   Where a person sells or offers for sale goods under a false description then he is guilty of a criminal offence. The matter should be reported to the local authority Trading Standards or Fair Trading Department who may prosecute, leading to a fine if conviction follows. The false description can be given orally. The disappointed buyer may have his own civil remedy for misrepresentation: see **9.19**. The Weights and Measures Act 1985 also makes it a criminal offence to sell a lesser quantity than that contracted for.

Misrepresentation

9.19   Although in most cases of purchases which go wrong the Sale of Goods Act or other warranties will provide redress, it may be that the seller or his advertising material has induced the purchaser to enter into a contract which she or he would not have done had the facts about the product been accurately stated or not falsely put over. Under the Misrepresentation Act 1967, s 2(1) the courts can grant damages for negligent misrepresentation as well as ordering rescission of the contract in appropriate cases. So, if a plant is advertised or represented as 'quick growing' or 'frost resistant' or seeds are sold as 'Sutton seeds' and are not, the garden owner may be able to take action for misrepresentation.

SEEDS AND PLANTS

9.20   In addition to the general sale of goods rights outlined above, there is further legislation which may assist the garden owner who buys seeds and plants:

The Plant Varieties Act 1997 and the Seeds (Registration, Licensing and Enforcement) Regulations 1985

9.21   The Seeds (Registration Licensing and Enforcement) Regulations 1985, and other Orders made under earlier legislation,

provide for the Ministry of Agriculture, Fisheries and Food (MAFF) to keep a register of seed merchants and set up seed testing stations at which all seeds are to be tested by sample. After the testing a 'statutory statement' as to the type of seed, growing potential, other varieties accidentally included by percentage generated etc, is to be displayed on all seeds and packages for sale. But note that the Plant Varieties Act 1997 is intended mainly for the protection of the arable farmer and although sales of packeted seeds for garden centres are covered, small seed sales and sales of unpacketed seeds are exempted.

The Agriculture and Horticulture Act 1964, s 11

9.22 This provides for the grading and marketing of certain agricultural and horticultural produce and it may be that the vegetables such as seed potatoes bought in bulk would have to be labelled, graded and packed as prescribed by the Act, the sanction being criminal proceedings.

The Weights and Measures Act 1985

9.23 The Weights and Measures Act 1985, mentioned above, provides that sale by weight or size must be accurate.

The Endangered Species (Import and Export) Act 1976

9.24 It should also be noted that buying rare seeds or endangered plant varieties or importing them from abroad (outside the EU) is prohibited and a criminal offence under the Endangered Species (Import and Export) Act 1976, details of which are set out in Appendix B.

TIME LIMITS

9.25 By the Limitation Act 1980, legal proceedings on any contractual term must be brought within six years of the right of action accruing. This will be either the date of the contract or of the first opportunity of examining the goods supplied. If the contract is 'under seal,' ie in a deed (which is unlikely), then the period is twelve years. It is important to act quickly in taking legal advice and if necessary issuing a writ before the end of the six year period. Where personal injury is involved the period is reduced to three years from the date upon which the right of action accrued, ie the date upon which the accident causing the injury happened or the identification of the injury. It is also important in the short term to notify the buyer or complain to

the local authority promptly. Failure to do so in the former case may mean that the court may presume that the buyer has accepted the goods and waived his right to rescind or to claim damages.[1]

1   See Sale of Goods Act 1979, s 11(1)(c) as to the buyer not being able to reject the goods where he has accepted them and s 35 as to when acceptance is deemed to happen, eg the buyer keeping the goods for more than a reasonable time.

Pesticides, plant foods and fertilisers

9.26   There are a number of widely drawn provisions in statutes and subsidiary regulations controlling the sale, display for sale, supply, storage and use of garden chemicals, biological products and fertilisers. Some paints and wood preservative liquids are also dangerous and subject to restrictions. The garden owner will be concerned to know that these provisions, which are for his protection, are complied with. In some cases, however, the garden owner may be purveying such items (eg fertiliser) to his neighbour and in some cases gardeners may have formed a club to buy chemicals etc in bulk and will then pass them on to the individual garden owners. In the latter case the organiser may have to comply with the legislation as to storage, labelling etc. Such items should be kept secure, eg in a locking garden shed, as the garden owner may be liable himself (and to others) if the substances are negligently stored allowing free use.

What may not be used in the garden

9.27   Under the following legislation (see **9.28** and **9.29**) certain chemicals used for pest control, such as DDT are banned, and all have to be packaged, stored and labelled with details of the chemical or biological preparation and a 'statutory statement' giving directions as to use, eg 'Use on gardens only' or 'Irritant' etc.

Farm and Garden Chemicals Regulations 1971

9.28   These regulations (SI 1971/729) make it a criminal offence to sell, offer for sale etc for use in the garden for controlling the growth of plants or destroying weeds any product not registered with the MAFF and properly labelled. Such products must be sent for testing. Eighteen days are required for analysis and a further 18 days for sample testing. After that the type, nomenclature etc will be prescribed and it is an offence not to use this on the label. Samples must be sent to the defendant in any legal action for enforcement seven days before any hearing, and must be produced at the hearing.

Food and Environment Protection Act 1985

9.29 Section 16 makes it an offence to sell, offer for sale, supply, use or advertise any pesticide (except eg for export, in skin preparations for the tropics, swimming pool cleaners etc) which has not been tested and labelled etc under a similar procedure to that mentioned in **9.28**. The local authority is responsible for enforcement and its inspectors have power of entry into garden sheds to see if there are non-complying products and to prosecute if so.

9.30 The prohibited pesticides are those prescribed under the current subsidiary legislation:

(a) Control of Pesticides Regulations 1986, SI 1986/1510;

(b) Plant Protection Products (Basic Conditions) Regulations 1997, SI 1997/189; and

(c) Control of Pesticides (Amendment) Regulations 1997, SI 1997/188.

Fertilisers

9.31 Under the Agriculture Act 1970, Pt IV and the Fertilisers Regulations 1991, SI 1991/2197, Fertilisers (Amendment) Regulations 1997, SI 1997/1540, and the Fertilisers (Sampling and Analysis) Regulations 1996, SI 1996/1342, SI 1990/887 and there are MAFF testing and 'statutory statement' requirements for fertilisers similar to those for pesticides. It is a criminal offence under ss 80–82 (for which there is a maximum £2,000 fine or three months in prison) to sell, supply etc non-complying, unmarked or adulterated fertilisers. Buyers requiring fertilisers to be tested must do so within six months of delivery or supply of the statutory statement, whichever is the later.

EQUIPMENT

9.32 The warranties provided by the Sale of Goods Act 1979 and other legislation will apply to garden tools, ladders, hedge clippers etc and if the equipment is electrical.

9.33 Many garden owners who refer to this section of the book first may find it disappointing not to have the detail of what the courts will and will not regard as a breach of a term of a contract but the general contract cases[1] as to car sales and machinery, etc provide a useful parallel. It is likely that the following will all be in breach of condition, enabling the items to be taken back and the price refunded:

(a) a garden fork which breaks after three weeks;

(b) a motor mower which repeatedly fails to start;

(c) a ladder with loose rungs or a bracket which can easily entrap fingers; and

(d) a chain saw with no guard or a missing saw tooth.

If injury or loss has resulted from any of the above the seller/ manufacturer will be liable for damages under the Sale of Goods Act and (if it applies) the Consumer Protection Act 1987. Also under the Consumer Credit Act 1974 where the goods have been purchased by use of a credit card, the credit card company or 'credit broker' will be treated as the seller and will be liable.

1   Eg *Bernstein v Pamson Motors (Golders Green) Ltd* [1987] 2 All ER 220; *Laurelgates v Lombard North Central Ltd* [1983] 133 NLJ 720 (cars); *Lexmead (Basingstoke) Ltd v Lewis* [1982] AC 225 (trailer coupling); *Varley v Whipp* [1900] 1 QB 513 (reaping machinery).

9.34   If the place of business of the seller or person advertising unsatisfactory goods is a shop or garden centre the local Trading Standards Officer should be complained to as the shop may have a bad record. If it does, this may help a case against them.

RETENTION OF TITLE CLAUSES

9.35   In connection with buying seeds, plants, pesticides, plant food, fertilisers, equipment etc the garden owner may come across a retention of title or *Romalpa*[1] clause. As mentioned in Chapter 13, if he is going into the business of selling garden plants or produce etc he may want to use one himself. Such a clause is usually found in the sale order form or on a notice in the garden centre/shop to this effect:

> 'The ownership in all goods (to be) delivered will only be transferred to the purchaser when he has met all sums that are due to (the supplier).'

The usual contractual situation is that the purchaser takes title to the goods *when* the contract is made in the shop (or on the telephone followed by delivery or by mail order) and pays after he has the goods. The normal rule means that if the buyer goes bankrupt without paying, the seller/supplier may lose his money. If a retention of title clause applies by being incorporated into the contract, the usual contractual situation does not apply: the title to the goods is

reserved until payment and the seller can trace the goods or money deriving from them by:

(a) re-taking the goods (and in this respect there may be a right of entry onto the garden owner's property in the clause); and/or

(b) going against any sub-buyer or separate account which the buyer may have with regard to the goods.

1   Named after the *Romalpa* case: *Aluminium Industrie Vaassen BV v Romalpa Aluminium Ltd* [1976] 2 All ER 552.

9.36   Where the goods have been mixed with other goods or turned into a different product, eg seeds sown in a lawn, (a) (in **9.35** above) may not be possible: see *Borden (UK) Ltd v Scottish Timber Products Ltd* [1979] 3 All ER 961 where an unpaid seller of resin was not allowed to trace the proceeds of sale of products made from it.

9.37   The retention of title clause was intended for large commercial contracts but can also apply to simple garden purchases. The legal position may run into complications where the (putative) buyer is a company, as it may create a charge over the assets of the company which would need to be registered at the Companies Registry to be valid.[1] But, without going into such complications, if a purchaser contracts subject to such a clause he may find that if he does not pay or pays late for garden goods, the seller may retake the goods or sue the persons to whom the purchaser has passed on the goods or the purchaser's bank.

1   *Re Bond Worth Ltd* [1980] Ch 228.

Hire

9.38   In the Consumer Credit Act 1974 and the Supply of Goods and Services Act 1982, there are implied conditions and warranties and provisions disallowing exclusion clauses in respect of hire purchase and hired goods which roughly correspond with those referred to above with regard to sales. It is not proposed to go into the position in detail, but similar warranties as to the items hired being of satisfactory quality and free of defects are given in respect of equipment, plant etc and other goods hired in the course of business by the Supply of Goods and Services Act 1982, s 9 as amended by the Sale and Supply of Goods Act 1994, s 7 and Sch 2 and 3. See also the *British Crane Hire* case in **10.5**.

10

Experts in the garden

SPECIALIST WORK IN THE GARDEN

10.1 Where a garden owner seeks the specialist services of an architect, professional landscape gardener or local expert from the garden centre, he is entitled to rely on the terms of any contract he has with the expert. The contract may include an express or implied term that the expert holds himself out as exercising a particular specialist skill and judgment in matters in respect of which he purveys services—the garden owner can sue for breach of these terms and, alternatively, for negligence in respect of loss or damage suffered by any lack of skill or incompetent act or omission.

EXPERT'S DUTIES

10.2 For example, if an architect is engaged to put in a swimming pool or garden feature, or a garden contractor employed to re-turf a lawn or put up a greenhouse or install heating there, then there are implied conditions and/or warranties:

(a) that he is not infringing any copyright in the plans he is using;

(b) that he will inspect the site and carry out such investigation that needs to be done as to stability, contamination, etc;

(c) that any architect's designs and the execution of the contract will be done in a good and workmanlike manner and with sound materials;

(d) that he will perform the contract within any agreed timetable and cost limit and will warn if any agreed cost limit is about to be exceeded;

(e) that if an architect he will issue his certificate for payment of contractors with skill and judgment;

(f) to make good any default in defective design or workmanship within a period as agreed or a reasonable period;

(g) that the architect will (possibly for a further payment) issue or assign such guarantees to a purchaser or mortgagee.

10.3 Builders, drainage engineers and other specialists, eg pond or tree felling experts are all taken to offer similar skills and

warranties. Often the JCT (Joint ConstructionTrade) standard form of contract used in the building trade, which has more detailed versions of the terms and warranties etc above, is signed between the parties.

10.4 So, in *Ruxley Electronics and Construction Ltd v Forsyth* [1996] AC 344 where a contractor installed a swimming pool six feet nine inches deep where one of seven feet six inches had been prescribed, the garden owner could sue the builder and was awarded damages of:

(a) £2,500 for the loss of amenity,

(b) £1,500 for inconvenience, but

not £21,561 being the cost of installing a new seven feet six inches deep pool. The difference in value between his house and garden with a seven feet six inches deep pool and of it with a six foot nine inches deep pool was held to be *nil*. Although this case is a House of Lords case, the decision seems to be at fault in not taking into account the fact that a seven feet six inches deep swimming pool can be used for adults diving and gives a greater value to the house and garden than only a six foot nine inches deep pool but that was the valuation evidence. Also, their Lordships seemed overly concerned about the garden owner getting double value, ie he already had a six foot nine inches deep swimming pool *and* if awarded £21,561 he might not use this to rebuild the pool. It is an accepted position that a plaintiff does not have to apply damages won towards 'making good'.

10.5 The garden owner will therefore be able to sue:

(a) a pond expert for wrongly installing a filter pump resulting in the death of his koi;

(b) a garden centre which has sent an expert to implement a planting scheme for the garden which wholly fails;

(c) a specialist tree feller who fells trees so as to obstruct the highway next to the garden resulting in local authority action;

(d) a hired driver of garden machinery, eg a JCB, who damages his flower beds or wall;

but a written contract with the service provider may attempt to exclude liability. However, the Unfair Contract Terms Act 1977 and the Supply of Goods and Services Act 1982 apply and such exclusion is only allowed insofar as this is reasonable. In a case where a land owner hired a crane which got bogged down in marshy ground because the driver refused to obey orders, it was held that

the hirer's exclusion clause was reasonable and applied to exclude damages for the days the crane could not be used.[1]

1   *British Crane Hire Corpn Ltd v Ipswich Plant Hire Ltd* [1975] QB 303.

10.6   Where the contract has involved physical damage resulting from work in the garden, damages are limited to *direct physical injury* and its consequences, not financial loss.[1]

1   *Murphy v Brentwood District Council* [1991] 1 AC 398.

Garden owner's duties

10.7   The garden owner's duties, in contrast, are only to give clear instructions, to allow access and to pay the agreed price as contracted. Thus when ordering services in such circumstances, the garden owner should write to the specialist detailing exactly what he is are asking for, eg 'landscaping of 1.25 hectares at the west end of the garden, with suitable plants for shade or spring display' or 'a pond of 80 gallons complete with filter for koi'. A timetable should be given and payment details should be specified (the number of instalments and when payable). Also, a warranty that they will remedy all unsatisfactory work within three months of completion of the contract should be requested.

10.8   Where the expert is to obtain planning permission and building regulation or other consents, this should be stated, also saying whether the expense is to be included in the price.

10.9   In all cases the contract should also specify a 'longstop' date by which if the works are not finished or planning permission not obtained (or from the contractor's point of view the instalments of price are not paid) the contract can be ended.

Taking action and settling claims against experts

10.10   The Limitation Act 1980 will apply and so legal action must be taken within six years of the act in breach of contract otherwise the courts will consider it out of time. However, some architects' and professional warranties are given by deed and where this is the case the period within which action can be taken is 12 years.

10.11   A Joint Contract Trades ('JCT') contract and often other written contracts will provide for any dispute to be referred to an architect or surveyor acting either as arbitrator or expert with power to determine the matter. The Arbitration Acts 1947–1996 lay down

the detailed procedure for an arbitration, ie the submission of evidence, timing etc and the contract should say who pays his fees and who pays for the whole exercise (often it is 'as the arbitrator/ expert shall decide').

10.12 Although this procedure should be simpler and less expensive than a High Court action, such dispute determination can be almost as expensive and it may be better to settle or at least to limit the cost in dispute by agreement to an amount which is justiciable by the County Court (under £25,000 for money claims and £50,000 for personal injury claims).[1]

1   High Court and County Courts Jurisdiction Order 1991, SI 1991/724, arts 5 and 7(3) .

10.13 A decision of an arbitrator can only be challenged in the courts if there has been some fundamental legal defect in his hearing the case, eg only taking one side's evidence, or misconduct.

11

Restrictions on garden use and building: (1) planning

11.1 After disputes with neighbours the next most likely legal problem driving garden owners to take legal advice and legal advisers to law books like this one is the planning legislation and its applicability to their gardens.

11.2 The current planning system in England and Wales has been with us since 1947 and has developed an ever increasing control over the activities of most average householders and garden owners. Parliament has given the main responsibility for planning legislation and its enforcement to the local authorities and thus the garden owner should contact his local planning authority and seek advice and co-operation from them concerning any problem as to his own garden or a neighbour's.

11.3 The purpose of the planning system is to protect amenity and the environment in the public interest. It is not meant to persecute or to pander to the interests of a particular garden owner. Too often householders come to the local planning authority expecting them to support their own proposal or reject that of their neighbour (NIMBY—'not in my back yard'—being a widespread British disease). But the local planning authority is there to police a highly complicated system for the general public good, not to help or hinder the individuals under their sway and should be indifferent, ie neutral, to all parties.

11.4 Unfortunately, 'indifference' has a pejorative meaning as well and the planning system at worst can lead to the kind of bureaucratic absurdities behind such recent press headlines as:

'Garden created from dump must be ploughed up' *The Times* 12 December 1997; and

'Nature lover fined for pruning tree' *The Times* 30 December 1997.

Is planning permission required?

11.5 Planning permission is required for 'development'. This can be either:

(a) putting up a new building or alterations to an existing one and other works; or

(b) change of the planning use (a technical term under the Act), for example, from garden to housing building plot, agricultural land to garden, garden to caravan park or car park etc (hence the 'Garden created from dump must be ploughed up' headline).

11.6 Many alterations and changes of use are permitted under subsidiary legislation under the Planning Acts, namely the Town and Country (General Permitted Development) Order 1995 ('GDO') and the Town and Country Planning (Use Classes) Order 1987 ('UCO'). These concessions for 'permitted development' are suspended in areas which are regarded as having a particular amenity such as:

(a) conservation areas;

(b) areas of outstanding natural beauty (AONB);

(c) national parks; and

(d) The Norfolk and Suffolk Broads.

(All of these will be referred to as 'conservation, etc areas' below.) Garden owners in any conservation area, national park or the Norfolk and Suffolk Broads may have to seek permission for matters permitted by the GDO or UCO elsewhere.

11.7 If development takes place without the consent of the planning authority where it is required (and this may mean consent to things which are permitted in other areas) then the garden owner can be the subject of an enforcement notice from the planning authority requiring information or ordering him to desist from building or using his garden for a particular activity ('a stop notice'). Failure to comply with an enforcement notice within the period prescribed in it (or with a stop notice within 28 days of service), will lead to criminal prosecution and a fine, and the planning authority can obtain a court order to remove offending work or for reinstatement and their legal costs.

Appeals

11.8 The garden owner can appeal as can anyone 'aggrieved by' a refusal of planning permission (note: it is not possible to appeal

against the *grant* of a permission) to the Secretary of State (in practice this will be a professional planning inspector) and the case may be heard at a public enquiry or can be dealt with by correspondence.

11.9   Certain important applications or appeals can be 'called in' to the Secretary of State for a public enquiry. No appeal will lie from the decision of the Secretary of State (in practice, his inspector) except where there has been an error of law, in which case application can be made to the High Court for judicial review of the decision which may be quashed with an order for costs for the applicant.

Listed buildings

11.10   There is even more stringent control over certain buildings which are of special architectural or historical importance. Buildings may be desinated as listed Grade I, such as St Paul's Cathedral, Grade II★ such as numerous Tudor, Stuart and eighteenth century country and town houses, and Grade II which can be old street lamps, minor buildings etc. It should be noted that the listing designation may include a garden wall or steps.

11.11   It is a criminal offence to demolish or alter a listed building (inside or out). No enforcement notice need be given. A separate application for listed building consent is needed for even minor alterations. Applications are advertised in the local papers and may be referred to English Heritage for comment. A grant may be available to private owners for preservation and maintenance of Grade I and Grade II★ buildings.[1]

---

1   Local Authorities (Historic Buildings) Act 1962. Pigeon crees (ie lofts for keeping pigeons) on an allotment in County Durham have recently been 'listed' see (1998) Times, 26 March.

11.12   Following is an outline of whether planning permission, and listed building consent where relevant, are required in a variety of cases which may concern garden owners:

Additions or extensions to a house

11.13   It is not appropriate to set out full details here, but basically additions or extensions are permitted up to 15% of the original house volume up to a maximum of 115 cubic metres except for terraced houses and in conservation, etc areas. If there is another building within five metres of the house, this is included as part of the house and reduces the volume against which the percentage and cubic metre allowance (as mentioned above) are allowed.

Garden buildings

11.14 In gardens and land around the house, planning permission is not required for:

(a) tool sheds;

(b) garages;

(c) septic tanks and cesspools;

(d) greenhouses;

(e) accommodation for pets and domestic animals;

(f) summer houses and saunas;

(g) stables or loose boxes;

(h) swimming pools;

(i) ponds;

(j) tennis courts;

(k) bird baths;

(l) statues;

(m) tents for 'recreation or instruction' for use by members of an organisation, eg Scouts;

(n) dovecots and pigeon lofts;

(o) bird tables;

(p) bird or bat refuges;

(q) beehives;

(r) gnomes.

Except where:

(a) the 'building' is nearer to the highway than the present buildings or within 20 metres of the highway;

(b) more than half of the open area around the original house would be covered;

(c) the building is not going to be used for domestic purposes, eg a hut to be used as an office;

(d) if more than four cubic metres high, then not within two metres of the boundary;

(e) the building is more than four metres high with a ridged roof or three metres with a flat roof.

Fuel storage tanks

11.15 Planning permission is not required except for tanks:

(a) with a capacity of more than 3,500 litres;

(b) more than three metres above the ground;

(c) nearer the highway than the original house unless at least 20 metres away;

(d) for gas or liquid petroleum.

Porches

11.16 Planning permission is not needed for a porch unless it:

(a) would have an area of more than three square metres;

(b) would be higher than three metres;

(c) would be less than two metres from a highway.

Fences, walls and gates

11.17 Planning permission is not required except if the fence, wall or gate is:

(a) over one metre high next to a highway; or

(b) over two metres high elsewhere.

Note that a planning permission cannot be granted for gates conditional upon the stopping up of a public right of way.[1]

1   *South Lanarkshire Council v Secretary of State for Scotland* (1997) 1998 SLT 445, OH.

Trees

11.18 No planning permission is required to plant or maintain any trees or shrubs unless they offend a restriction in a planning permission, eg for an open sight line for an access, but for trees covered by a Tree Preservation Order or in a conservation, etc area see Chapter 4.

Parking and hard standing

11.19 Planning permission is not needed for a car parking area or hard tennis court except where:

(a) the hard surface is not going to be used for domestic purposes, eg it is to be for commercial parking; or

(b) it is for an access to the highway (as to which see **1.6**).

Satellite dishes, television and radio aerials

11.20 Apart from certain instances (concerned mainly with height, interference with exterior etc), planning permission is not required for satellite dishes, TV and radio aerials.

Repairs, maintenance, windows, skylights, solar panels

11.21 In general planning permission is not needed for repair or maintenance of a house, or for new windows, skylights or solar panels, but in conservation, etc areas it may be required as to the colour and type of cladding used, etc.

Demolition of buildings

11.22 Building demolition was made the subject of planning permission recently (it was always required in conservation areas and for listed buildings). Permission is not required for pulling down a garage or shed of less than 50 cubic metres or gates, fences or walls or if the demolition is required for health and safety or other legislation.

Permission always required in conservation, etc areas or for listed buildings

11.23 Note that in all the cases in **11.13–11.22,** if they are in conservation, etc areas or if they relate to listed buildings permission is required.

OBTAINING PLANNING PERMISSION

11.24 This is usually done in two steps:

(a) outline permission; followed by

(b) detailed planning permission (with plans and specifications etc).

Procedure[1]

11.25 Forms should be requested from the local planning authority. If the property is held under a lease or a tenancy agreement, it will be necessary to serve notice of the application on a freeholder or superior landlord. If the property is tenanted, notice should be served on the tenant(s). After the completed forms have been lodged with the appropriate fee, the council has a duty to deal with the application within eight weeks, beyond which time the applicant may appeal (see **11.8–11.9**).

1 Town and Country Planning (Applications) Regulations 1988, SI 1988/1812; Town and Country Planning Act 1990, s 71.

11.26 The application will be registered as a local land charge and notice will be given (and must be given in a conservation,

etc area) to neighbours and by local display. Neighbours, the local amenity group and the public have time (usually 21 days) to put in their objections.

11.27   When the matter (including objections) has been considered by the relevant council committee (which the applicant as a member of the public can attend but not speak at) the council will issue its decision, which will be either:

(a) Unconditional consent;

(b) Consent subject to conditions;

(c) Refusal.

11.28   Applicants can appeal (see **11.8–11.9**) against unreasonable conditions or against refusal but their neighbours cannot appeal against the grant of consent. It is open to an applicant to consult with the planning officers and put in another application (eg satisfying any criticism) immediately and there will be no charge if this is done within 12 months.

Trees

11.29   As to the planning legislation about trees, Tree Preservation Orders etc, see Chapter 4.

BUILDING REGULATION AND BYELAW CONSENT

11.30   If the proposed works in a garden involve buildings which are to be inhabited or will be over 30 square metres in size or will involve digging up or changing the direction of a drain or sewer or the roof line of a building or in certain other situations, a separate building regulation approval[1] or byelaw consent may be required from the building control section of the local authority. This is separate from planning permission and the grant of planning consent does not exempt the garden owner from having to apply for and get building regulation consent where this is required.

1   Building Act 1984 and Building Regulations 1991, SI 1991/2768 (and later Building Regulations amending the latter) (greenhouses and agricultural buildings used for retailing, packing or exhibiting need building regulation consent).

WALLS

11.31   As to the special rules which apply to demolishing, altering or building or rebuilding party walls see **2.15ff.**

ADVERTISEMENTS

11.32 If a person wants to put up an advertisement which is in excess of 0.3 square metres in size on the side wall of his house or garden or free standing in his garden, then Special Advertisement Control Consent is required. This includes large house name plates and 'Beware of the Dog' notices.

11.33 Temporary notices up to 0.6 square metres may be put up outside, except in National Parks etc for local events such as fetes etc and election posters at elections. There are also special rules as to estate agents' boards.

GARDEN EXTENSIONS

11.34 At the moment, the taking over of adjacent agricultural or common land or land with an industrial use (eg for waste tipping) as part of a garden is *not* covered by the General Development Order. The Law Commission has invited public comment on this as a result of criticism—see the news items referred to in **11.4**. The Department of the Environment is proposing to amend the GDO Sch 2 to cover this, but it has not yet happened and until it does, such breaches may result in an enforcement notice, fines and costs.

11.35 As to acquisition of a legal title to land adjacent to one's own, see **1.16ff**. It should be noted that while it may be possible to establish a possessory title to such additional land through fencing it off etc, it may not be possible to plant it as a garden because of planning control!

WINDOW BOXES AND HANGING BASKETS

11.36 There is no reason for the owner of that most modest of gardens, the window box, to go without proper legal advice and it may be helpful to mention matters which particularly apply to window boxes and plant pots kept on window ledges.

Planning

11.37 Where the property is in a conservation area or is a listed building then the installation of bars, brackets etc may be an alteration to the exterior of a building for which planning consent is required. Otherwise no consent is required.

Leases

11.38 If the window box, plant pots or hanging baskets are to be put outside windows of a leasehold property or a property to which a management scheme under the Leasehold Reform Act 1967 or Leasehold Reform, Housing and Urban Development Act 1993 applies, eg an upper flat in a block, the covenants in the lease or management scheme should first be checked. There may well be one 'Not to put out any plant pot on the window ledges' or, more likely, 'Not to make any alterations to the exterior of the building' or 'Not to allow any poster, placard, notice to be put or any display which shall be able to be observed outside the flat'. The second of the three prevents the attachment of brackets etc but not the putting out of plant pots, and the last would probably not be breached by the 'display' of flowers, but each covenant must be read carefully. The covenant may add 'without the landlord's written consent (not to be unreasonably withheld)' or some such wording. If so, the lessee/tenant *must ask* the landlord before putting up the box. It may be that he cannot reasonably refuse to give a licence (a written document) permitting this under the lease. The lessee/tenant will be expected to pay the landlord's legal costs for preparation of the licence, but should qualify any undertaking given in this respect to paying his solicitor's 'reasonable charges' only.

Window boxes and hanging baskets fronting highways

11.39 By the Town Police Clauses Act 1847, s 28 (as amended by the Criminal Justice Act 1967, Sch 3) which applies in all urban areas, it is a criminal offence to fix or place any flower pot or box or other heavy article without sufficiently guarding the same from being blown down in any street (including yards, alleyways, passages etc) or to cause obstruction, annoyance or damage to a resident or passer-by, which is subject to summons in the magistrates' court and a fine. Note that it only prohibits window boxes etc *not properly secured.*

11.40 If the window box, pots or the hanging baskets fall down injuring a neighbour or passer-by or they suffer damage by water or pesticides the person reponsible will be liable for damages.

11.41 By the Highways Act 1980, ss 79, 132 and 152, the highway authority has power to require removal of any 'projection' or 'danger' (and boxes, pots and baskets may come into these categories) or can do so and charge the person responsible.

12

Restrictions on garden use and building: (2) leases and restrictive covenants

Leases

12.1 As we have seen, sometimes a garden is held under a lease whereby a tenant pays rent and enters into certain obligations to a landlord for a term of years. These tenant's covenants are legally binding on:

(a) the original tenant;

(b) his successors in title who take over the lease (by it being assigned to them); and

(c) where the covenants are passed on by the tenant in an underlease to his sub-tenant (ie the person holding the garden on a later lease for a shorter term from him), that sub-tenant.

12.2 The tenant's covenants in leases may be *positive* (requiring something to be done), or *negative* (eg 'not to .....'). Following are some examples:

'To keep the fence on the northern and eastern boundaries of the land (garden) in good repair and stock proof condition'

'To plant the land (garden) with flowers and shrubs and to mow the lawn and maintain the same in a neat and tidy condition'

'Not to plant any tree or shrub or allow any tree or shrub to grow over a height of three metres'

'Not to use the demised premises (garden) except as open land for recreation of the tenant as owner of (house) ....'

'Not to put up any building on the demised premises (garden) without the landlord's prior written consent'

Landlord's remedies for breach of covenants

12.3 Under the above examples, if the tenant does not keep up the fences, plant and mow, or trim trees and shrubs or puts up a

house then he is in breach of covenant and the landlord has a number of rights of legal redress against him. First, the landlord can sue for damages for breach of the covenant. These might be, for example, the cost of the garden work which the tenant has not done or the value by which the landlord's or the adjoining house owner's own interest is diminished through the wrongful use of the garden.

12.4   In the case of negative covenants only (and therefore *not* the covenant to fence, plant, etc) he can go to court and seek an injunction to stop the tenant using the garden communally or stop the building work on the new house.

12.5   If the tenant does not comply the landlord can forfeit the lease after serving a three month notice requiring remedy and he can get a court order evicting the tenant. The tenant usually has a right of 'relief', ie the court will give him the opportunity of putting things right and paying compensation.[1] In all cases the landlord is likely to obtain an order for payment of his legal costs from the tenant. It will therefore be seen that the tenant of a garden who fails to keep a covenant in a lease is in an invidious position.

1   Law of Property Act 1925, s 136.

RESTRICTIVE COVENANTS

12.6   Where the tenant owns the garden freehold there may nevertheless be 'covenants' rather like those in a lease which apply between him and another land owner. Although he is not liable to be evicted like the leasehold tenant, a freehold garden owner may nevertheless be prohibited on pain of legal proceedings from doing certain things in the garden. The covenants could arise, for example, if the owner of a house with a large garden sells off part of it and in the conveyance or transfer of the land the purchaser (who may pay a lesser price because of this) covenants with him and his successors in title, the owners of the house, eg 'not to put up any building or erection on the land edged red (the garden) ...' or 'not to use the land edged red (the garden) for any use or permit the same to be used for any use otherwise than as a garden used with the new house'.

12.7   Under the old equitable rules of the Court of Chancery it became established that a negative covenant of this nature could be binding not only between the original seller and purchaser but, in certain circumstances, between the persons who bought the house or the land (garden) from them.[1] These circumstances are:

(a) that the covenant must relate and be annexed to the land retained by the seller;

(b) that the benefit or burden of the covenant must be expressly assigned; or

(c) if the land is part of a 'building scheme' when the covenant is to protect later purchasers.

1   *Tulk v Moxhay* (1848) 2 Ph 774 (the restrictive covenant in dispute was that which still preserves the centre of Leicester Square, London W1 as a garden!).

12.8   Since 1925 a covenant has to be registered at the Land Charges Registry as a 'Land Charge'[1] or if the land has a registered title it has to be noted on the register so that any future purchaser will have notice of it. Covenants can only be legally binding on successors in title to the garden/house in this way if they are negative (ie restrictive) covenants as 'not to ... do something', so a positive covenant 'to repair the front gate' would not be legally binding on a successor (although it would be between the original seller and the original buyer). A covenant to fence is an exception because although it is a *positive* covenant, ie 'to erect and maintain a fence on the northern and eastern boundaries ...' it is construed as a legal easement (see **1.5**) and is binding on successors in title.

1   Land Charges Act 1925, ss 10(1), 13(2) and 20(8).

Protecting a view

12.9   It will be seen that when open land is let or sold it will be possible to obtain a covenant from the tenant or purchaser 'not to put up any building or erection and not to allow trees or shrubs to grow above three metres' etc and this covenant should preserve the garden as open land for ever. So, if for example the landlord/seller enjoys a view over it from an adjoining house, the view will be preserved and leylandii would not be allowed to grow above three metres so as to interfere with light to the part of the garden which he retains.

12.10   This is an effective way of preserving a view and stopping the planting of high trees and shrubs to interfere with the enjoyment of a garden in the right circumstances, and the Lands Tribunal will not modify the covenant if there is anyone detrimentally affected in such a case.

Gardens in the suburbs and on housing estates

12.11   Where building plots are sold off by a developer restrictive covenants are often imposed in identical terms for all plots, and

some may affect the area intended to be the garden of the individual house. This is a building scheme: see **12.7**(c). For example:

'Not to put up any building or erection on the land hatched black (other than a garden shed not exceeding 3 metres in height).'

'Not to build but to keep open the area between the front of the house (shown by a dotted line on the plan) and the public highway.'

12.12　The covenant may be expressed to be not only for the benefit of the developer but also for the benefit of each and every part of the land owned by him at the date of the lease/sale and if so it may be enforceable by the individual plot owners against each other. If a land owner wishes to stop a neighbour building on his garden under such circumstances, he must prove that:

(a) there was a common landlord/seller (ie the developer);

(b) the covenants were taken for the benefit of retained land and for the part of it which he now owns;

(c) the covenant is a negative covenant (see **12.7**);

(d) the neighbour whom it is sought to stop building on his garden is affected by the covenant against building and has notice of it (ie it is registered as a land charge or at the Land Registry against his title).[1]

1　*Elliston v Reacher* [1908] 2 Ch 374.

What if a neighbour wants to build on his garden?

12.13　If a neighbour wants to build on his garden and the restrictive covenant comes into the above category, then the land owner affected may apply to the court for an injunction to stop the neighbour building. The applicant will be expected to pay money into court as security for the neighbour's legal costs and damages for the delay in stopping him building should the application be unsuccessful.

12.14　The expense can be shared if other neighbours join in on the application. If the application is successful, the court will grant an injunction stopping the building as stated in the restrictive covenant. Alternatively, it may refuse to grant an injunction and instead award damages, ie a sum to compensate for the loss in value of one's house with the new building next door.

12.15　It is important to take action promptly to object to an unlawful use of land in breach of covenant. In a recent case where a neighbour delayed for three years in complaining against use of land for a bungalow and as a riding school in breach of covenant

the Court of Appeal held that he could not get an injunction because of his acquiescence (but he was still entitled to damages).[1]

1   *Gafford v Graham* [1998] 21 LS Gaz R 36, CA.

Building on one's own garden

12.16   On the other hand a garden owner whose garden is subject to a restrictive covenant against building may wish to take the initiative in getting this removed so that he can build there. He may want to have the covenant *discharged* (ie cancelled altogether), or *modified* (changed to allow eg one bungalow for granny at the end of the garden only). How does one go about it?

Agreement of the covenantee

12.17   If the benefit of the covenant is vested in the landlord or the original developer/seller only, he should be approached to see what he will accept to waive or partially release the covenant. He is entitled to ask for money and a market situation prevails. If the restrictive covenant says 'consent not to be unreasonably withheld' then there may be a legal argument as to what is 'reasonable'. Some of the points below may help. The covenantee will also make the person requesting a release pay his legal costs for the deed of release which will be necessary.

12.18   It is important to ensure that the person with whom one is dealing is the *only person* entitled to the covenant. Otherwise it could happen that the matter is resolved with one covenantee, only to find that other neighbours can still go against the modification/ discharge of the covenant, for example as entitled under a separate covenant or if it is part of a building scheme.

12.19   It is possible to insure with specialist insurers against the possibility of persons coming forward in future who can enforce the covenant. A single premium appropriate to the risk will be payable. How much will depend on the insurer's view of the risk and the amount insured against by way of indemnity. If the covenants are old nineteenth century covenants and there have been other local breaches minimum cover can be relatively cheap, eg £100-£500. It is advisable to do this even if the person releasing the covenant appears to have a 'cast iron' title.

Law of Property Act 1925, s 84

12.20   If the person entitled to the benefit of the covenant does not wish to negotiate on the matter, one can apply to the Lands

Tribunal which has powers under the Law of Property Act 1925, s 84 to wholly or partially discharge or modify the restriction where:

(a) because of a change in the character of a property or the neighbourhood or other material circumstances, the covenant ought to be deemed obsolete; or

(b) that the continued existence of the covenant would impede some reasonable use of the land for public or private purposes and, in doing so, either

    (i) would not secure to the persons entitled to the benefit of it any practical benefit of substantial value or advantage to them; or

    (ii) would be contrary to the public interest;

(c) and that money will be an adequate compensation to them for any loss or disadvantage they will suffer for the discharge or modification; or

(d) that the persons of full age and capacity entitled to the benefit of the restriction in respect of estates in fee simple or lesser estates or interests to which the benefit of the covenant is annexed have agreed either expressly or by implication to it being discharged or modified; or

(e) the proposed discharge or modification will not injure the persons entitled to the benefit of the restriction.

12.21 The Lands Tribunal can make an order discharging or modifying the covenant and an order for payment of compensation and costs as appropriate. There are exceptions for certain public covenants or where the government is involved, eg defence, Forestry Commission etc, and the Lands Tribunal cannot discharge or modify covenants taken by the National Trust (for heritage land) or planning obligations entered into under the Town and Country Planning Act 1990, eg 'Section 106' agreements entered into by developers.

When will the Lands Tribunal discharge or modify a covenant?

12.22 This will depend upon the expert and local evidence produced to the Tribunal. It is of course advisable to use a barrister who specialises in this work, and evidence such as the following should be brought:

(a) a local surveyor stating that development has taken place on similar gardens with details and evidence of the valuation of the land with and without the restriction and other relevant values;

(b) neighbours to say that they do not object;

(c) a local councillor who supports the case.

12.23 Such development will probably need planning permission, which can be obtained without reference to the restrictive covenant. If planning permission is obtained and a copy and details of the planning brief preceding the decision are produced to the Tribunal, this will be very valuable evidence.

12.24 It is notable that the Land Tribunal will respect a view over a garden and other amenities which an open garden offers and has refused to discharge covenants in the following cases:

(a) *Re Collett* (1963) 15 P & CR 106 (view from Babbacombe to Portland Bill);

(b) *Re Saddington* (1964) 16 P & CR 81 (view of River Tees);

(c) *Re Whiting* (1988) 58 P & CR 321 (National Trust property);

(d) *Re Bushell* (1987) 54 P & CR 386 ('loss of air and spaciousness' in Wimbledon).

What infringes the restrictive covenant?

12.25 To prepare for attacking or defending a breach of a restrictive covenant against putting up a building, in persuading the other party or the court what is 'reasonable' where this applies, and before the Lands Tribunal under the Section 84 procedure, it is useful to look at a number of cases where the court has considered what infringes the restriction. It should of course be noted that the decision in every case will depend on the detailed wording of the covenant and no two cases are the same, so the following information is for guidance only.

12.26 A covenant against putting up any building was held to be infringed by:

(a) a bay window: *Western v Macdermot* (1866) LR 1 Eq 499;

(b) a portico: *Doe d Palk v Marchetti* (1831) 1 B & Ad 715;

(c) an advertising hoarding 156ft x 15ft: *Nussey v Provincial Bill Posting Co* [1909] 1 Ch 734;

(d) a railway embankment: *Long Eaton Recreation Grounds Co v Midland Rly* [1902] 2 KB 574;

(e) a wall 5ft high: *Child v Douglas* (1854) 1 Kay 56;

(f) a lean-to shed: *Bowes v Law* (1870) LR 9 Eq 636;

(g) a trellis screen 58ft long x 12ft high; *Wood v Cooper* [1894] 3 Ch 671.

but not by:

(a) electric pylons and cables: see dicta in the *Long Eaton* case above;

(b) a fence: *LCC v Allen* [1914] 3 KB 642;

(c) a coal shed 6' 8" x 7' 5": *Gardiner v Walsh* [1936] 3 All ER 870.

12.27   The Court of Appeal case of *Windsor Hotel (Newquay) Ltd v Allen* [1981] JPL 274, CA is perhaps the most interesting relevant decision. It concerned a garden in Newquay whose hotelier garden owner infringed a covenant against building by putting up a brick barbecue 8 feet high with 10 feet chimneys at either end projecting above the boundary wall. It was held that this was a breach of covenant and an injunction was granted ordering him to pull it down.

12.28   In another case concerning a garden, a covenant against use except as a private dwelling-house was held not to be infringed by the building of a swimming pool: *Harrow v Strong* (1977) 25 EG 140.

WHAT MAY NOT BE GROWN IN A GARDEN

12.29   There are plants and the like which are not allowed to grow in a garden. Poisonous plants will also be considered here.

12.30   The Misuse of Drugs Act 1971 provides:

Section 6(1) '... it shall not be lawful for a person to cultivate any plant of the genus cannabis'.

Section 6(2) 'Subject to section 28 it is an offence to cultivate any such plant in contravention of section 6(1) above.'

Section 28 provides a defence where the accused person proves that he neither knew nor had reason to suspect the existence of some fact which the prosecution must prove and other similar circumstances, eg if some teenagers had planted cannabis in an old person's allotment without him knowing.

On summary conviction the penalty is six months' imprisonment or the maximum fine of £5,000 or both, and on indictment, 14 years or a fine, or both. The growing of coco leaf or poppy straw is also an offence.

12.31   As to other potential drugs such as the opium poppy (papaver somnifer) or mushrooms containing psilacybin ('magic mushrooms') it is not an offence to grow them, but it is to dry stalks or freeze or process them.

12.32   In the Act there is a lengthy list of drugs which the garden owner must not produce, supply or offer to produce or supply them (s 4) and as an occupier of premises (which includes a garden) he must not allow or permit activities involving drugs there. So a garden owner should not allow anyone (including his own teenage children) to hold a party in his garden which drug users may attend. The penalties for these offences are graded by reference to the type of drug (A, B and C), but for Sch A can be six months' imprisonment (on summary conviction) or life (on indictment) plus fines etc. By s 25 the police have full powers of entry, search and arrest in a garden.

12.33   There is no law preventing the growing of tobacco, hops or grapes in a garden. The controls on tobacco and alcohol apply at a later stage of manufacture, so the Customs and Excise cannot raid a garden for these!

POISONS

12.34   The law as to poisons and 'hazardous substances' (which includes poisons and pesticides) affects the garden owner less directly. Certain poisons are illegal in the sense that they may not be sold, offered for sale, supplied and used, but there are exceptions for certain poisons used for killing specific pests. For example, some very dangerous poisons such as strychnine can be used against moles. Note as to gardens that:

(a)   There is a general duty not to use artificial poisons etc to kill wild birds or animals under the Wildlife and Countryside Act 1981 and the Protection of Animals Act 1911, but this is modified for certain animals and certain poisons: see the legislation for details.

(b)   As to naturally poisonous plants in a garden, the garden owner's liability to visitors to the garden and trespassers and animals is as outlined in Chapters 6 and 7. Here it may be noted certain plants have certain adverse affects on humans and animals:

   (i)   giant hog weed, chicory (cichorium) and achillea cause skin allergies;

   (ii) sedum and the sweet smelling shrub cionura and some figs and laburnum are all poisonous if taken in excess. Yew is poisonous even in moderate quantities and can kill.

12.35   The most common poisonous plants are as follows. laburnam, honeysuckle[1], cotoneaster[1], deadly nightshade, woody nightshade, yew, sweet peas[1], pyracantha[1], elder[1] and mahonia[1].

Where poisonous plants are grown the grower should ensure that the labels etc are kept and displayed and that visitors are warned. It is important that where a child or animal has to be rushed to hospital or treated that the doctor/vet knows what has been eaten. Note the case of *Hastie v Edinburgh Magistrates* 1907 SC 1102 where a garden owner was held liable for death of a young child who ate deadly nightshade berries: see **7.16**.

1   Eating the fruit of these plants is not expected to cause harmful effects unless taken in substantial quantities: 'Beware the peril of poison ivy (and the rest)' *The Times* 9 August 1997, Weekend section p 6.

12.36   With regard to liability in negligence and occupiers' liability it is interesting to compare the cases of:

Ponting v Noakes [1894] 2 QB 281 where a horse reached over the hedge and ate leaves from a land owner's yew tree, it was held that the land owner was *not* liable for damages for the death of the horse as he had no duty to prevent the horse having access to the tree by leaning across the boundary; and

Crowhurst v Amersham Burial Board (1878) 4 Ex D 5 where a yew tree in a cemetery grew over the boundary railing by approximately four feet and the plaintiff's horse grazing in the adjoining field ate from it and died, where it was held that the cemetery owner *was* liable as the yew branches trespassed beyond the boundary and he should have known of this and of the risk to the neighbour's animals.

So if a neighbour's cat eats poisonous leaves while trespassing in another's garden the garden owner would not be liable to its owner for its death.

OTHER POINTS ON GROWING PLANTS

12.37   Certain wild plants are identified by the Wildlife and Countryside Act 1981 as being rare and it is a criminal offence to pick, uproot or destroy them, punishable by a fine. The plants are set out in Appendix A.

12.38   Under the Wildlife and Countryside Act 1981 and the National Parks and Access to the Countryside Act 1949, s 17 certain areas of the country are designated as:

(a)   national parks;

(b)   areas of outstanding natural beauty (AONB);

(c)   nature reserves;

(d)   sites of special scientific interest (SSSI).

12.39   The National Park authorities and local authorities have powers in these areas and if a garden owner's garden is in a National Park or an AONB or in a conservation area for planning purposes (see Chapter 11) he may be subject to legislation which restricts his use of his land, restricts felling, planting trees etc. Where a site is designated as an SSSI (which can include a part of a garden or grounds), there is a duty on the owner to give details to the Secretary of State for the Environment of all 'operations' on the land which may damage the flora and fauna protected, eg orchids, red squirrels.

12.40   By the Wildlife and Countryside (Amendment) Act 1985, s 2 the owners of such land must be given nine months' notice of 'notification' as an SSI site and have three months to object.

12.41   Once a site is designated, however, a land owner has to give four months' notice of 'operations', eg ploughing etc affecting the area of SSI, and must enter into a 'management agreement' with English Nature or get its consent to the operations. Should plants etc be damaged then the owner is guilty of a criminal offence (for which there is a maximum fine of £2,500) unless the operations are within the widely-drawn exceptions. By April 1996 English Nature had drawn up approximately 2,300 management agreements but lacks the funds to 'police' the system.

12.42   There are further powers under the Wildlife and Countryside Act 1981 to set up 'Super SSSIs' by Nature Control Orders and the MAFF has powers under the Agriculture Act 1986 to establish and enter into management agreements regarding 'Environmentally Sensitive Areas' and to pay grants for management. It is unlikely that a domestic garden would be included but part of a large land owner's grounds may well be covered.

12.43   In addition to not picking, uprooting or damaging wild plants in his own garden or grounds, the gardener should be wary of buying bulbs or plants of wild varieties on the doorstep or in the pub. It may be that the plants, eg bluebells (hyacintoides nonscripta) which have recently been included in the 'rare wild plant' category under the Wildlife and Countryside Act 1981, have been dug up illegally and such a purchase could be aiding and abetting the crime. Needless to say listed wild plants should never be harvested even if they grow in profusion in one's garden.

13

Produce of the garden

13.1 This book is intended to assist in advising the amateur gardener rather than the professional market gardener or garden centre retailer and still less is it concerned with the farmer and food manufacturer. However, many garden owners will want to sell or purvey the produce from their gardens whether by putting leeks into the annual leek show, opening their vegetable garden to local visitors and letting them buy the produce, or by setting up a road-side stall. In these cases the legal position will be as follows.

FLOWERS AND NON EDIBLE PLANTS

Commercial sale

13.2 If it is proposed to use the garden for the commercial sale of flowers, plants and vegetables on a long term basis, this may involve 'development', a change of use from residential, and planning permission may have to be obtained: see Chapter 11.

In the course of business

13.3 If the sale is 'in the course of business', and the garden owner is dealing with potential purchasers as consumers, note what is said in Chapter 9 about the Sale of Goods Act 1979 and the Consumer Protection Act 1987. The garden owner will be liable to the buyer for the implied conditions and warranties as to title, satisfactory quality, fitness for purpose etc and could find that his customers:

(a) bring back the flowers/plants with some complaint and ask for their money back; or even

(b) keep them and threaten to sue for breach of warranty (eg that the plants have died or have failed to flourish).

He must therefore take a view on his legal position, eg:

(a) Has the contract for the sale of the flowers etc been accepted by the buyer?

(b) Has the buyer kept them long enough to examine? Or over a 'reasonable time'?

(c) What is a 'reasonable time' when seeds and seedlings are bought in the winter and the plants are to come up in the spring?

Note the Scottish case of *Wilson v Carmichael & Sons* (1894) 21 R
732 where a buyer of 'Enfield market cabbage' which he had been
told would grow early in the year but was, in fact, late growing was
given limited damages as he could have found out before the growing
season.

13.4 It may well be that in most cases a refund should be allowed
for good customer relations, if not for legal reasons.

13.5 The seller could, and should if he is to go into business
properly (having accepted the planning and tax consequences
for a business warned of above), draw up an order form/receipt
for goods sold. If he is to take credit cards (thereby being almost
certainly a 'business') or pay VAT he will have to document his
sales. A notice or clause should be put in the documentation
stating that 'no responsibility is accepted for the condition or
suitability of any plant or seeds etc' but of course this will be
subject to the Supply of Goods and Services Act 1982.

13.6 He may even include a *Romalpa*[1] clause to try and secure
payment of sales on credit but most garden owners will want to
take cash. He can also insure against paying damages etc to
customers and against his legal costs and should do this if the
business justifies it. If the sale is not 'in the course of business' then
it is unlikely that the 'buyer' will have any redress except in cases of
a flagrant breach of contract or negligence.

1   See **9.35**.

FOOD

13.7 If he is to sell vegetables, mushrooms, honey or jam from the
garden, the garden owner is into deep water. The days of a principal
local garden owner (the Squire or his wife?) giving cakes, jam etc to
the local village fete for sale in a good cause without any legal
consequences arising are, sadly, over!

13.8 The Food Safety Act 1990 (replacing the Food Act 1984)
and associated UK and EU legislation affect all transactions
involving food. 'Food' does not include live animals and birds, live
fish or shell fish or fodder for animals so these can be sold without
the consequences below. Nor does the Act apply to 'primary
agricultural or fish products' where no industrial process has taken
place. What is 'an industrial process'?

(a) Is washing a leek an industrial process?

(b) Is spraying apples, fruit etc whilst growing?

(c) Is cutting cucumbers for sandwiches for the village fete?

All could be, in which case a leek show competitor and Women's Institute jam queen would be within the Act.

13.9   Under the Act:

(a) 'Any land or buildings' used for the sale, offer for sale or supply of food must be licensed. This could include a garden.

(b) Mobile shops need not be licensed but the place from which they operate must.

(c) Hospitals, staff canteens, schools etc are all included.

(d) Premises used for village fetes, church halls etc used only occasionally do not have to be registered (does this include once a week?).

(e) 'Bed and breakfast' hosts with fewer than three rooms do not have to be registered but those with more rooms do.

13.10   The local authority is the registering authority and the Act provides that failure to register and the sale, offer for sale or supply of food without registering are criminal offences. So is the sale of food which does not comply with food safety requirements or is not as described: see **13.12ff**.

13.11   It is important to note that no money need pass to the seller for a 'sale' under the Act. The proceeds can go to the charity for which the fete is being run or, eg a cake can be given as a prize in a raffle. The cake would still be within the Act (but if the event is in a village hall used only occasionally, the hall would be exempt from registration).

Food Safety Act 1990

13.12   Details of specific provisions of the Food Safety Act 1990 and the Orders made under it which may apply should the garden owner display, offer for sale, deliver or market food and not be within the exemptions are as follows. Reference is also made to the relevant EU legislation which has been adopted by the UK.

13.13   The display, sale etc with the intention of sale of:

(a) Food 'not fit for human consumption' (s 7);

(b) 'Not complying with food and safety standards': see the Orders below (s 8); and

(c) Selling etc 'to the purchaser's prejudice any food which is not of a nature, substance or quality demanded by the purchaser' (s 14)

are criminal offences. The local authority is responsible for sending inspectors, testing, sampling, prosecuting etc offenders and if convicted they will be fined. By s 35 the sanctions for offences under ss 7, 8 and 14 are:

(a) On summary conviction before the magistrates—fine: up to £20,000;

(b) On indictment (eg second offence or serious infringement) unlimited fine and up to two years' imprisonment.

13.14 Section 15 provides that it is an offence to label or adulterate food in a way so as to falsely describe it or likely to be misleading as to the nature, quality or substance of the food. Note for example the case of *Amos v Britvic Ltd* (1984) 149 JP 13 where imported orange juice which had water added in the UK was not allowed to be called 'fresh' but could be called 'made with concentrated orange juice'.

13.15 Section 35 provides for fines of:

(a) on summary conviction up to £5,000; and

(b) on indictment the same as in **13.13**, ie unlimited fine and up to two years' imprisonment.

13.16 The same fines are prescribed for offences under the regulatory orders, the most important of which are the:

(a) Food Safety (General Food Hygiene) Regulations 1995, SI 1995/1763 (eg washing of food, washing hands and overalls etc for food handlers);

(b) Food Safety (Temperature Control) Regulations 1995, SI 1995/2200 (eg milk at below 8°C);

(c) Food Labelling Regulations 1996, SI 1996/1499.

These Orders and Regulations apply to 'any undertaking whether carried on for profit or not and whether public or private carrying on any or all of the following operations, namely, preparation, processing, manufacture, distribution, handling or offering for sale or supply of food'. This includes private houses and therefore, presumably, their gardens.

Training must be given to staff in all the above regulations.

13.17 There is no power in the Food Safety Act 1990 for the magistrates' court to compensate the victim of a breach of the Act, who will have to pursue a separate right of civil action for breach of contract or negligence. As to a person's civil law rights to sue for negligence mention should be made of what is probably the most

famous case in English legal history, *M'Alister (or Donoghue) v Stevenson* [1932] AC 562, 'the slug in the ginger beer bottle' case which establishes that there is a right of action in negligence against the manufacturer as well as the seller of adulterated food and drink which causes injury.

Defences

13.18   The main defences available under the Act are:

(a) that the infringement was the act of a third party (eg someone has tampered with the food); and

(b) 'due diligence', ie that all reasonable precautions had been taken.

EU Regulations

13.19   The main EU Regulations in parallel to the above are:

(a) EC 1053/72 as to offer for sale etc; and

(b) EC 2257/94 as to labelling.

13.20   There also exist even more detailed regulations, both European and domestic, relating to, eg:

(a) Honey—the Honey Regulations 1976, SI 1976/1832, Sch 2 (purity of honey, labelling etc);

(b) Jam, bottled fruit, chutney etc—see the Jam and Similar Products Regulations 1981, SI 1981/1063 (fruit content to be 45%, fruit derived solids content 65%, labelling etc);

(c) Cauliflowers—EEC Regulation 23/1962 and Annex 11/1 and 211/16 and Annex 1 (there are similar regulations relating to onions, artichokes, celery, headed cabbage etc and UK legislation as to potatoes, apples, pears etc (Horticultural Produce Act 1986, s 1 and regulations under the FSA);

(d) Eggs, milk, cream and cheese

It is not proposed to go into detail about these, but the following should be noted:

   (i) As the garden owner may keep hens and want to sell eggs, the legal position should mentioned. With regard to the Food Safety Act 1990 and roadside stalls etc: see **13.23ff**. Sale of produce from the premises etc is lawful, but as to the eggs themselves the delegated legislation under the Act will apply as to hygiene, grading, marking and packaging and as to the 'sell by date'. No one is to sell eggs from a domestic fowl or duck except in accordance with

the Eggs (Marketing Standards) Regulations 1985, SI 1985/1271 which provide for registered packers and approved methods of packaging etc. Failure to comply will lead to criminal prosecution with a fine of £2,000.

(ii) 'Cream' is milk of a cow separated by skimming which is intended for sale for human consumption and contains not less than 18% milk fat.

(iii) 'Clotted cream' is cream which has been scalded, cooled and skimmed once or more and contains not less than 55% milk fat: Cream Regulations 1976, SI 1976/752. See also Dairy Products (Hygiene) Regulations 1995, SI 1995/1086 and Cheese Regulations 1970, SI 1970/94. So if 'cream' or 'clotted cream' is offered, it must comply with these descriptions and otherwise with these regulations and the Food Labelling Regulations 1996, SI 1996/1499. Milk put out on the table for use in tea is 'exposed for sale' and must comply.[1]

13.21 The responsibility for sending inspectors, taking samples, testing and prosecuting offenders is that of the local authority (District Councils for minor matters, County Councils for more serious) and they have powers of entry. They can also make 'Improvement Orders' prescribing what must be done, requiring shops, restaurants and indeed any place of sale (which could include a garden) eg to improve hygiene, and can close down any food 'business'.

1   *McNair v Terroni* [1915] 1 KB 526 (the offence under earlier legislation was 'exposing for sale' unfit etc food, but such display of milk would still contravene the current law).

Enforcement

13.22 As we have already seen, the Agriculture and Horticulture Act 1964 and orders under it prescribe the grading and labelling of fresh horticultural produce, eg sale of potatoes by weight, jam by weight and description etc. There is an exception for direct sale by the producer where produce is or is to be delivered to the customer at the premises where it is produced or at any stall or vehicle from where it is to be sold.

So it will be seen that the sale, offering for sale etc of food (with or without flowers and plants) is a highly regulated operation which may require form filling and expense with the local authority and expose the food supplier to criminal proceedings and fines.

Does all this really apply to the amateur gardener? Answer: yes it does, but, if, for example, the occasion is the sale of untreated vegetables grown in the garden at an annual fete the registration and most other formalities need not be complied with, but the hygiene requirements, if breached, could lead to prosecution. In practice, local authority inspectors have more to do than prowl around village halls and gardens open to the public every summer Saturday afternoon; nevertheless they do have the power to enter, inspect and take proceedings against offenders.

ROADSIDE STALLS

13.23   A permanent stall may need planning permission if it involves a change to commercial use. Under the Highways Act 1980 the local authority has a power to require the removal of 'obstructions', which a roadside stall may be. As well as being liable to be removed, a stall in a dangerous position by the highway could expose the person setting it up to a claim for negligence from a road user who is distracted by it and crashes.

13.24   Under the Local Government (Miscellaneous Provisions) Act 1976, s 7 the highway authority may make an order prohibiting roadside sales and give seven days' notice to an offender who will be liable to a fine on scale 3 if he does not comply, but this provision is meant not to apply to:

(a) sale by or on behalf of the owner or occupier of agricultural land on that land of agricultural produce produced on that land; or

(b) sale of refreshment or facilities for recreation in lay bys: Highways Act 1980, ss 115 A–115E.

'Agricultural land' in 'produce of agricultural land' however appears to mean a farm or market garden only and *not* a domestic garden so the highway authority might be able to make an order against a stall on the road run by a non-commercial gardener.

'PICK YOUR OWN'

13.25   The invitation of the public into your orchard or vegetable field to 'pick and pay' may be a change of use and require planning permission: see Chapter 11. The fruit or vegetables are probably outside the Food Safety Act 1990 as not having been subject to an 'industrial process' but see above. The Agriculture and Horticulture Act 1964 provides an exception for grading, labelling etc in sales of

produce at the place where it is grown (see **13.22**), so a 'pick your own' would be outside these provisions.

Access from the highway

13.26   A 'pick your own' operation should ensure that it has a right of way with vehicles for the number of cars which will be coming. Also the gate or turn off may need planning permission: see Chapter 11.

ORGANIC FOOD

13.27   Organic food also has a specific legal meaning in EC and UK law, and local authorities have a duty to enforce relevant labelling, advertising etc legislation. Food is 'organic' only if a MAFF inspector approves the farm or garden from which it comes.[1] This must be free of pesticides, weed killers and artificial fertilisers etc and the soil is likely to have had to rest from these for at least two years before the description 'organic' is authorised.

1   EU Regulations 2042/98, EEC 1935/95 EC. The local authority will also enforce labelling, advertising controls.

14

Garden design and copyright

COPYRIGHT

14.1 It should be noted that where an architect or garden designer is engaged the plans which he prepares belong to him (unless agreed otherwise). Once a client has paid his fees, the plans may then become the client's property, but in principle the ideas and designs will remain the expert's.

14.2 In many cases, eg diagrams in gardening books as to what flower bed or features go where and what plants are to be put where are put forward and can be implemented without any legal consequences, but an author and garden designer has a right under UK and EU law to register a copyright or registered design and assert his legal ownership of the intellectual property involved.

14.3 Such ideas and inventions may be protected and the garden owner using them must be wary of infringement where a work of art such as a sculpture or a garden feature is involved. As long ago as the Sculpture Copyright Act 1814 and Industrial Designs Act 1833 (both now replaced) artists have had the right not to have their work copied without being paid for and the Copyright, Designs and Patents Act 1988 now applies: see **14.5ff**. Where a copyright or design is registered the garden owner cannot use it without a licence, for which he may have to pay.

14.4 With regard to garden tools and equipment, here again designs and the object itself may be registered as a patent or have a trade mark in the UK and EU and the gardener who sells or copies the equipment without licence may be guilty of a criminal offence. He will also be liable to the copyright owner in damages. He may also be committing the civil wrong of passing off, for which he could be the subject of proceedings for an injunction and for damages.

COPYRIGHT, REGISTERED DESIGNS AND PATENTS

14.5 These are now dealt with in EU law under the European Patent Convention of 5 October 1973 which deals with copyright, trade marks etc. (Designs have yet to be covered.) In UK law the

relevant legislation is the Registered Designs Act 1949 and, more importantly, the Copyright, Designs and Patents Act 1988. The latter covers all artistic work, graphic work, sculpture, design work of an architect and work of architectural craftsmanship and would therefore include garden designs, sculptures, features etc. These can be protected by registration provided that:

(a) they satisfy standards by being:

    (i)   original;

    (ii) fixed; and

(b) the author qualifies.

14.6   Registration for UK patents etc is dealt with in London and in Munich and The Hague for the EU.

14.7   The intellectual property in patented or copyright material has, of course, a pecuniary value and is transferable. The registered right lasts for 20 years (10 years for designs).

15

Propagation of plants and seeds

'Bio copyright'

15.1 A gardener who breeds a new variety of plant is entitled to exploit his discovery and his plantsman's skill and care for his own benefit. Although this is a highly technical area, the basic legal position as to new varieties and plant propagation should be noted by both the gardener who develops a new variety (who may want to record and sell rights in the new variety or sell the plants themselves), and by the garden owner who may be offered new varieties etc by persons not entitled to exploit and sell them.

Plant varieties

15.2 Plant breeders' rights are a form of intellectual property similar to patents and were so recognised under UK legislation 34 years ago in the Plant Varieties and Seeds Act 1964. Commercial or amateur gardeners can obtain protection of any new variety of plant or vegetable which they might develop and the income through royalties derived from their commercial exploitation. Since then the protection has been extended to include the European Union and beyond. The Convention for the Protection of New Varieties of Plants ('UPOV') 1961 was ratified by Parliament on 17 September 1965, and by amendments to the 1964 Act and orders made under it there is statutory control throughout the European Union (and for some other countries which have adopted the UPOV) extending to the latest developments in plant breeding technology and the whole field of plant and living organisms. This is now consolidated in the Plant Varieties Act 1997.

Scheme of protection of plant varieties

15.3 Under the Plant Varieties Act 1997 (and its predecessor, the Plant Varieties and Seeds Act 1964) and the orders made under their protection is available when a scheme has been made by Order by the Minister concerned (the Secretary of State for Agricultural Forestry and Fisheries or the Secretary of State for the Environment)

relating to the genus or species to which the plant, seed or vegetable variety belongs. Adaptation can be made by later order to cover later features or characteristics within the variety.

Initial registration

15.4 Registration gives the plant breeder a European Community Trade Mark and European Plant Variety Right ('EPVR') entitlement to use the variety and the name[1] registered and to prevent others from doing anything infringing or wrongfully using that variety name during the period of development.

1 Plant Varieties Act 1997, ss 18 and 19.

Development

15.5 Following the initial registration the plant breeder has two years under this provisional protection in which to develop the variety. The legislation sets up a testing agency (the Plant Varieties Office) under the direction of a Controller who will consider the permanent protection of the variety judging such characteristics as to whether the variety is:

(a) new;

(b) distinct, ie the variety has one or more morphological, physiological or other characteristic(s) setting it apart from other varieties;

(c) uniform—the variety must have developed its own characteristics, sexual reproduction or vegetative propagation;

(d) stable, ie it must not have been a freak development but remain distinctive after reproduction or cycles of reproduction.[1]

'Prior commercialisation', ie the fact that someone else has developed and sold a similar variety, will defeat a claim for permanent protection.

1 Plant Varieties Act 1997, s 4 and Sch 2.

Criminal sanctions

15.6 Once a right is granted it is a criminal offence to infringe it by selling or exploiting the variety or harvesting it or making products from harvested material.[1] Directors of a company which is guilty of any offence can themselves be convicted and fined.[2]

1 Plant Varieties Act 1997, ss 13 and 14.

2   Plant Varieties Act 1997, s 36.

The varieties currently licensed

15.7   Extracts from the Plant Varieties Act 1997 and the Plant Health (Great Britain) Order 1993 are set out in Appendix A to give an idea of the many varieties of plants and vegetables protected by schemes under the 1964 and 1997 Acts. The registered names are too great in number to be listed but the reader is referred to the details of the Order and to the Plant Varieties Office. The Royal Horticultural Society's testing centre at Wisley has full details and is most helpful in guiding plant breeders.

15.8   The Controller will, if satisfied, license the variety.[1] He can, however, revoke the licence if the evidence of the above characteristics is no longer available (eg distinct reproductive material no longer produced to him) or if prior commercialisation is later proved.[2] When a new scheme for a variety is applied for only prior sales or offers for sales by the applicant count against him but sales abroad in the previous four years are disregarded.

1   Plant Varieties Act 1997, s 3.
2   Plant Varieties Act 1997, ss 21 and 22.

Period of licence

15.9   The UK licence and the EPV right will be co-extensive and will last for:

(a) 25 years for plants and seeds; and

(b) 30 years for trees and vines.[1]

1   Plant Varieties Act 1997, s 11.

Effect of a licence

15.10   The holder of a licence has a duty to maintain the new variety in existence. He can sub-license it, assign his rights and generally exploit it for money or in exchange for other rights.[1]

1   Plant Varieties Act 1997, s 16.

Exceptions

15.11   There are exceptions to the plant breeder's rights to cover cases such as use of seed of a particular variety which a farmer has saved on his own holding, and, to prevent monopoly, it is a principle of the legislation that the right should only be for selling reproductive

material (eg seeds, bulbs etc for propagation) not for consumption (eg seed for milling). If the Controller finds that a licensed plant breeder has unreasonably failed to grant rights to an applicant he may compulsorily grant a licence to such a person.[1] EU law will also apply to prevent the grant of an over-restrictive exclusive licence which prohibits seeds and plants being produced and sold by other licensees.[2]

1   Plant Varieties Act 1997, s17.
2   *LC Nungesser KG* and *Kurt Eiele v EEC* Case No 258/78 (a maize seed licence granted in Germany was held to be contrary to Article 85(1) and could not be exclusive as this distorted competition).

Fees and challenges to licensed rights

15.12   The licence is also conditional upon payment of the prescribed fees to the Office of Plant Varieties and to the Controller and if these are not paid or any conditions attached to the licence are not kept to the licence will be revoked.

15.13   Anyone who has previously commercially dealt with the variety, or has a new, distinct, uniform and stable version of the material can take proceedings to challenge the licence in the Plant Varieties and Seeds Tribunal. Set up by the 1997 Act, the Tribunal can make decisions and award costs.[1]

1   Plant Varieties Act 1997, ss 42–46.

Development of a unique variety

15.14   A gardener who has developed a unique variety complying with the above requirements and who wishes to exploit it commercially should seek specialist advice. He should apply to the Plant Varieties Office, which will prescribe the procedures and requirements for testing. This can be an expensive process, involving as it does the Plant Varieties Office's fees, growing cultivars and submitting reproductive material etc for laboratory testing in quantity and preparing technical information in great detail. It is, of course, perfectly lawful to develop one's own varieties and do grafting in one's own or a friend's garden without infringing the Act, which is aimed at commercial sales.

What benefits will a licence give to the holder?

15.15   In addition to being able to sell and sub-license the new variety at home and abroad the holder of a licence can sue anyone who infringes his right in the civil courts.

Genetically modified organisms

15.16   Under the Environmental Protection Act 1990 and the Orders made under it the development and exploitation of genetically modified organisms, that is plants or vegetables or indeed animal based products which have had their growth or flavour enhanced by artificial means, are subject to government control. Section 106 of the Act limits the sale, supply etc of any genetically modified organisms and by s 110 the Secretary of State (the MAFF) can issue prohibition orders banning them subject to criminal sanctions (s 118).[1]

1   Environmental Protection Act 1990 and Regulations, eg SI 1992/3217 and SI 1993/15.

15.17   The genetic modification of plants, vegetables etc is unlikely to be something which the amateur gardener will want to do, and if he does, provided that his experiments are confined to his own garden and its results are not sold commercially then he should not breach these provisions. The commercial gardener should refer to more specialist books on food and drugs.

EU LAW AND GARDENS

15.18   The European Union has laws applying in the UK against importing goods including plants, bulbs and seeds from outside the EU. There are also laws as to the free movement of goods including plants, bulbs and seeds within the territory of the Union, which apply in the UK. The garden owner should not therefore bring plants, bulbs, seeds etc from any territory outside the EU without authorisation. However, it is possible for those within the EU to deal in the plant types etc now existing and developed under the UPOV and European Plant Variety Rights (indeed, one is encouraged to do so—see **15.19**). It is to be hoped that innovative amateur plantsmen and women will not be discouraged from seeking out new strains abroad, but they should remember to get official consent. In addition to the restriction on plant, seed etc imports from outside the EU, each EU Member State has its own controls against pests and possibly diseased plants coming within its borders. In the UK the Plant Health Act 1967 empowers Customs and Excise to stop people bringing in plants etc and to confiscate them without compensation. An extract from the Act and a summary of the Plant Health (Great Britain) Order 1993, SI 1993/1320 is given in the Appendix. The import and export of certain species are also prohibited under the Endangered Species (Import and Export) Act

1976. Except for commercial gardeners buying plants, bulbs etc officially under EU rules with a 'plant passport' as provided for in the Act, no-one should bring plants, bulbs (or even cut flowers) into the UK.

15.19 There is a conflict between the principle of free movement of goods and the right of Member States to ban plants on health grounds. This was exemplified in the case of *EEC v Italy*[1] in which Italy was held to have infringed art 30 of the Treaty of Rome as to free movement of goods by banning plants susceptible to Erwinia amylovora (fire blight) and was fined substantially for doing this. This case involved the most elementary confusion of principles and policy and has resulted in uncertainty for commercial gardeners.

[1]   Case 294/92, ECJ, [1994] ECR I-4311 (the plants banned were Chaenomelis Lindl, Cydonia Mill, Malus Mill, Pyracantha M J Roem, Pyrus L, Sorbus L other than Sorbus Intermedia L and Stranvaesia Lindl (other than fruits and seeds)).

15.20 In the United States new life forms can be patented. In the EU this is excluded by art 53(9) of the European Patents Convention 1973. A Council Directive as to extending the EU patent law to cover bio-technical inventions (Council Directive of 16.2.1993) was rejected by the European Parliament on 1 March 1995 and is not currently proceeding. However, as mentioned above, it may be possible to patent techniques involved in the propagation of organisms under existing EU rules and UK law.

16
Burial in the garden

16.1 It is pertinent to consider who (or what) can be buried in the garden and the legal position of this particular use of the garden.

HUMANS

16.2 Contrary to popular belief, it *is* possible to be buried in one's garden. This is to be distinguished from having a religious service for burial and being buried in consecrated ground which under Church of England rules (and other denominational rules) is *not* possible except in very rare circumstances (eg the burial of the Princess of Wales at Althorp in 1997 where special consecration took place). The legal position is dealt with in the Burial Laws Amendment Act 1880. Local authorities and religious bodies have a duty to provide burial grounds which are to be used for burial of all dead who are notified to the authorities. They may also provide cremation facilities, but are not obliged to do so. Deaths must be registered with the local registrar under the Births and Deaths Registration Act 1874 and orders under it (currently SI 1987/2088).

16.3 The Registrar's office is provided by the local authority and the Registrar must be informed by a person (usually a relation) with knowledge of the circumstances of the death who must provide a certificate as to the cause of death signed by a registered medical practitioner. Where there has been a violent or unnatural death or where the cause of death is unknown, a Coroner's Inquest will be held to ascertain the cause of death. It is the duty of the executor of the deceased to cause the body to be buried or cremated.

16.4 Cremation, which is dealt with under the Cremation Regulations 1930, SR & O 1930/1006, and Cremation (Amendment) Regulations 1985, SI 1985/153, can only happen in a registered crematorium, with the requisite two doctors' certificates or order of the Coroner.[1] However, there is no reason why ashes should not be scattered or an urn containing them be buried in the garden, which is frequently done.

1   Coroners Rules 1984, SI 1984/552.

16.5 What generally stops human burial in the garden being legal is the law relating to waste: see Chapter 22. A dead body is 'clinical waste'

and cannot be disposed of except by a licensed operator in accordance with the Control of Pollution Act 1974 and Environmental Protection Act 1990. It is a criminal offence to dispose of controlled waste except as under the Act. In practice, however, the local authority may grant a waiver to enable burial to take place in a garden in special circumstances.

16.6 There is also a further public health aspect to burial in the garden. No grave is to be dug under a building: Public Health Act 1975, s 343. Also, where the deceased has died of an infectious disease, the local health authority has a duty (with power of entry) to remove and dispose of the body: Public Health (Control of Diseases) Act 1984, s 48.

ANIMALS

16.7 In the case of animals only the public health law is concerned. Dogs and cats and other animals (other than those dying of infectious diseases: see the Animal Health Act 1981, s 23) can be buried or their ashes scattered or buried in the garden.

16.8 There is a specific exemption from the provisions as to controlled waste in the Waste Management Licensing Regulations 1994, SI 1994/1056, Sch 3, para 37. Activities exempted from the rules prohibiting disposal of waste include: 'Burial of a dead domestic pet in the garden of domestic property where it lived so long as it is not hazardous (ie clinical[1]) waste with the consent of the owner.'[2] Strictly since 1 January 1995 even such exempted waste should only be disposed of in a place registered with the local authority but realistically it is up to the pet owner/garden owner whether they comply by temporarily registering their garden under the 1994 Regulations, reg 18(1). It is a criminal offence not to do so.

1   'Clinical waste is (a) human and animal tissue or excretions, drugs or other medicinal products, swabs and dressings, syringes and other sharp instruments which unless rendered safe may prove hazardous to any person coming in contact with it and (b) any other waste from various health care, retailing or research activities or the collection of blood for transfusion being waste which infects any person coming into contract with it': 1994 Regulations, reg 14.

2   This would appear to mean that a pet cannot be buried in the garden of a property in which it did not live.

TOMBSTONES IN A GARDEN

16.9 Tombstones will probably be within the General Development Order 1988 unless they are very high or too near the highway, in which case planning permission will be required: see Chapter 11.

17

Leasehold gardens

17.1 The tenant of a garden may hold the garden on a tenancy either:

(a) let with a house, other building or land, eg office, shop, farm or agricultural land etc, and his garden will be dealt with as an adjunct to the house or other unit under, for example, the Rent Acts or the Landlord and Tenant Act 1954, Pt II; or

(b) separately, let by itself, eg a market garden, allotment or smallholding, when the tenancy may be the subject of special legislation such as the Agricultural Holdings Act, Allotments Acts etc.

17.2 Where the unit is a residential house to which the garden is ancillary and is held on a long lease, usually over 21 years, at a low rent, then the legislation as to leasehold enfranchisement may apply to the garden.

17.3 Finally, where the garden is held with a council house or flat the 'right to buy' legislation giving council tenants the right to buy their house from the local authority may apply to the garden as well.

SECURITY OF TENURE

17.4 The normal legal position under the common law is that when a lease or tenancy for a term of years expires or is determined by notice, the tenant must give the property let back to the landlord with vacant possession. Where the tenancy is periodic (ie weekly, monthly, yearly etc), notice of at least one week, month or of one half a year respectively determining at the end of a completed period of the tenancy must be given. Statute has modified this in some cases, as indicated below.

Residential occupiers

17.5 For lawful residential occupiers the Protection from Eviction Act 1977 provides that at least one month's written notice must be given (even if the tenancy is weekly).[1] Also, particular notice provisions may apply under the Rent Acts and Housing Acts.

1   Protection from Eviction Act 1977, s 7.

Allotments

17.6   Tenancies of allotments to which the Allotments Acts apply can only be determined by 12 months' notice (or three months' where specified in the tenancy agreement) which generally must determine before 6 April or after 29 September. The same applies to agricultural holdings: for more details see **17.9ff**.

Gardens held with other property

17.7   Whether the garden is held with another unit, eg a house, shop or farmhouse, or held separately, the key issue which will apply to security of tenure is:

> 'Is the garden used by the tenant for recreation and growing of flowers, fruit and vegetables for himself and his family only or is it used for a business?'

Use as family garden

17.8   If it is used as a family garden, then the only security of tenure which a garden owner tenant will have will be as follows:

(a) If the garden is held with his house or flat then it may enjoy with that house the protection which the Rent Acts/Housing Act 1988 gives to residential tenants (see **17.33ff**).

(b) If the garden is held separately it may be an allotment or allotment garden or 'cottage holding' in which case the Allotments Acts 1908–1950 may apply (see **17.60ff**).

Agricultural holdings

Business use

17.9   If the garden owner tenant is using his garden (whether in conjunction with his house or other unit, eg farm building, or not):

(a) for agriculture; and

(b) is so using it for the purposes of a trade or business

he may have security of tenure of the land (and house, etc) as an 'agricultural holding' as outlined below.

17.10   There are two separate regimes which may apply:

(a) Agricultural Holdings Act 1986;

(b) farm business tenancies.

In both cases the definition of 'agriculture' is as provided in the Agricultural Holdings Act 1986, s 96(1):

'Agriculture' includes 'horticulture, fruit growing, seed growing, dairy farming and livestock breeding and keeping, the use of the land as grazing land, meadow land, osier land, market gardens and nursery grounds and the use of land as woodlands when the use is ancillary to the farming of land or other agricultural purposes.'

17.11 'Livestock' includes 'any creature kept for the production of food, wool, skins or fur or for the purpose of its use in the farming of the land or the carrying on in relation to land of any agricultural activity'. So keeping bees, deer, foxes for fur, a fish farm, cultivating snails or frogs in a garden for business might make it an agricultural holding. The keeping of pheasants for shooting is not within the category.[1] Note that horticulture, fruit growing, seed growing and market gardens are all specifically included.

1   *McNeill v Duke of Hamilton's Trustees* 1918 SC 221.

17.12 'Market garden' means a garden where flowers, fruit, vegetables etc are grown for the market,[1] ie for sale, but an ordinary domestic garden will not be included merely because of the incidental sale of produce[2] including flowers or bulbs.[3] The use may be non-agricultural but must be related to agriculture. For example, in *Dow Agrochemicals Ltd v EA Lane (North Lynn) Ltd* (1965) 115 LJo 76 (county court) land was used for crops in order to test weed killer and this was held to be used for 'agriculture'.

1   *Lowther v Clifford* [1927] 1 KB 130.
2   *Bickerdike v Lucy* [1920] 1 KB 707.
3   *Watters v Hunter* 1927 SC 310 (garden used as bulb farm was held not to be within the Agricultural Holdings Acts—but query this decision: surely growing bulbs is 'horticulture'?).

17.13 There is no minimum size for what can be an agricultural holding so an area as small as a domestic garden or allotment could be included.[1]

1   *Stevens v Sedgman* [1951] 2 KB 434; *Craddock v Hampshire County Council* [1958] 1 All ER 449 (land of 0.229 acres).

Agricultural Holdings Act 1986

17.14 If the garden (or unit with the garden on it) is used for agriculture *and* is used for a trade or business then the Agricultural Holdings Act 1986 may apply, with the following consequences.

(a) Section 2: a tenancy of less than a year is converted into a tenancy of two years.[1]

(b) Section 25: a landlord must give at least 12 months' notice to quit.[1]

(c) Sections 63-70: where notice to quit is given the tenant is entitled to compensation for improvements, fixtures and value of crops etc.[1]

(d) Section 26: the tenant can give a counter notice which will suspend the effect of the landlord's notice to quit until the matter has been considered by the Agricultural Lands Tribunal.

(e) There are cases where the notice which will take effect without consent: s 26(1)and Sch 3, Cases A–F. There are also cases where the consent of the MAFF is required or where the Agricultural Lands Tribunal must confirm the notice to quit and order possession, such as bad husbandry, unsound estate management etc and(Case B) where use is required for a purpose other than agriculture.

(f) Section 12 and Sch 8: if the landlord or the tenant requires the rent to be varied then either may refer to arbitration by the Agricultural Lands Tribunal.

Until 12 July 1984 on the death of the tenant a successor within the family had a right to succeed to the tenancy (limited rights still apply).[1]

1   This also applies to farm business tenancies: see **17.19ff**.

17.15 As noted concerning fencing of gardens (**2.20**) the Agricultural (Maintenance Repair and Insurance of Fixed Equipment) Order 1948, SI 1948/184 contains implied covenants affecting both landlord and tenant in respect of the repair, improvement, contribution to the cost of repair and improvement of barns, stalls, agricultural buildings, machinery, ditches, hedges, fences, gates etc.

17.16 A tenant has a right to remove agricultural fixtures and compensation will be payable for any not removed and for improvements.

17.17 Note that for market gardens, greenhouses will be among 'fixtures' which the tenant is entitled to remove. Compensation for fixtures and improvements for market gardens is dealt with in the Agricultural Holdings Act 1986, s 79(2) and in Sch 8 and a holding can be directed to be treated as a 'market garden' for compensation purposes by the Agricultural Lands Tribunal upon application (s 80). An extract from s 79 is set out in Appendix A.

17.18   The garden tenant who uses his garden for agriculture for a business will also be subject to the general legal consequences under the immense volume of legislation in the Agriculture Act 1970 and other legislation (EU and UK) concerning farming (eg milk quotas, set aside etc) and reference should be made to Rodgers, *Agricultural Law* (2nd edn 1998) on these matters.

Farm business tenancies

17.19   The second regime which a garden tenant who uses his land for agriculture, horticulture, food growing, market garden etc and as a business may find that his tenancy falls under, or may wish by agreement with his landlord to bring into play for his holding, has recently been established by the Agricultural Tenancies Act 1995: 'the farm business tenancy' ('FBT'). This applies to lettings of land used for 'agriculture' (see definition in **17.10**) since 1 September 1995 and includes all or part of land farmed at the beginning of the tenancy (thus avoiding the highly complicated Agricultural Holdings Act rules as to notice to quit *part* of a holding). To be an FBT two conditions must be met:

(a) the *Business Condition*: it must be land used for agriculture farmed for the purpose of trade or business; and

(b) the *Agriculture Condition*: the character of the tenancy must be primarily agricultural having regard to:

   (i)   the terms of the tenancy;

   (ii) the use of the land comprised in the tenancy;

   (iii) the nature of the commercial business carried on any other relevant circumstances; or

   (iv) if it is agreed between the landlord and the tenant (by exchange of notices) that it is to be an FBT.

17.20   The FBT will incorporate certain implied conditions as to quiet enjoyment, repair etc and will provide for *some* only of the protection given to the tenant by the Agricultural Holdings Acts: see footnote 1 in **17.14**:

(a) A limited security of tenure only but the tenant's interest must still be determined by not less than 12 nor more than 24 months' notice: s 6.

(b) Rent to be determined by rent review (direct negotiation between landlord and tenant): s 9.

(c) There are still provisions as to the tenant's right to take fixtures and for compensation: ss 8, 15 and 16.

17.21 It is the 1995 Act, and therefore the FBT, which will apply to current lettings of market gardens, smallholdings etc and its provisions should be carefully noted. The 1995 Act was intended to take away some of the more restrictive fetters on the landlord in the Agricultural Holdings Acts which kept agricultural land off the market (eg rent arbitration and successor's rights) and to widen the scope of lettings to include modern 'agri business' such as sale of non-agricultural goods, horse riding, motorcycle racing etc which would have been outside the protection of the Agricultural Holdings Acts.

17.22 Note that market gardens, nurseries, fruit growing etc are all within 'the agriculture condition' and the garden could be combined with other non-gardening activities and still be the subject of an FBT.

Other commercial use

17.23 Assuming that the garden owner tenant:

(a) does not use his garden for recreation, growing of flowers, fruit and vegetables for himself and his family; and

(b) uses it for a trade or business but *not* such as to fall within the Agricultural Holdings Acts or FBT,

is there any other protection which may apply?

17.24 The Landlord and Tenant Act 1954, Pt II ('the 1954 Act') applies to 'premises', which could include a garden used for the purposes of a trade or business by the tenant. There is a regime with which most practitioners are familiar in ss 24–40 whereby:

(a) when the tenancy expires it is deemed to continue unless determined under the 1954 Act;

(b) the landlord (ss 24 and 25) and the tenant (s 26) can serve notice (in the landlord's case not more than 12 nor less than six months before expiry, in the tenant's case not more than six nor less than three months before expiry) followed by taking court proceedings for a new lease of up to 14 years at a market rent;

(c) the court may grant the landlord possession on certain grounds such as non-payment of rent, breach of covenant etc and (subject to compensation) for the landlord's own occupation or for demolition or reconstruction of any buildings.

17.25   It is provided by the Landlord and Tenant Act 1954. s 43(1)(a) that the Act does not apply to tenancies protected as an agricultural holding and by the Agricultural Tenancies Act 1995, s 40 and Schedule, para 10 it is not to apply to land the subject of an FBT. Therefore most market gardens, fruit farms etc will have Agricultural Tenancies/FBT protection, and the 1954 Act will not apply.

17.26   In *Short v Greeves* (1988) 08 EG 109 (CA) it was held that a garden centre which began by selling its own produce and was protected by the Agricultural Holdings Act still remained within that regime and did not become a business tenancy under the 1954 Act even though by the time of the proceedings 60% of the produce sold was brought in from outside.

17.27   Examples of business premises which might be protected are garden centres, gardens used for horse training, breeding of dogs etc, a 'gnome reserve' or a specially let arboretum all of which would be covered by the 1954 Act.

17.28   There is no problem about a garden being 'land' or 'premises' in terms of the 1954 Act. The following were held to be premises under the 1954 Act and therefore the subject of a business tenancy:

(a) a field for a riding school: *Bracey v Read* [1963] Ch 88;

(b) a right to train racehorses: *Watkins v Emslie* (1982) 1 EGLR 81; and

(c) gallops for racehorses: *University of Reading v Johnston-Houghton* (1985) 2 EGLR 113.

17.29   In *Wandsworth London Borough Council v Singh* (1991) 2 EGLR 75, CA it was held that an open area of approximately 500 square metres used for recreation and leisure by Wandsworth Council was 'occupied' by the Council even though their only interest was 'passive' except for infrequent maintenance. The Council had spent money on planting trees and on seats and could prevent members of the public from having access by locking gates. It was held that presence and control through its servants and agents was sufficient occupation to give the Council's leasehold interest under a tenancy at £150 per month determinable on three months' notice the protection of the 1954 Act. An earlier case in which a tenant of 46 garages who had no office, electricity or water on the premises were held not to have sufficient 'occupation': *Trans-Britannia Properties Ltd v Darby Properties* (1986) 1 EGLR 151 was distinguished.

17.30 So a tenant of a garden used for the purposes of his or her business may be protected by the 1954 Act even though the premises have no accommodation on them and even if there is no water or electricity connected, provided the tenant exercises control and carries out minimal maintenance there. An isolated garden or one held under a separate lease used for business purposes could therefore be within the 1954 Act where the tenancy is not excluded by s 43. By the Law of Property Act 1969 it is now possible to obtain a court order contracting out of the Act before the tenancy is entered into.

17.31 Where a mansion house is used as offices, hotel or health farm, or a purpose built block of offices has a garden for office workers, a 'sitting out' area at a supermarket, school grounds etc will all be cases of gardens held with business premises and may be within the 1954 Act even though the use, ie recreation of office staff or customers, is not literally for the business concerned.

17.32 A lease of 'a right to use a garden' alone could not itself be the subject of a business tenancy.[1] However, where 'a right to use a garden' (as opposed to the garden itself) is included with the main premises in the previous lease it is thought that the courts would include it in any new lease.[2]

1   *Land Reclamation Co Ltd v Basildon District Council* [1978] 2 All ER 1162 (separate lease of a right of way could not be renewed under the 1954 Act).

2   *Re No 1 Albemarle St* [1959] Ch 531 (1954 Act renewal could include right to use advertising sign) but see *Nevill Long & Co (Boards) Ltd v Firmenich & Co* (1983) 268 EG 572 (where the court refused to grant a right of way not included in the previous lease) and see also *G Orlik (Meat Products) Ltd v Hastings & Thanet Building Society* (1974) 29 P & CR 126 (where a right to park was not included in the new lease).

Residential use

17.33 If the garden tenant is not using the garden for the purposes of a trade or business it may be that it is held in the same tenancy as a house, flat or cottage. If this residential unit is 'a dwelling house' (which expression includes flats, duplex flats, chalets, nissen huts etc (but *not* caravans) as well as a 'house' in the literal sense) then the Rent Acts (various Acts commencing with the Rent and Mortgage Interest (Restrictions) Act 1919 and culminating in the Rent Acts 1977 and 1988 which consolidated the earlier legislation) may apply if the letting was before 15 January 1989, or if the letting was after that date the Housing Act 1988 may apply to give the tenant security of tenure of the 'dwelling house' and of the garden held with it.

17.34 Under the Rent Acts, the tenant will have a personal right to remain notwithstanding expiry of his tenancy or notice to quit. Under the Housing Act 1988 the residential tenant who qualifies gets an 'Assured Tenancy' or 'Assured Shorthold Tenancy' which continues until determined by notice under the Act or an order of the court.

Gardens held with residential tenancies

Those let before 15 January 1989: the Rent Acts

17.35 The tenant of a garden held under a separate letting of the garden from the 'dwelling house' would not be covered unless the tenancies of both units can be regarded as one letting.[1]

1 *Pender v Reid* 1948 SC 381 (rent originally separate for house and garden to be assessed as one rent).

17.36 A dwelling house held with agricultural land exceeding two acres cannot be protected. The Rent Act 1977 provides in s 26(1):

'For the purposes of this Act any land or premises let together with a dwelling-house shall unless it consists of agricultural land exceeding 2 acres in extent be treated as part of the dwelling-house.'

And in s 6(1):

'Subject to section 26 of the Act a tenancy is not a protected tenancy if the dwelling-house which is subject to the tenancy is let together with land other than the site of the dwelling house.'

17.37 'Agricultural land' within s 26 is defined by reference to the General Rate Act 1967, s 26(3) (although this applies to rating and has now been repealed) includes arable pasture, woodland and cottage gardens exceeding 0.10 hectares (¼ acre) but *not* land occupied with a house as a park, gardens, pleasure grounds or land kept mainly or exclusively for sport or recreation or land used as a racecourse. So:

(a) A separate garden eg over the road from the house (and not on the site of the house) would not be protected (see s 6);

(b) A house held with more than two acres of land used for agriculture would not be protected. It might, however, be the subject of protection under the Agricultural Holdings Acts (see **17.14ff**) (because of the 'agriculture' definition), but not, presumably, if the gardens or grounds are used for sporting, recreation etc.

However, most gardens, ie those less than two acres (or larger, but not of agricultural land, will share the 'dwelling house' protection.

17.38 'Garden land' held with a dwelling house and subject to a Rent Act protected tenancy has been held to include:

(a) an orchard: *Chubb v Ford* (1947) 143 EG 1911;

(b) one and a half acres of meadow land and one acre of garden: *Hill v Morland* (1946) 147 EG 245;

(c) four acres of land used for grazing and recreation: *Stanhope v Bashford* [1942] EG 134 EGD.

17.39 A conflict may arise between protection under the Rent Acts of a dwelling house and garden, and premises with a garden which are the subject of a business tenancy under the Landlord and Tenant Act 1954, Pt II (as to which see **17.52**). In *Gurton v Parrott* [1996] 1 EGLR 98, CA a tenant who held a house and whose late widowed mother had used the rear garden for dog breeding and kennels was held not to be a business tenant, but had the protection of the Rent Acts—the dog use was a hobby only and did not detract from the use of the house as his residence. But in *Pender v Reid* 1948 SC 381, a Scottish case, where a house, coal yard, garage and workshop were let under one lease, and as these comprised three quarters of the premises and were used for a business, it was held that the Rent Acts did *not* apply to the house.

Those let on or after 15 January 1989: the Housing Act 1988

17.40 The Housing Act 1988 applies to gardens held with residential tenancies let on or after 15 January 1989. Section 2(1) provides that the Act applies 'if under a tenancy a dwelling-house is held together with land' and s 2(2) 'if and so long as the main purpose of the letting is the provision of a home for a tenant or, if there are joint tenants, at least one of them'. Under the Housing Act 1988, which applies to most short term residential lettings to individuals, an 'Assured Tenancy' or 'Assured Shorthold Tenancy' will include 'land held with the dwelling house' and so a garden held with the house will clearly be included in an assured tenancy.

OTHER RIGHTS

Gardens held with residential property on long leases

17.41 Where the garden is held with a lease from a private landlord of a house or flat which is for a term of over 21 years[1] then the tenant, if he uses the house as his only or main residence, may be

able to buy the freehold from his landlord compulsorily by giving appropriate notices at a price fixed under the Act. Leasehold Reform Act 1967, s 1—the right to buy the freehold of flats is collective. See the Leasehold Reform, Housing and Urban Development Act 1993, s 1.[2]

1   It formerly had to be at a low rent and below a particular rateable value and these rules may still be relevant but we do not propose to deal with the detail here.

2   The right is exercisable by the tenants' nominee of one thirds of the total number qualifying tenants and one half of the number of flats in the building must be involved: s 13.

Leasehold reform legislation

17.42   The Leasehold Reform Act 1967 and Leasehold Reform Housing and Urban Development Act 1993 each give alternative rights for individual tenants to apply for a lease extension of the house or flat for terms of 50 or 90 years respectively at a premium (price) fixed under the relevant Act at a nominal rent.

Houses

17.43   In the Leasehold Reform Act 1967, which relates to houses, s 2 (3) provides that:

'subject to the following provisions of this section, where in relation to a house let to and occupied by a tenant reference is made in this Part of the Act to the house and premises, the reference to premises is to be taken to referring to any garage, outhouse, garden, yard and appurtenances which at the relevant time are let to him with the house and are occupied and used for the purposes of the house or any part of it by him or by another occupant.'

So a garden included in the lease or indeed held under a separate lease but used with the house would be included. It should be noted, however, that where there was a house with an immediately surrounding garden and an area of rough ground used as a garden but divided by a fence, it was held that although the garden was part of the house, the area of rough ground was not.[1]

1   *Methuen-Campbell v Walters* [1979] QB 525, CA.

Flats (1)

17.44   Section 13 of the Leasehold Reform, Housing and Urban Development Act 1993 provides for the service of the initial notice from tenants commencing the collective enfranchisement procedure

pursuant to their rights on the landlord's holding to buy the superior interests in their block. The notice must:

> 'specify and be accompanied by a plan showing ... (1) the premises of which the freehold is proposed to be acquired'.

If the block of flats has a garden it is therefore vital that the tenants exercising this right should show this on the plan.[1] So too the procedure in s 42 for an individual tenant to claim an extension lease provides for submission of a plan and it is vital that any garden should be shown on it.

1 The failure to annex *any* plan makes the initial notice invalid: *Mutual Place Property Management Ltd v Blaquiere* [1996] 2 EGLR 78.

17.45 The 'premises' to which the collective right applies in s 1 of the 1993 Act are not defined but where the block has the right to use a garden it seems clear that all easements are to be conveyed to the tenants' nominee.

17.46 There are cases, eg where there is a resident freeholder, or there are local authority secure tenants in the block, in which the tenants' nominee must grant a lease back to the freeholder: s 36. In this case it is clear that the lease back is to include easements 'as nearly as may be for the benefit of the demised premises the same rights as exist for the benefit of those premises immediately before the enfranchisement', and 'all such further easements and rights (if any) as are necessary for the reasonable enjoyment of' the leased back premises (Sch 9, para 10). So the right to use a garden would certainly be included.

Flats (2): Landlord and Tenant Act 1987

17.47 The Landlord and Tenant 1987 also gives tenants of flats to which the Act applies a right of first refusal to buy the freehold and superior leasehold interests when the landlord is seeking to sell, at the same price. Criminal sanctions now apply to landlords who fail to give notice.[1]

1 Housing Act 1996.

17.48 It is not proposed to give the highly complicated details of this legislation but it should be noted that a garden held with the flat or the right to use the garden would be included in the transfer of the freehold or extended lease.[1] However a garden let under a series of short leases was held not to be included in the property

the freehold of which the tenants had the collective right to enfranchise.[2]

1   *Kay Green v Twin Sectra Ltd* [1996] 2 All ER 546 (Landlord and Tenant Act 1987: tenants had right to purchase freehold of block of flats: held they were entitled to rights over gardens and utility areas held with the existing leases of the flats and these rights could not be severed and determined by the freeholder).

2   *Burr and Anor v Eyre and Others* (1998) 20 EG 132.

Gardens held with council properties: 'the Right To Buy'

17.49   Under the the Housing Act 1985, s 119 the secure tenant of a local authority who qualifies by reason of three years' residence has the right to buy the freehold of a house or to a 125-year lease of a flat at a discounted price. Section 184(1) states that the land let together with the dwelling house shall be treated as part of the dwelling house unless it is agricultural land exceeding two acres (to tie in with the Rent Acts). By subs (2) if land is or has been used for the purpose of the dwelling house, eg as a garden, and the tenant puts it in his notice and it is 'reasonable in all the circumstances' then the tenant may acquire this 'land' as well.

17.50   So, where the tenancy includes a garden he will get the garden. He will also get the garden if he uses it separately, even, it seems, if held on licence, but he must put it in his notice and may have to justify that it is reasonable in all the circumstances.

17.51   However, the author has known cases where gardens have been held separately on licence and the local authority has determined the licence before the 'right to buy' notice was served with the successful intention of not allowing its tenant to include the garden in the freehold conveyance/125-year lease. Thus a council tenant in this position would be well advised to get in first and to mention use of the garden in the notice.

Gardens let separately

Used for business

17.52   As already seen, gardens let separately used for business may be the subject of security of tenure under the Agricultural Holdings Act 1986, Agricultural Tenancies Act 1995 or Landlord and Tenant Act 1954, Pt II. It is not proposed to deal further with gardens used for horticultural purposes, market gardens, fruit growing land etc which will be covered by one or other of the above regimes but small commercial gardens will be dealt with briefly.

Smallholdings

17.53 Smallholdings are similar to and dealt with in the legislation relating to allotment gardens. However, 'smallholdings' are used for the purpose of a trade or business and allotments cannot be.[1]

1   Smallholdings and Allotments Act 1908.

17.54 'Smallholdings' are a unit of land let by a smallholdings authority (the county or district council) and by the MAFF as a 'smallholding', meaning an agricultural holding exceeding one pole (an old measurement) now 0.405 hectares but not exceeding 20.2 hectares or having a annual letting value of more than £100.[1] Reference to the relevant parliamentary debates shows that it was intended that 'smallholding' was to be the minimum area of land which could be worked by one man full time with another as assistant within certain conditions.

1   Agriculture Act 1970, s 38.

17.55 The smallholdings authority used to have power to acquire land by agreement or compulsorily but the power for the latter has been repealed[1]. The Ministry of Agriculture, Fisheries and Food has similar powers but these are no longer exercised in practice.

1   Agriculture Act 1970, s 48(2).

17.56 The smallholdings authority must once a year advertise for tenants of vacant smallholdings and keep records and select tenants with agricultural experience (usually five years full time or three years with agricultural college experience). If a smallholder dies they must consider his family as new tenants first.[1]

1   Agriculture Act 1970, s 44 and Smallholdings (Selection of Tenants) Regulations 1970, SI 1970/1049.

17.57 Smallholdings are 'agricultural holdings' and are used for a trade or business, and as such are subject to security of tenure and rent regulation.

(a) As to security of tenure, lettings before 1 September 1995 and their continuation are subject to the Agricultural Holdings Act 1986 (see **17.14**) but there are special provisions as to the MAFF approved scheme for co-operative farming, which is more restrictive than the open market situation which exists for other agricultural holdings.[1]

(b) On or after 1 September 1995 smallholdings are to be held on farm business tenancies: see **17.19ff**.

1   Agricultural Tenancies Act 1995.

17.58   With regard to rent, the smallholdings authority must have regard to the rent reasonably expected to be determined as an agricultural holding and also to other local lettings (disregarding improvements, dilapidations and deterioration or damage to the holding for new lettings).[1] In other agricultural lettings before 1 September 1995 the rent is referred to arbitration by the Agricultural Lands Tribunal, whereas for FBTs a normal contractual rent review provision with private arbitration is acceptable—however, the legislation permitting this does not appear to apply to smallholdings. It is to be hoped, nevertheless, that the courts would accept a FBT rent review provision if accepted by both parties.

1   Agriculture Act 1970, s 45.

17.59   Notices to quit must be for at least 12 months expiring at the end of the current term.[1] As in the case of agricultural holdings the tenant can suspend operation of the notice by counternotice and application to the Agricultural Lands Tribunal. The cases set out in **17.14**(e) apply where, with certain variations as to smallholdings, the notice to quit will be allowed to operate. These include an extra case (Case A) which applies to smallholdings in the following circumstances:

(a) the tenant has attained 65; and

(b) if the holding includes living accommodation, that alternative accommodation is provided; and

(c) it is acknowledged that this case (Case A) was incorporated in the tenancy.

In certain other cases, the MAFF or the Agricultural Lands Tribunal may give consent if it is fair and reasonable to do so.[2]

1   Agricultural Holdings Act 1986, s 25.
2   Agricultural Holdings Act 1986, s 26 and Sch 3.

Gardens not used for business

Allotments, allotment gardens, cottage holdings and poor, field gardens and fuel allotments

17.60   The common characteristic of all these types of gardens is that they are *not* used for a trade or business and they must, as

stated by the Allotments Act 1922, s 22(1) (as amended) be 'cultivated by the occupier for the production of vegetables or fruit crops for consumption by himself or his family'.

17.61 It would be interesting to write a social history of the influence of war and returning soldiers on English land law, from the Crusades (which led to land owners putting their land 'in the dead hand' of others (ie 'mortgages') while they went to the Holy Land), to the pressure on government (in particular Liberal governments) to provide work on the land for soldiers and sailors returning from the Boer War and the Great War of 1914–1918. Certainly it was the latter which was responsible for the allotment movement. As a result the plot for 'the little man' has had special protection, and these arrangements still exist.

17.62 'An allotment garden' is an allotment, ie plot of land not exceeding 1011.72 square metres which is wholly or mainly cultivated by the occupier for the production of vegetable or fruit crops for consumption by himself and his family. The land measurement was originally 40 poles, but this old English unit of 30¼ square yards is no longer used.

17.63 The legal power of acquiring land for allotments is one of the few cases in English law where the State (through a local authority) has powers to compulsorily acquire land for private use by another. Under the Allotments Acts 1908 to 1950 it is the duty of the local authority (the parish council and county council have the duty: compulsory acquisition powers are vested in the district council):

(a) to consider representations from local inhabitants who want allotment gardens for themselves and their families. Note that local state schools can be required to be used for public meetings: Small Holdings and Allotments Act, 35(1).

(b) to let or sell its own land or to acquire by purchase through agreement or compulsorily or hire land for that purpose.[1] The consent of the Secretary of State of the Environment is required, and he must go through a procedure of advertisement and public enquiry and will confirm the hiring. The compulsory acquisition or hiring is subject to payment of compensation.

1   Land Settlement (Facilities) Act 1919, s 17.

17.64   Once the land is available the local authority has powers to manage the allotments, improve them, buy and hire garden tools, and will advertise, select and let to tenants, who can be an association or one or more individuals. There are standard terms for a tenancy, for example, not more than one quarter's rent can be required to be paid in advance (unless it is under £1.25 pa) and for rules of allotment holders associations, which again may be set up by the local authority. Lettings must be at the best rent reasonably obtainable with no premium and recovery of possession must be able to take place within 12 months. Subletting without consent is not allowed.[1]

(a) Notice to quit must be at least 12 months expiring on or before 6 April or on or after 29 September in any year (to enable the tenant to have the summer on the holding).[2]

(b) However, there may be provision for re-entry on four months' notice by agreement for certain purposes (eg development) and on bankruptcy, non-payment of rent etc.

1   Smallholdings and Allotments Act 1908; Allotment Act 1950.
2   Allotments Act 1922, s 1(1).

17.65   On determination of his tenancy, the tenant:

(a) is entitled to compensation for his crops and manurial value;

(b) has the right to remove crops;[1] and

(c) is entitled to compensation for disturbance (equal to one year's rent) if re-entry is on certain grounds, eg for development.[2]

1   Allotments Act 1922, s 2(6) and (9).
2   Allotments Act 1950, s 3(2).

17.66   Before a local authority gives notice to quit to allotment holders it needs the Secretary of State's consent. This will only be given where adequate alternative provision for the displaced allotment holders is made.[1]

1   *R v Secretary of State, ex p Gosforth Allotments etc Association* [1995] 70 P & CR 480.

Cottage holdings, poor, field garden, and fuel allotments

17.67   These are very obscure and rarely found as they are obsolete and are no longer likely to be created.[1] Under nineteenth century and earlier Poor Law and Enclosure Acts plots were allocated to 'the labouring poor' by the local parish church officers or parish council. There are powers of compulsory acquisition, exchange, letting and management in the legislation setting up the category

of tenancy, eg the Enclosure Act 1845. 'Fuel allotments' were to enable poor people to cut wood and turf for heating and cooking.

1   Most of the relevant law (and much surplus allotment law) was abolished by the Statute Law (Repeals) Act 1993, s 1 and Sch 1, Pts II and III.

Allotment societies

17.68   Allotment holders associations are frequently set up and are useful in sharing expenses of seeds, plants, tools etc and of the facilities at the site, eg sheds and the provision of water. Note that the water authorities do not have a duty to supply water to an isolated garden (see Chapter 21) and water supply will have to be acquired by agreement. Such associations are often run as co-operatives or Friendly Societies[1] on a non-profit making basis and the local authority has power to make them loans and grants for expenses, as may the Secretary of State.[2]

1   Industrial and Provident Societies Act 1965.
2   Smallholdings and Allotments Act 1908, s 49(2) and (4) as amended; Agriculture Act 1947, s 58.

17.69   For more on allotments or for precedents for the forms required to set up such a society or deal with lettings, notices and the like, see the Encyclopaedia of Forms and Precedents Vol 3(2) 1998 issue, which has an excellent set of all forms required.

18

Disposal of a garden

18.1 If a garden is held with a house and the owner wishes to sell or dispose of the garden or part of it (whether disposing of the freehold or by way of lease), he would be well advised consult both his lawyer and his accountant. Whether the land is sold for development or is disposed of by way of gift within the owner's family, there will be tax and other considerations to take into account. This is particularly the case where the disposal is outside the owner's family, but also for disposals with the family, eg by way of gift.

18.2 It should be checked whether consent of a mortgagee is required, and whether any of the land is subject to a tenancy or licence which must be terminated. The rights to be reserved to the house or to other parts of the garden must also be considered, along with the nature and detail of any restrictive covenants to be released or new restrictions to be imposed over the area to be sold. Where the land is to be developed it must also be checked whether planning permission is necessary and if so who is going to apply for it (the vendor or the purchaser), what is to happen if it is refused or granted subject to onerous conditions (for example, would there be an appeal, if so by whom and at whose cost?), and the effect of any planning permission obtained on the value of the land and the proposed price.

LEASEHOLD GARDENS

18.3 Where a garden is leasehold it is likely to be necessary to apply to the landlord for consent to any sale or disposal. Assignments of part of land held under a lease are usually prohibited because of the difficulties of rent apportionment and the exercise of landlord's remedies, such as distress or forfeiture, against part only of the original premises. Consequently it may be necessary for the vendor lessee to grant an underlease of the part being sold which, again, may need consent. If a lease or underlease is being granted the covenants to be given by the landlord or by the tenant must be agreed and other aspects of the transaction, for example, whether the tenant is to have a right to renew the lease or an option to purchase the freehold reversion, must be considered.

158

BUILDING PLOTS

18.4 If part of a garden is to be sold as a building plot, it may have to be released from any mortgage over the house and garden, and a deed of release may be required. The mortgagee may require the entire proceeds of sale to be paid to it in reduction of the loan. Again, where the garden is leasehold the consent of the landlord, or where the lease is an underlease that of the head landlord, may also have to be obtained.

18.5 As seen in Chapter 12, the garden may be subject to a restrictive covenant against building and action will have to be taken to approach those entitled to the benefit for release or application made under the Law of Property Act 1925, s 84. Indemnity insurance should also be considered, in particular if the mortgagee landlord or covenantee is no longer the same person originally entitled or cannot be traced.

SPECIAL CONSIDERATIONS

18.6 In the sale of garden land there may also be other special features which should be dealt with in the sale contract such as the seller's right to retain that season's fruit or vegetables and the removal of garden fixtures such as statues, ponds and the fish in them, which may give rise to problems if not anticipated (see Chapter 19).

TAX CONSEQUENCES

Capital gains tax

18.7 In addition to deciding the description of the land being disposed of (with plan), price, title, easements and covenants etc, the tax consequences of the transaction must be anticipated. A sale of land is a chargeable event for the purpose of capital gains tax and the disposal is treated as having taken place at the date of contract of sale, unless the sale is conditional in which case it is deemed to have taken place when the condition is satisfied. The capital gain upon which tax will be paid is computed by deducting from the disposal value:

(a) the expenses of finding a buyer and professional fees involved in the disposal;

(b) the cost of acquiring the asset or, if it was acquired before 1 April 1982, market value on 31 March 1982;

(c) any allowable expenditure on improvements;

(d) the indexation allowance;[1]

(e) any part of the sale price attributable to income tax; and

(f) the consideration for trees felled or cut or woodlands managed by the occupier on a commercial basis with a view to realisation of profit.

1   Under the Finance Bill introduced by the government on 17 March 1998 it is proposed that indexation of gains should cease with effect from 5 April 1999 and a time of ownership basis of relief will apply.

18.8   There are technical rules for land held before 6 April 1965 and concerning adding back half of a gain between 1 April 1982 and 5 April 1998.[1] On disposal of part of the original asset (which will generally in the case of the sale of a garden or part of it be a house with the garden), then the value of the asset and costs of acquisition and of improvements are apportioned.[2]

1   Taxation of Chargeable Gains Act 1992, Schedule.
2   Taxation of Chargeable Gains Act 1992, ss 38 and 42.

Reliefs

Capital gains tax

18.9   Where a garden is an asset used in connection with a business, payment of capital gains tax can be deferred and the gain 'rolled over' into the value of an asset acquired with the proceeds or the charge to tax relieved completely. The garden owner may be entitled to roll-over, replacement or retirement relief. It is not proposed to deal with these in any detail here. The most important reliefs likely to be available on the sale of a garden or part of one are:

(a) small land sales—sales at a price below £20,000 where the amount or value of the consideration for the transfer does not exceed one fifth of the value of the holding as it subsisted immediately before the transfer;[1]

(b) private residence relief—where the disposal is of an individual's only or main private residence or of the garden and grounds held with it not exceeding half a hectare (one acre).[2]

In both cases no capital gains tax is payable.

1   Taxation of Chargeable Gains Act 1992, s 242.
2   Taxation of Chargeable Gains Act 1992, s 222(2).

Private residence relief

18.10   Private residence relief is in respect of the house itself so if a garden is sold with the house the 'house relief' applies to the house and garden.[1] 'Garden relief' is a separate relief which applies on the sale of the garden or grounds or part of a garden or grounds

held with a house up to the half hectare limit. Where a garden exceeds half a hectare then the relief may be allowed if the larger area is required for the reasonable enjoyment of the house as a residence tested objectively. Where the house held with the garden or grounds is sold before the garden or grounds then the relief is not available, as it is the house which 'qualifies' the garden or grounds and once that has been sold the sale of the remaining land is treated as an unrelieved disposal of a chargeable asset on its later sale.[2]

1   Taxation of Chargeable Gains Act 1992, s 223(2)(a) (42–44 *Halsbury's Statutes* (4th edn) Taxation).

2   *Varty v Lynes* [1976] 3 All ER 447; but it was stated in the Inland Revenue Tax Bulletin of 18 August 1995 that they would not be taking this point in future.

18.11   Where the garden is a separate piece of land, eg on the other side of a road, then it may not be regarded as a garden or part of a garden held with the private residence unless it is shown objectively that the land has been 'naturally and traditionally' the garden of the house.[1]

1   *Wakeling v Pearce* [1995] STC(SCD) 96 (garden 30 feet away from house across road: relief was available as it was always naturally and traditionally the garden of the house).

18.12   It should be noted that the private residence relief and the separate relief for gardens are only available if the house has been the taxpayer's main private residence for the whole of the period of ownership, except for:

(a)   a period of up to 36 months immediately before the disposal (this is intended to cover persons moving to a new house without having sold their previous house, but is of general application);

(b)   a period of up to three years in total throughout the period of ownership;

(c)   periods of absence when the taxpayer has worked in employment abroad;

(d)   periods totalling four years when the taxpayer was prevented from residing in the house because of his place of or conditions of work.

18.13   The position concerning a genuine period of residence in the house must therefore be documented in detail and proved to the Inland Revenue in order to obtain the relief for the garden or part of it.[1] The residence must have been for 'private use', so use for business purposes even of one room in the house, or if the owner has taken in lodgers, may deprive him of the relief, or may mean

that a proportion of the value of the house used for business purposes will be the subject of capital gains tax.

1   See *Goodwin v Curtis* [1996] STC 1146 (residence for five weeks pending sale not enough).

18.14   Where a person has more than one private residence he must give written notice to the Revenue before the sale opting for one of them to be his main private residence in order to qualify any sale of the garden of that house for relief.

Income tax charge

18.15   If the garden has been used for business purposes (or if the garden is land held for development with the sole or main object of realising a gain from disposing of the land when developed) the gain can be taxed as income at the vendor's highest rate as taxpayer under the Income and Corporation Taxes Act 1988, s 776.

18.16   It is often provided in the sale contract that the buyer should pay an 'overage payment' being an additional sum payable upon the buyer obtaining a price in excess of an agreed figure from sub-buyers. Although this might seem to be evidence of an intention to realise a development gain, it has been held that such a provision does not apply so as to put the disposal within s 776 and take it out of the private residence garden relief.[1]

1   *Page (Inspector of Taxes) v Lowther* [1987] STC 799.

18.17   Income arising from rents, licence fees or parking fees for the use of a garden and for sale of flowers or produce is part of the owner's income and is taxed under the normal income tax rules.

VAT

18.18   Value added tax is chargeable on transactions in land as from 1 April 1989 but there is an exemption for the sale of residential property[1] and land held for 'relevant residential purposes', which includes a garden. A garden sold with a commercial property or used for business purposes or agriculture could be subject to VAT, but there is a relief for assets of a business being sold as a going concern provided the buyer and seller are registered for VAT, apply to HM Customs and Excise before completion of the transaction so to treat it, and HM Customs and Excise accepts that the relief applies.[2]

1   Value Added Tax Act 1994 (Sch 8 groups 5, 6).
2   Value Added Tax Act 1994 , s 49, Value Added Tax Regulations, 1995 1995/2518, reg 6.

19

Rights of removal of departing owner or tenant

19.1 At the end of the lease or on a sale with vacant possession the garden owner or tenant will hand the garden back to the landlord or on to the new owner. What can he take with him and what must he leave?

CROPS AND FRUIT

19.2 In many contracts for the sale and purchase of freehold and leasehold gardens and in leases there will be an express provision that the seller/tenant may take any crops, fruit and plants for the current growing season; indeed there may be a right reserved for him to come back and harvest the crop or pick the fruit in the autumn, making good all damage caused, if completion of the sale takes place or the holding is quit in the spring or summer.

Agricultural Holdings Acts

19.3 Where the land is held under a tenancy for agriculture or horticulture to which the Agricultural Holdings Acts 1947 and 1986 apply then there is a statutory right for an outgoing tenant to take fruit bushes or other crops or be compensated[1] and also to be compensated for fixtures and buildings erected for the purpose of the trade (eg greenhouses). There is a similar right in respect of allotments.[2]

1　Agricultural Holdings Act 1986, s 63 (compensation for disturbance), ss 64 and 65 (compensation for tenant right) and s 79 and Sch 10 (smallholdings and market gardens).

2　Allotments Act 1922, s 2(6) and (9) and Allotments Act 1950, s 3(1).

FIXTURES AND FITTINGS

19.4 A well-drafted contract for the sale of a garden should specify in detail what is to be taken, eg greenhouses, statues, shrubs and plants etc. If the contract does not, then the seller

who has been paid and who has moved has no right to come back and take any item. If the issue arises after exchange of contracts but before payment of the full purchase price on completion, the argument may be over a deduction from the purchase price to cover the 'missing' items. Where the contract or lease does not specify what can be taken, the courts deal with the dispute according to whether the item is a 'fixture', ie does it adhere to the land or is it enjoyed separately from it? If they are fixtures the items should be left for the buyer/landlord, but if not there may be a right to take the disputed items. The number of cases of this type which do result in litigation is perhaps surprising, and emphasises the importance of careful drafting of leases and contracts for sale of gardens.

Garden ornaments and statuary

19.5   In *D'Eyncourt v Gregory* (1886) LR 3 Eq 382 it was held that executors of a tenant for life could *not* remove stone lions and garden seats because they were fixtures. In *Hamp v Bygrave* (1982) 266 Estates Gazette 720 the court held that garden urns, a statue and patio lights were fixtures. In each case they had to be left for the reversioner/purchaser.

Greenhouses

19.6   Greenhouses (even those which rest by their own weight on a concrete base or which attach by bolts) have been held not to be fixtures and are removable in the absence of agreement to the contrary.[1]

1   *HE Dibble Ltd (Trading as Mill Lane Nurseries) v Moore* [1970] 2 QB 181 (two greenhouses resting on their own weight did not pass to purchaser) and *Deen v Andrews* (1986) 52 P & CR 17 (greenhouse bolted to plinth was a chattel, not a building, and the vendor could enter and dismantle it).

Other cases on fixtures

19.7   In the most recent case regarding fixtures which went to the House of Lords, *Elitestone Ltd v Morris* [1997] 2 All ER 513, chalets free-standing upon concrete bases were held to have become fixtures. But in *Mears v Callender* [1901] 2 Ch 388 certain glasshouses were held to be removable. Also the seller was allowed to take a crop from the apple trees on the property with the consent of the court. In *Berkley v Poulett* (1976) 120 Sol Jo 836 a statue of a Greek athlete 5' 7" high weighing 10cwt and a sundial were held to be removable by the seller. In the next most recent and 'senior' case to the *Elitestone* case, *TSB Bank plc v Botham*

[1996] EGCS 149, CA, which concerned taps, light fittings, gas fires etc, the intention of bringing in the items and fixing them in position and whether they were to be permanent or not was held to be decisive. It was held that they should be left.

20

Taxation

20.1 For a charge to income tax or capital gains tax to arise with regard to a garden some activity (eg a business) or event (eg a sale) has to happen to generate the tax. The other main tax on land owners, which has been much longer established than either of these, is 'rates'. Rates are local government taxes, and were originally raised by the parish officers or 'vestry' of each church area to pay for repairs to streets and bridges, administering the poor law etc, and continue today to be based on the 'occupation' of land in the local government area, which can include a garden. There are now two types of local tax:

(a) rates; and

(b) council tax.

RATES

20.2 By the Local Government Finance Act 1988, s 64(4) rates are charged on 'lands' and there are extensive old statutes and case law as to what constitutes a rateable 'hereditament' (ie land unit) and whether it is capable of occupation. The unit will probably be a building, eg offices, house etc and adjoining land such as its garden which will be assessed at a value (the 'rateable value') by the District Valuer and will be recorded on the local authority's list.

20.3 A mere easement such as the right to use a garden or other incorporeal (ie 'disembodied') rights are not regarded as capable of occupation and will not be subject to rates. Neither will a common holder's rights in common land, eg a right to graze one cow, unless there is a specific unit of land on which the common holder's rights can be valued with regard to this.[1] Sporting rights are rateable.

1 *R v Tewkesbury Trustees for Burgesses* (1810) 13 East 55; *Lincoln Corpn v Holmes Common Overseers* (1867) LR 2 QB 482 (where Blackburn J held that the collective value of the commoner's rights were nil, so no rates payable).

20.4 The 'rate' is a percentage figure on each pound of rateable value and is now a uniform rate set by the government and charged throughout England and Wales on business property (the Non-Domestic Business Rate), which is paid to the local authority.

20.5 Prior to 1988 rates were also charged on domestic property and were fixed individually by each local authority and the law of rates as to gardens goes back to the previous legislation and case law.

20.6 Domestic rates were chargeable on a garden which was included under the description 'a yard, garden, outhouse or other appurtenance belonging to or enjoyed with the property' (Local Government Finance Act 1988, Sch 5), and if a garden is held with a commercial building, eg a hotel or dog kennels, it will be valued with the building and the Non Domestic Rate will be payable on the total rateable value. Under Sch 5, 'agricultural land' is exempted from rates. This includes 'a market garden, nursery grounds and allotments'. 'A market garden' is a holding cultivated for the purpose of the business of market gardening even though the occupier takes most of the produce for home consumption.[1] Under Sch 5, para 2 agricultural land does *not* include:

'(a) land occupied together with a house as a park

(b) gardens (other than market gardens)

(c) pleasure grounds...'

Hence a garden is by implication subject to non-domestic rates and council tax. In *Hood Barrs v Howard (Valuation Officer)* [1967] RA 50, 13 RRC 164 it was held that an orchard was *not* subject to agricultural relief as it was part of a 'garden' and should therefore be included in the rates. An 'agricultural building', ie a building used for agriculture and which is not a dwelling also subject to relief from non-domestic rates. These include greenhouses, sheds, broiler houses, buildings for cultivating mushrooms and bee hives. See Local Government Act 1988, Sch 5, paras 5–8.

1   *Bickerdyke v Lucy* [1920] 1 KB 707.

COUNCIL TAX

20.7 There is now a separate tax payable by domestic property owners under the Local Government Finance Act 1992, s 1: council tax. Council tax was introduced as a more acceptable alternative to the community charge. The latter (known as 'the poll tax') was a tax on individuals within a local authority area—brought in in 1988 by Margaret Thatcher's government, it proved extremely unpopular and was later withdrawn. As with the old rates, council tax is not charged at a uniform level throughout England and Wales; rather it is fixed by each local authority.

20.8 The council tax is charged in respect of all 'dwellings' in a local authority's area: Local Government Finance Act (LGFA) 1992, s 1. It is based on the value of the dwelling, ie the house or flat, and would include any garden held with the dwelling. However, neither 'a yard

garden, outhouse or appurtenances belonging to or enjoyed with property used wholly for the purpose of living accommodation' (nor garages or stores) are 'dwellings' except in so far as they form part of a larger property which is itself a dwelling: LGFA 1992, s 3(3). This seems to mean that a garden held separately from a house or flat would not be valued or liable for council tax and that a garden would only be liable for council tax if it is included with a larger unit, ie the house with which it is held.

20.9   The valuation of the 'dwelling' (and garden) is decided by the District Valuer. The amount of the tax will depend upon into which of eight bands (A–H) of increasing value the property fits. The actual charge can vary by reference to the number of people living in the house, whether it is a weekend cottage etc, and is payable by the resident(s). Council tax also applies to caravans and boats: LGFA Act 1992, s 7.

20.10   The Secretary of State of the Environment has power to amend by Order in Council the definition of 'dwelling': LGFA 1992, s 3(6). or to make regulations to deal with the alteration of the council's valuation lists. This can include whether or not a dwelling has a 'domestic use in such a manner so as to constitiute it a domestic property for the purposes of Part III of the 1988 Act': LGFA 1992, s 4. It might not be possible for gardens to be reclassified as separate units for council tax under these provisdions but this seems likely.

APPLICATION OF TAXES AND AGRICULTURAL RELIEF

20.11   The value of the garden will therefore usually be included in the unit with which it is held for both rates and council tax valuations. The right to use a garden would not be separately assessed but such right might enhance the value of the property enjoying it.

20.12   The question of whether an isolated garden or one held separately would be subject to rates or council tax is not expressly dealt with in the legislation. If the garden was held with a house but separated from the latter, for example by a road, it would be 'enjoyed with a dwelling' and therefore included with the value of the dwelling and subject to council tax: see *Wakeling v Pearce* [1995] STC(SCD) 96.

20.13   An isolated garden could certainly be 'lands' and capable of rateable occupation. Many such gardens will be market gardens or allotments and subject to agricultural relief. It is difficult to think of an example of an isolated garden which would be separately valued and chargeable for non-domestic rates.

21

Entitlement to things found or dug up in a garden

21.1 Sometimes the garden owner may 'strike lucky' by finding jewellery, old artefacts or other valuables in his garden. Or his guest or someone he has licensed to use a metal detector there may do so. What is the legal position?

MINES, MINERALS AND FOSSILS

21.2 If the garden is leasehold the lease may provide that the mines and minerals under the garden or even any stone or sand excavated belong to the landlord, in which case anything in the minerals, stone etc such as fossils will be his property. Similarly, freehold land may be subject to a reservation in favour of an earlier owner. If there is no reservation in the lease or sale/ownership documents then mines, minerals and the like will be the leaseholder's or freeholder's property.

COAL, GAS AND OIL

21.3 If coal reserves or oil are discovered in a garden, the garden owner cannot exploit it. The Coal Industry Act 1949, ss 5–9 nationalised all coal, and the Petroleum (Production) Act 1934 vested all oil in the State. It is possible that a garden owner might be licensed to dig it up or pump it out, but this is unlikely as specialists in the field are more likely licensees. However, the garden owner does own the land surface and can charge for anyone entering his land for exploration or exploitation of these substances. He can also claim compensation if underground workings cause his garden to subside.

PIPES ETC

21.4 The pipes, wires and cables laid under the garden pursuant to an easement to lay and maintain water pipes and sewers belong to the owner of the pipes etc who put them in, *not* to the garden owner.[1]

1   *Simmons v Midford* [1969] 2 Ch 415.

FINDS OF JEWELLERY OR VALUABLES

21.5 Usually items found in a garden belong to the garden owner, who can sell them, give them to the British Museum and generally exercise rights of ownership. There are, however, exceptions:

(a) If stolen goods, eg a car wireless or wallet with cash is thrown over the fence into A's garden, the property is not A's, and A has a duty to hand it in to the Police—if A does not do so he will be guilty of receiving stolen goods or other offences under the Theft Acts.

(b) What if the finder claims the item? A number of cases establish the following position:

   (i) If the item is buried or submerged in a pond and has 'acceded to the soil', ie become thoroughly dug in, it is then subject to 'treasure trove' (see **21.6ff**) and it will be the land owner's.[1]

   (ii) If the item is casually on the land, ie just lying about, then it will depend whether the land owner asserts his rights to exclude others by exercising care and control over the land which he occupies: if he does, the item found belongs to him. If however the garden is open land, and the owner allows the public or neighbours on it and does not maintain it, then the finder may be able to keep the item as 'finders keepers'. In the case of *Parker v British Airways Board* [1982] QB 1004 the Court of Appeal held that the finder of a bracelet in the Executive Lounge at Heathrow (a passenger in transit) was entitled to the £850 value of the bracelet (which he had handed in to BA) and not BA, as beyond cleaning the lounge, BA seemed not to exercise care and control and did not supervise the activities of passengers there. However, it is unlikely that this point could be taken against a garden owner whose garden is fenced, and even if it is not, where the owner cuts the grass etc and keeps trespassers out.

(c) Treasure trove and the Treasure Act 1996: see below.

1   See *Elwes v Briggs Gas Co* (1886) 33 Ch D 562 (pre-historic boat found in building work by lessee was held to belong to the land owner) and *SouthStaffordshire Water Co v Sharman* [1896] 2 QB 44 (two rings in mud in pool were held to belong to land owner not finder).

Treasure trove and the Treasure Act 1996

21.6 Under English law everything has an owner. If no one claims it or is alive to claim it, it belongs to the Crown as 'bona vacantia'— this stems from the Norman idea (dating from 1066) that the Crown owns everything which it has not graciously allowed over the years other people to acquire. Thus the ancient rule of law of treasure trove presumes that any coins or chattels containing a substantial amount of gold or silver (eg rings, cups, bangles etc) buried or hidden by an unknown owner were concealed by him with a view to recovery; as he never came back to recover them and it can be assumed from the age of the coins etc that he must be dead without heirs, property in them reverts to the Crown. So old gold coins or silver found in a garden are likely to be treasure trove.

21.7 All finds must be reported to the Crown, via its officer the Coroner within 14 days and it is a criminal offence not to do so.[1] The Coroner will hold an inquest, which is likely to be open to the public, and will decide if the find is treasure trove and therefore reverts to the Crown.[2] If it does, the Crown will often compensate (or get the British Museum to compensate) the finder. The legal position is now governed by the Treasure Act 1996.

1 Treasure Act 1996, s 8.

2 See William Blackstone *Commentaries* p 295. 'A man, that hides his treasure in a secret place evidently does not want to relinquish his property, but reserves a right to claiming it again, when he sees occasion and if he dies and the secret also dies with him, the law gives it to the King in part of his royal revenue.'

21.8 The items which now revert to the Crown include items which were previously 'treasure trove', but also now include anything the owner of which cannot be identified:

(a) if the object or coin is at least 300 years old at the date of the find, and when found

(b) if not a coin (eg a bangle, cup etc), if it is at least 10% gold or silver in its metallic content, or

(c) if a coin

   (i)   is one of at least two in the same find having that content of gold etc (see (b)), or

   (ii) when found is one of at least ten coins in the same find.[1]

Objects can be in the same find even if discovered at different times.[2] Objects in this category now belong by statute as well as common

law to the Crown or its franchisee, and the rights of the land owner or occupier are expressly extinguished.[3] The Secretary of State for Heritage has the power to designate classes of objects which would not otherwise be treasure.[4]

1   Treasure Act 1996, s 1(1).
2   Treasure Act 1996, ss 1(1)(d).
3   Treasure Act 1996, ss 4 and 6.
4   Treasure Act 1996, s 2.

21.9   Only if the treasure is transferred to a museum can the Secretary of State decide to pay a reward, but such a payment can be made to the land owner as well as to the finder, if they are different people.[1] There is no right to sue the Crown or the museum for non-payment of a reward.[2]

1   Treasure Act 1996, s 10.
2   Treasure Act 1996, s 10(6).

21.10   If the artefact or buildings or the remains of them found in a garden are of significant archaeological or historical interest the Secretary of State may schedule the site under the Ancient Monuments and Archaeological Areas Act 1979 as such an area. When a site is scheduled, no digging or interference with the soil, stones etc is allowed, and the Secretary of State's consent is necessary for any works (repair, alterations, tipping etc). There is a right to claim compensation from the Department of Heritage for any loss suffered as a result.[1]

1   Ancient Monuments and Archaeological Areas Act 1979, ss 7, 8 and 9.

22

Garden waste, water and electricity supply

22.1 There is nowadays detailed law applying to every household, business, office, hotel, restaurant, hospital etc in the country as to what one can do or cannot do with one's rubbish. In most cases the waste from a garden will be 'household waste' and dealt with accordingly.

22.2 The Controlled Waste Regulations 1992, SI 1992/588, Sch 1 define 'household waste' as waste issuing from (inter alia):

> 'any land belonging to or used in connection with a domestic property, caravan or residential home'

and garden rubbish will be covered by this in most cases. 'Household waste' is exempted from the highly detailed and onerous regulations made for other types of waste, which can only be disposed of by a licensed waste operator with the appropriate waste management licence in an authorised place, eg tip or land fill site. Similarly, the exemption is repeated in the Environmental Protection Act 1990, s 33 which prescribes these 'waste disposal operations' which excludes:

> 'household waste from domestic property which is treated, kept or disposed of within the curtilage of the dwelling or with the permission of the occupier of the dwelling.'

So such disposal, which would seem to include bonfires of leaves and the keeping of compost heaps, is quite lawful.

22.3 The local authority has a duty to collect and dispose of household waste under the Environmental Protection Act 1990, s 45(1) but can require the householder to provide waste receptacles of a particular kind, eg plastic bags or 'wheelie bins', and pay for them: s 46(3). However, there is a defence to the offence of not complying where the requirement is unreasonable or the existing receptacle is adequate: s 46(7)(a), so any exceptional requirement or payment as to the removal of garden waste may be able to be challenged on this basis.

173

WASTE FROM A COMMERCIAL GARDEN OR 'CONTROLLED WASTE'

22.4 If the waste is, for example, from a garden centre or other trade premises or is 'controlled waste' within the Control of Pollution Act 1974 and the Environmental Protection Act 1990 (eg 'clinical waste') then it may be necessary to comply with the additional provisions of the Act as to removal by a licensed waste operator by a prescribed method to a licensed tip and to pay for the service over and above council tax/rates. A conviction for breach of s 33 of the 1990 Act can lead to a substantial fine, or a prison term, or both. However, it is a defence for the defendant to show that due diligence was exercised (ie he took all reasonable steps to comply) or that he was acting on the instructions of a third party.

22.5 Even if a garden is commercial or its waste exceptional, certain activities are outside the waste management licensing provisions, for example, 'burning as fuel straw, poultry, litter, wood, waste ...' and 'spreading compost' or 'sludge' or if the waste is 'biodegradable waste'.

22.6 Accumulation of the wrong kind of waste or unauthorised disposal of it can also give rise to liability for a civil claim by a neighbour or the person affected under s 73(6) of the Environmental Protection Act 1990.

LITTER

22.7 It is a criminal offence to deposit litter in an open public place under the Environmental Protection Act 1990, s 87 and the local authority, which has a duty to collect litter, can by a Street Litter Control Notice under SI 1991/1324 require the occupiers of premises (which could include a house but it is unlikely) such as fast food restaurants or shops to make arrangements to collect and dispose of the litter or to pay for them to do so. This may help a garden owner whose front garden is used as a dumping ground for fried chicken boxes, papers etc and he should take up such a problem with his local authority direct or through his local councillor. As noted earlier, the local authority also has powers to collect errant supermarket trolleys, but only from the public street.[1]

1   Environmental Protection Act 1990, s 99 and Sch 4.

22.8 There is a separate power under the Public Health Act 1936, ss 79–80[1] to require the owner or occupier of premises to remove any noxious matter, manure etc in an urban district. This can include removal from a pond, pool, ditch or watercourse.

1   The 1936 Act has been mostly replaced by the Environmental Protection Act 1990, but this power still exists.

WATER

22.9 The position as to riparian rights of garden owners along a river and as to private water supplies has been dealt with in Chapters 2 and 3. It is vital that a garden should have water for irrigating plants and vegetables and for watering the lawn and thus the legal position as to when this has to be provided, who pays for it and who can stop the supply and when, is important.

22.10 Under the Water Industry Act 1991, s 39(1) it is the duty of each water undertaker (ie the water company licensed for water supply in an area) to connect the premises in its area for domestic supply. An owner or occupier can serve notice requiring the water undertaker to connect his premises with the water main.[1]

1   Water Industry Act 1991, s 45(1) as amended by the Competiton and Service (Utilities) Act 1992, s 43(1).

22.11 The Water Supply and Sewerage Services (Customer Services Standards) Regulations 1989, SI 1989/1159 and SI 1989/1383 regulate the interruption and cutting off of water supplies.

22.12 Certain standards are contracted for between the undertaker and the Director of Water Services, eg water pressure, and these must be kept to. A complaints procedure under s 86A of the Water Industry Act 1991 is available to all customers and any duty in that Act can be enforced by the Director or the Secretary of State.

Water for the garden: is it a 'domestic supply'?

22.13 By s 218(1) of the Water Industry Act 1991 'domestic purposes' means 'drinking, cooking, central heating and sanitary purposes' so does not strictly include garden purposes. Domestic supply is to any building or part of a building occupied as a dwelling house whether private or not and if unoccupied likely to be so occupied. However, water for the garden will be treated as a domestic supply provided that the water is to a tap *in the house* and is taken

from there to the garden and it will be considered to be for domestic purposes and must be provided and charged and paid for within the domestic tariff. The position is otherwise if the supply is direct to a tap in the garden or by a hose pipe.[1] Where the supply is for non-domestic purposes, eg to a market garden, an isolated garden or an allotment, the undertaker does not have to supply water where it would have to incur unreasonable expenditure which would put at risk its existing or probable future obligations.[2] The matter is subject to agreement and the water authority may require payment to provide a supply. Any dispute can be determined by an arbitrator or by the Director.[3]

1   Section 218(2)(b).
2   Section 55.
3   Section 56(2) and (3).

Water charges

22.14   Under the 1991 Act undertakers must put forward a charges scheme and where this has been approved by the Director of Water Services as a condition of being given the monopoly of the service the scheme must be kept to. This will usually be expressed as a 'water rate' each year for the area concerned. Currently it can be based on the rateable value of the property but this is not to apply after 31 March 2000.[1]

1   Water Industry Act 1991, s 145(1).

22.15   Section 142(2) of the Water Industry Act 1991 provides that, by agreement with the customer, the water undertaker may install and charge on the basis of supply through a water meter installed at the property supplied. The water undertaker has a right of entry to read any such meter[1] and must charge according to the readings.[2] It is a criminal offence to tamper with a meter.[3]

1   Water Industry Act 1991, s 172(2)(d).
2   Water Industry Act 1991, s 18.
3   Water Industry Act 1991, s 175(1).

22.16   There can be and is a separate charge made for 'non-domestic supply', ie water coming direct to the garden or for use of a hose pipe or irrigation system. The customer must pay these charges when agreed under threat of discontinuance of the supply on seven days' notice.[1]

1   Water Industry Act 1991, s 61.

Interrupting or stopping water supply

Drought orders

22.17 The water undertaker has a duty to assess and manage its water resources and has a statutory power to cut off the supply without breach of duty under the Water Industry Act 1991, s 52 if it considers it reasonable to do so (with a defence of 'due diligence' available against any claims against it for so doing). It will therefore do so in the event of a threatened drought. Orders to cut off the supply can be either ordinary or emergency orders. In either case, the undertaker must apply to the Environmental Agency or the Environmental Agency, may initiate it under the Water Resources Act 1991, ss 74 and 75 and Sch 8. Orders can be made for particular areas and for types of user and for any duration.

Hose pipe bans

22.18 The garden owner may also be subject to interruption or stopping of his own individual supply by a 'hose pipe ban'. This is a power under the Water Industry Act 1991, s 76(1) for a water undertaker, where it considers that there is a serious shortage of water available for distribution or that such a situation is threatened, for so long as it considers necessary to prohibit or restrict the use of hose pipes or similar apparatus for watering private gardens or washing private motor cars in all or part of the area which it supplies. The undertaker must advertise the proposed ban and the date upon which it is to take effect in at least two local newspapers 21 days before the relevant date.

Criminal offences

22.19 Failure to comply with a drought order or hose pipe ban will result in prosecution and on conviction a fine on scale 3 (presently £1,000). Each contravention, eg each day, could lead to another fine.[1]

1   Water Industry Act 1991, s 76(3).

22.20 In a recent High Court case it was held that the water undertaker's general power to suspend a water supply, eg for non-payment of water rate, is unlawful where it operated automatically when a credit card ran out.[1]

1   *R v Director General of Water Services, ex p Oldham Borough Council* (1998) Times, 6 March.

Refund of charges

22.21   Where the undertaker makes a special charge for non-domestic supply such as the use of a hose pipe and a drought order or hose pipe ban is introduced then it must refund the consumer the appropriate proportion of the extra charge for any period for which the ban applies.[1]

1   Water Industry Act 1991, s 76(4).

Spray irrigation

22.22   There is also power for the Environment Agency to restrict the abstraction of water for irrigating crops and market gardens etc by notice specifying the proposed reduction and duration[1] and for the general supply.[2] Devices for watering plants under cloches or in pots in a garden centre or in greenhouses and mixed manure/pesticide sprays are excluded.[3]

1   Water Resources Act, s 57(2).
2   Ibid, s 33.
3   Spray Irrigation (Definition) Order 1992, SI 1992/1096.

Escape of water

22.23   It should be noted that under the Highways Act 1980, s 245 it is a criminal offence to allow the escape of water or sewage etc on to the highway and water undertakers and householders will be liable. On the other hand, the highway authorities have a duty to repair highways and prevent flooding onto adjacent land.[1]

1   Highways Act 1980, s 41. See also *Burnside v Emerson* [1968] 3 All ER 741.

ELECTRICITY

22.24   A 'licence holder' (ie statutory provider of electricity—the local electricity authority) has a compulsory power of acquisition which can be used to take over any land or acquire an easement for pylons, cables etc over and under ground: Electricity Act 1989, s 10 and Sch 3. There is another statutory right which may affect garden owners: by the Electricity Act 1989, s 10, Sch 4, para 9 the authority can on 21 days' notice to the owner require trees which interfere with its lines to be felled or lopped, paying expenses, or do the work itself in accordance with good arboricultural practice doing as little damage as possible (Sch 4, para 1). The authority must pay compensation both for the value of the timber and for the loss of amenity.

22.25 As to the electricity authority's obligation to supply electricity, under the Electricity Act 1989, s 16 a licence holder has a duty to supply 'premises', which includes electricity to light a public highway and a private road. Whether an authority would have to provide a supply to an isolated garden or allotment has never been decided but it is thought that it would. But note that the authority can refuse when the applicant's own system or wiring is in a dangerous condition: Electricity Supply Regulations 1988, reg 27.

22.26 Running the supply from a house to a garden shed is, of course, a matter for the property owner's electrician to do, subject to compliance with the regulations.[1]

1   Electrical Equipment (Safety) Regulations 1994, SI 1994/3260.

22.27 With regard to electric lawnmowers and other devices, the relevant electricity safety regulations must be complied with. As to interference with radio and television reception the standards in the Electromagnetic Compatibility (Amendment) Regulations 1994, SI 1994/3080 must be complied with.

23

Rights of entry and acquisition

23.1 From the previous chapters it will have been noted that various persons have a right by law to go into a private garden and see what is going on there, eg local authority planning department officials, police under their powers as to drugs, food inspectors and MAFF officials where the garden is a market garden etc. In addition to the State, the local authority and what used to be called 'statutory undertakers', ie the water, electricity and gas utilities, have power to acquire a garden or part of it or rights over it by agreement or, failing agreement, compulsorily.

23.2 There are listed in the *Encyclopaedia of Compulsory Purchase and Compensation* (looseleaf) no less than 71 statutory provisions giving various authorities power to take over land, ranging from the Children and Young Persons Act 1933 (for a children's home) to the Merchant Shipping Act 1995 (for a lighthouse)! Set out below are the provisions most likely to apply to a garden.

Act	*Acquiring authority*
Highways Act 1980: s 239 road widening; ss 238–246 construction of highways, motorways and generally	Local Highway Authority or Department of Transport (the Highways Agency)
Road Traffic Regulation Act 1984 (parking places)	Local Authority
Environment Act 1995: s 65(7) and Sch 8 (picnic areas, rights of way etc)	Local Authority
National Parks and Access to the Countryside Act 1949: ss 12, 17, 18 (picnic and camp sites, rights of way and management etc)	National Parks Authority

Planning (Listed Buildings and Conservation Area) Regulations 1990 (and the NPACA 1949, s 70) (repair of listed buildings, eg walls, gates etc)	Local Authority
Local Government Act 1972: s 121; Housing Act 1985, ss 17, 27, 300; Housing Act 1988, s 77 (general acquisition for housing, amenities etc)	Local Authority
Land Drainage Act 1991: ss 12 and 14 (prevention of flooding)	Land Drainage Authority
Town and Country Planning Act 1990: ss 226 and 228 (development, car parks etc)	Local Planning Authority
Electricity Act 1989: s 10 and Sch 3 (electricity sub-stations, pylons, cables and easements for them)	Licence holder of statutory powers, ie the local electricity company
Gas Act 1986: s 9(3) and Sch 3 (gas pipes, filling stations and easements for them)	Gas undertaker, ie local gas company
Pipelines Act 1967: ss 11, 12 and 14 (gas pipelines)	
Water Industry Act 1991: s 155(1) (pipes and sewers), s 188 (easements)	Water undertakers, ie water companies and local authorities re sewers
Telecommunications Act 1984: s 34 (acquisition of land (with consent of Secretary of State)) and s 83 (easements for wires, cables, aerials etc)	BT and other telecommunication companies
Agriculture Act 1947, s 66 as amended by the Agriculture (Miscellaneous Provisions) Act 1954, s 7 (Smallholdings: see 17.55)	

In all the above cases the Land Compensation Act 1961 and the Acquisition of Land Act 1981 apply and compensation will be payable.

22.3   Compensation will be equal to market value as agreed between the owner's valuer and the District Valuer, and may also include:

(a) 'injurious affection' (eg the diminished value of the remainder of land cut off from the rest by a motorway);[1]

(b) disturbance, eg value of crops etc.[2]

There are also special rules for additional payment to residential occupiers and businesses.[3]

1   Land Compensation Act 1961, s 7.
2   Land Compensation Act 1961, s 10.
3   Acquisition of Land Act 1981, s 19 and Compulsory Purchase Act 1965, s 21.

23.4   Disputes are referred to the Lands Tribunal which has an informal procedure but expert valuation evidence, generally by a surveyor, will be required. The garden owner's legal costs and surveyor's fees are usually payable by the acquiring authority.

COMPULSORY ACQUISITION

23.5   There is a provision which garden owners subject to compulsory acquisition may find useful in the Town and Country Planning Act 1990, s 150 whereby if only a small part of a property is to be taken and the remainder will be blighted, the owner may require the acquiring authority to take and pay compensation for his whole unit.[1] This has been held to apply to a house and garden where only nine square metres of the garden was to be taken, as this would have adversely affected the owner's total amenities, and replacement of trees and fences would not have been adequate to make good these amenities.[2] In a recent case, it was held that the land owner could require the authority to take the whole of his property where it was acquiring the subsoil in the road in front of his house.[3]

1   A form of notice under s 150 is included in Appendix A.
2   *Smith and Smith v Kent County Council* (1995) 70 P & CR 669, Lands Tribunal.
3   *Norman v Department of Transport* (1996) 72 P & CR 210 (LT).

23.6   Common land, fuel or field gardens and allotments (as to all of which see Chapter 17) can only be compulsorily purchased if the Secretary of State certifies that equivalent land is being made available to the holders.[1]

1   *R v Secretary of State, ex p Gosforth Allotments etc Association* [1996] EGCS 112.

Appendix A

1

LICENCE/LEASE FOR USE OF A GARDEN

THIS LICENCE/LEASE is made the   day of

BETWEEN:

(1) [Name of Grantor] of [Address] ('the Owner') and

(2) [Name of Licensee/Tenant] of [Address] ('the Licensee/Tenant')

[**SUPPLEMENTAL** to a Lease dated the   day of   19[   ] whereby the Tenant is the tenant of premises known as number [   ] [   ] Square ['the Premises'] dated the   day of 19[   ] and made between [   ] (1) and [   ] (2) whereby the said premises were demised to the Tenant for a term of [   ] years subject to payment of the rents and observance and performance of the covenants on the part of the Tenant therein contained]

WITNESSES as follows

1. The Owner hereby grants to the Licensee permission to use the garden shown ('the Garden') edged red on the plan attached to this Agreement [with full title guarantee] hereby grants unto the Tenant the right to use the Garden shown edged red on the plan for the term of the said Lease [yielding and paying the additional rent referred to in clause 2] [but subject to determination on determination of the Lease] for the purpose of recreation only subject to the rules or regulations which are set out in the Schedule hereto and such other rules and regulations as shall be made by the owner from time to time and of which written notice is given to the Licensee/Tenant *or* is displayed on the notice board in the Garden for regulating the conduct of persons using the Garden [but not so as to exclude the Owner who may continue to visit the garden and use it for normal recreation jointly with the Licensee]

2. Payment. In consideration of the grant of this Licence/Lease the Licensee/Tenant must pay to the Owner the sum of £[   ] by equal quarterly payments in the usual quarter days as

provided by the Lease [by half yearly instalments on the [   ]
day of [   ] and the [   ] day of [   ] in each year]

3.   The Licensee/Tenant covenants with the Owner [to observe
and perform the covenants on the part of the Tenant in the
lease of the premises as if the rights hereby granted were
included in the Lease] to observe and comply with and ensure
that all persons authorised by the Licensee/Tenant to use the
Garden for the purposes aforesaid shall observe and comply
with the rules and regulations for the time being set out in the
Schedule or such other rules and regulations made by the Owner
for regulating the conduct of persons using the garden]

4.   The Licensee/Tenant must not do anything in the Garden that
may cause a nuisance damage disturbance inconvenience
discomfort or annoyance to the Owner or any occupant of
nearby premises

5.   The Owner is not to be liable for any accident loss or damage
suffered by the Licensee/Tenant in using the Garden

6.   Indemnity. The Licensee/Tenant must indemnify the Owner
against all actions proceedings or claims by any third party
arising from his use of the Garden

7.   This Agreement is to continue until terminated by one month's
[or as required] notice in writing given by either party to the
other *or*

8.   Determination. The Lease shall determine on the same date as
the determination of the Lease of the Premises but if the Tenant
shall fail to observe and perform the provisions of this Lease it
may be separately determined by the Owner on one month's
written notice as far as concerns the term hereby granted (but
not affecting the Lease of the Premises)

9.   Relationship. Nothing in this Licence is to create the
relationship of landlord and tenant

10. Personal Agreement. This Licence is personal to the Licensee and no person other than the Licensee   and his family may use the Garden *or*

11. Assignment. This Agreement being supplemental to the Lease may only be assigned to a person to whom the Lease of the Premises shall be assigned (subject to the prior consent in writing of the Landlord as therein provided) and no person other than the Tenant or his successors in title and families of such persons may use the Garden

IN WITNESS etc

THE SCHEDULE

Rules and Regulations relating to the Garden

[See form 2]

Signature etc.

2

RULES REGULATING USE OF A GARDEN BY THOSE ENTITLED[1]

RULES FOR USE OF .... GARDEN

1   *Entitlement to use*

The Garden is [owned by *(name of owner)* ('the Owner') *(or)* managed by *(details of garden committee)* ('the Garden Committee')] and the only authorised users of the Garden are the [owners *(or)* tenants] for the time being of *(describe properties)* [who comply with rule 2 below], their families and guests. No one else may enter and use the Garden.

2   *Payment condition*

[Owners *(or)* Tenants] and their families and guests are authorised users of the Garden only if and so long as the [owner *(or)* tenant] pays the sum of £...... a year or such other sum as is decided on from time to time by the [Owner *(or)* Garden Committee] [after consultation with the authorised users], to [the Owner or his authorised agent *(or)* the Treasurer of the Garden Committee].

3   *Walls, gates and railings*

Users of the Garden must not climb over the walls, gates or railings of the Garden or leave any gate [open *(or)* unlocked] at any time.

4   *Damage*

Users of the Garden must not:

4.1 climb, damage, pull down or destroy any tree, shrub or plant in the Garden;

4.2 break, deface or damage any seat or other property belonging to the Garden;

4.3 cut up or damage the surface of any gravel walk or lawn;

4.4 trample on or injure any planted or dug ground;

4.5 place or leave any obstruction on the walks or elsewhere;

4.6 cause any nuisance, annoyance, damage or injury to the owner or to the person or property of any authorised user; or

4.7 consume or carry alcohol or illegal drugs in the Garden.

5   *Bicycles etc*

Bicycles, tricycles, skateboards, rollerskates and rollerblades may not be used in the Garden.

6 *Nuisance*

Noisy and disorderly conduct and any other practice likely to interfere with the quiet use and enjoyment of the Garden is prohibited.

7 *Games*

[Tennis *(or)* Netball *(or as the case may be)*] may be played on the [tennis courts *(or)* netball courts *(or as appropriate)*] provided in the Garden, but not in any other part of the Garden, and no other games whatsoever may be played in the Garden.

8 *Rubbish*

The Garden must be kept clean and free of rubbish and no rubbish may be disposed of in the Garden [otherwise than in the bins provided].

9 *Dogs*

Dogs are not permitted in the Garden [except on a lead] [and only if the dog owner cleans up and disposes of the dog's excreta [in the bins provided]].

10 *Expulsion for unauthorised activities*

Anyone using the Garden without the right to do so or consuming or carrying alcohol or illegal drugs or acting in an anti-social or disorderly manner must leave the Garden immediately upon being requested to do so by the Owner or anyone acting with the authority of the Owner.

1   Similar rules may be promulgated as byelaws where a garden is vested in a committee of inhabitants under the Town Gardens Protection Act 1863, see vol 29 *Forms and Precedents* OPEN SPACES Form 4.

3

STATUTORY DECLARATION BY A GARDEN OWNER AS TO UNINTERRUPTED POSSESSION OF LAND FOR MORE THAN 12 YEARS[1]

I, *(name of declarant)* of *(address)*, do solemnly and sincerely declare as follows:

1   [I am *(number)* years old and by *(or)* By] a conveyance dated *(date)* and made between (1) *(name of seller)* and (2) myself ('the Conveyance') the freehold property known as *(address or description of property conveyed)* ('the Property'), which for the purpose of identification only was edged red on the plan annexed to the Conveyance ('the Plan'), was conveyed to me.

2   A copy of the Conveyance and the Plan is now produced to me and marked 'XY 1'.

[3   Since the date of the Conveyance I have always treated the area shown hatched red on the Plan, comprising ...... hectares of uncultivated ground, ('the Additional Land') as part of the garden to the Property, and I have planted trees there as indicated on the Plan and put up a [6 foot high close boarded fence *(or as the case may be)*] along the whole of the [northern *(or as the case may be)*] boundary of the Additional Land as is shown on the Plan.

4   I have also, as detailed below, landscaped the whole of the Additional Land and in particular have carried out the following works *(insert details)*.

(or)

3   At the date of the Conveyance, the area of land comprising ...... hectares shown hatched red on the Plan ('the Additional Land') was let to or occupied by *(name of occupier)* who paid a rent or licence fee of [£1 per year *(or as the case may be)*] in respect of his occupation, and as from that date for [a period of *(state period)* *(or)* upwards of 12 years] I have collected and have been in receipt of the said payment of [£1 per year *(or as the case may be)*] from *(name of occupier)* who has always regarded me as the owner of the Additional Land, and I have therefore been in receipt of the entire rent and profits arising from the Additional Land continuously for *(number)* years without any claim being made by any third party in respect of that land.]

[4 *(or)* 5]   I have occupied the Property since it was conveyed to me and I have [occupied *(or)* been in receipt of rent and profits in respect of] the Additional Land as detailed above up to the

present time. Throughout this period I have been in continuous, full, free and undisturbed possession and enjoyment of the Additional Land without giving any acknowledgement of the title to it or any part of it to any other person, without the consent of any other person and without any claim adverse to the title to the Additional Land.

AND I make this solemn declaration conscientiously, believing the same to be true, and by virtue of the Statutory Declarations Act 1835

DECLARED at .... this ...... day of ....

(signature of declarant)

Before me

(signature of person before whom declaration is made)

[A commissioner for oaths *(or)* A solicitor empowered to administer oaths]

1   If this declaration is to be used to found an application for first registration of the land in question (eg as an addition to an existing registered title), it will need to be lodged under cover of an application for first registration of the land in Form FR1. The Land Registry generally investigates carefully the evidence on which the claim is founded and normally arranges for inspection of the land in order to check the circumstances on the ground. If the land is already registered and a prima facie case is made out for claiming a title by adverse possession, notice is always served on the existing registered proprietor giving him an opportunity to object and show grounds why the application should not be accepted.

4

NOTICE AS TO TRESPASSING WHERE THERE IS NO RIGHT OF WAY

WARNING

This is private land and no right of way, public or private, is acknowledged over it. If you use it you are therefore trespassing and legal proceedings may be taken against you without further warning.

5

LETTER TO A NEIGHBOUR AS TO USING AN UNAUTHORISED ROUTE OVER A GARDEN—VARIATION FOR EXCESSIVE USE OF AN AUTHORISED ROUTE

(date)

Dear *(name of neighbour)*,

[1 Acacia Avenue *(or as the case may be)*]

I am writing to you as the owner of the above property. It has come to my notice that you [and your family] [*(unauthorised route)* have been taking a short cut over my garden between your property [3 Acacia Avenue *(or as the case may be)*] and the public highway. I have to point out that this route is not a lawful right of way for your property nor is it a public footpath and you are using it by my permission only.] [*(excessive use)* have been using the footpath across my garden between your property [3 Acacia Avenue *(or as the case may be)*] and the public highway with vehicles. I have to point out that this right of way is for foot passage only and that you are not allowed to use it for driving, parking or unloading cars and vans.]

I should therefore be obliged if you would desist from using the [route *(or)* footpath] unlawfully. Please would you acknowledge receipt of this letter and confirm that you will not continue with the use complained of above. Should you continue with such use after [7 days *(or as required)*] of receipt of this letter I shall refer the matter to my solicitor and legal proceedings may be taken against you to protect my rights without any further warning to you.

Yours faithfully,

(signature of owner)

6

LICENCE TO USE A WALL FOR GROWING ROSES[1]

THIS LICENCE is made the .... day of .... BETWEEN:

(1) *(name of grantor)* [of *(address)* *(or)* the registered office of which is at *(address)*] ('the Owner') and

(2) *(name of licensee)* of *(address)* ('the Licensee')

NOW IT IS AGREED as follows:

1   Definitions
In this agreement:

1.1 'the Plan' means the plan annexed to this agreement;

1.2 'the Red Land' means the property known as *(address or description)* shown edged red on the Plan;

1.3 'the Blue Land' means the property known as *(address or description)* shown coloured blue on the Plan; and

1.4 'the Wall' means the wall on the [south *(or as the case may be)*] side of the Red Land, between the points marked 'A' and 'B' on the Plan, forming part of the Red Land.

2   Recitals
2.1 The Owner is the owner in fee simple in possession [free from incumbrances] of the Red Land.

2.2 The Licensee is the [owner *(or)* tenant] of the Blue Land a portion of which is situated on the [south *(or as the case may be)*] side of and contiguous to the Wall.

2.3 The Owner and the Licensee have agreed to enter into this deed to regulate the use of the Wall by the Licensee for growing roses.

3   Grant
In consideration of the yearly sum mentioned below and the covenants on the part of the Licensee contained in this agreement the Owner grants to the Licensee, for the term of [10 years *(or as required)*] subject to the proviso for determination contained below, full right and liberty:

3.1 to train roses against the Wall by inserting in the Wall suitable flat pegs of approximately [7.5cm *(or as required)*] in length with eyes at one end through which wires are threaded for training and supporting the trees; and

3.2 to enter the Red Land with any necessary equipment and not more than [2 *(or as required)*] other persons at any one time for these purposes and to maintain, tend and replace the pegs, lines and rose plants and to gather the flowers, but for not other purpose whatsoever.

4   Payment

The Licensee must pay to the Owner during the continuance of this licence the yearly sum of £ ....[, if demanded,] on *(date)* in each year, the first such payment to be made on *(date)*.

5   Licensee's obligations

5.1   Licence fee

The Licensee must pay the licence fee in the manner mentioned above, if demanded.

5.2   Access

The Licensee must permit the Owner, at reasonable times in daylight between the months of October and March inclusive and on giving reasonable notice, to enter the Blue Land so as to have access to the [south *(or as the case may be)*] side of the Wall to inspect, point and repair the Wall but not for any other purpose, provided that the Owner must make good at his own expense all damage occasioned by the exercise of these rights.

5.3   Damage

The Licensee must exercise the rights granted by this agreement so as to do as little damage as possible to the Wall and the Red Land and must repair all damage done immediately. In particular the Licensee must cause as little damage as possible to the Wall by the insertion of the pegs and must cement the pegs in such a manner as to render the Wall impervious to moisture so far as possible where the pegs are inserted and must maintain the cement during the currency of this licence.

5.4   Removal of pegs

The Licensee must remove the pegs and all attachments from the Wall and must cease to use the Wall immediately on the termination of this licence.

5.5   Indemnity[2]

The Licensee must indemnify the Owner from and against all claims actions and demands that may be brought against the Owner by reason of the exercise by the Licensee of the rights and liberties granted by this licence.

6   Determination

If the Licensee is in breach of any of his obligations under this licence, including the obligation to pay the yearly sum of £...... if demanded, or any condition contained in this licence, the Owner may determine this licence by a written and signed notice served on or posted to the Licensee, and on the expiration of such notice this licence is to determine without prejudice to the remedies of the Owner in respect of anything previously done or suffered by the Licensee.

7   Declarations

7.1 This licence does not grant any right to support.

7.2 The Licensee attaches any peg to the Wall at his own risk.

7.3 The Owner is not liable for damage to or collapse of the Wall nor for damage to anything attached to the Wall.

8   Notices

The provisions of the Law of Property Act 1925 section 196 as amended by the Recorded Delivery Service Act 1962 are to apply to any notice to be given under this licence as if the Owner were a lessor and the Licensee were a lessee.

9   Relationship

Nothing contained in this licence is to create the relationship of landlord and tenant.

10   Personal agreement

This Licence is personal to the Licensee and no person other than the Licensee and his family may use the Wall.

AS WITNESS etc *(see vol 12 Forms and Precedents* (1994 Reissue) DEEDS, AGREEMENTS AND DECLARATIONS Form 90 [1691] et seq*)*

> *(signature (or common seal) of owner)*
>
> *(signature of licensee)*

1   As to the distinction between leases and licences see vol 22(1) *Forms and Precedents* (1996 Reissue) LANDLORD AND TENANT Paragraph 1 [1] et seq.

2   A person dealing as consumer cannot, by reference to any contract term contained in a contract made after 31 January 1978, be made to indemnify another in respect of business liability for negligence or breach of contract except so far as that term satisfies the requirement of reasonableness: see the Unfair Contract Terms Act 1977, s 4 (11 *Halsbury's Statutes* (4th edn) CONTRACT).

7

LICENCE IN RESPECT OF PARKING

(date)

Dear *(name)*

[1 Acacia Avenue *(or as the case may be)*]

I agree to allow you [and your employees] to park [1 *(or as the case may be)*] private car on the hard standing in my garden [shown edged red on the attached plan] on the following conditions.

1   You will pay me the sum of £...... per month on the [1st *(or as required)*] day of each month during the subsistence of this licence.

2   You are to have licence to park a car nominated by you by registration number between the hours of 0800 and 1900 on weekdays [and on Saturday from 0800 to 1200 only,] commencing on and from *(date)* and determining and including *(date)* ('the Expiry Date').

3   This licence is personal to you and cannot be assigned nor the benefit passed on by you to any other person.

4   The parking is to be at your own risk and I am not to be responsible for loss or damage of any car or contents or for death or injury or damages to persons or property arising from this licence or the use of my garden.

5   The hard standing area may be used for parking the car only, and no car repairs, filling or emptying of tanks or car washing may be undertaken, and the hard standing may not be used for any other purpose.

6   You must indemnify me against all actions, proceedings, costs, claims and liabilities arising from the parking of the car or use of my garden, and [you must insure against such liability, or ensure that such liability is insured against, with a reputable insurer to the amount of at least £...... against fire and other usual risks and third party liability in such sum as is approved by me *(or)* you must repay me the amount which I have to pay in respect of insurance or additional insurance in respect of fire and other usual risks and third party liability upon my producing details to you].

7   All sums payable under this agreement, unless otherwise stated, are exclusive of VAT and other duties or taxes. Any VAT or

other duties or taxes payable in respect of such sums are to be payable in addition to them.

8   This licence is to determine:

   (a) if you fail to keep any of the above terms;

   (b) upon the Expiry Date; or

   (c) upon the expiration of one month's written notice expiring at any time which may be served by you on me or by me on you;

and on any of the above events you must remove the car from the parking area and this licence is to determine, but without prejudice to any rights I may have against you for breach of the terms of this letter or otherwise.

To confirm your agreement to the terms of this letter please sign, date and return the additional copy and the arrangements in this letter will become legally binding.

Yours faithfully,

(on copy)
[I *(or)* We] agree to the above terms.

Signed:
Dated:

8

Notice warning that unauthorised vehicles may be clamped or removed

WARNING!

WHEEL CLAMPING AND REMOVAL OF VEHICLES IN OPERATION!

NO PARKING [IN FRONT OF THE CHAIN *(or)* BEYOND THIS POINT]

THIS IS A PRIVATE CAR PARK

By entering this private property you agree that:

1   any vehicle parked here without [my *(or)* our] prior written consent [may be restrained by wheel clamp *(or)* or towed away and held at [the *(name)* pound *(or)* *(name)* Garage] at *(address)*];

2   the vehicle will be released when you have paid [£35 *(or as the case may be)*] release fee in cash [or by credit card] to the owner whose address and telephone number appears below [and a storage charge of [£60 *(or as the case may be)*] per day for parking of vehicles towed away]; and

3   no liability is accepted for loss of or damage to any vehicle [, clamped or not,] or its contents whilst left here or for any delay in releasing vehicles.

(name of owner)
(telephone number of owner)
(address of owner)

9

GUIDANCE ON COMPLETION OF NUISANCE DIARIES

If legal action is to be taken, eg to stop a noise amounting to a nuisance, a court hearing may result. Irrespective of whether a local authority or an individual initiates the action, the court will want to know which residents have been affected by noise and will ask for details of specific incidents. It is therefore essential that an accurate, detailed record is kept of the noise. If there are any inaccuracies in the record the validity of the whole diary may be challenged.

It is suggested that the diary be done as a form, with columns containing the headings below. Along with notes on each entry, examples are also given. Full details of the person writing the diary should be included (full name, age (if over 21, write 'over 21'), occupation, address, contact telephone numbers (day and evening)), and at the foot of the 'diary' the following:

'I confirm that the details given above are true and accurate [Signature and name].'

Date noise occurs
Enter the date the noise happens.
Eg: Monday 21 May 1997

Time noise started/finished
Use either 'am/pm' or the 24 hour clock.
Eg: 11.15 pm/2 am

Location of listener
The complainant/listener should enter the room(s) in which he was when he heard the noise.
Eg: Front bedroom, Flat 2, 5 Barton House

Address noise came from
It is very important to establish the address from where the noise comes. This can be difficult when the noise is in a flat, as sound can travel through several floors and/or doors. The source must therefore be established while the noise is happening.
Eg: 7 Barton House—flat directly above

Description of noise
Eg: loud music, drums, shouting, machinery.

Disturbance caused/level of noise

The complainant/listener should state the level of noise and the disturbance it causes. Eg for rock music etc this could include: 'words of song audible; loud thumping bass; so loud I could not hold a conversation without raising my voice; could not hear my television; disturbed my sleep'—ie anything that in the complainant's/listener's own words would give an indication as to the level. (NB Exaggeration of the level will not help the case.)

Eg: could hear words of each song—made it impossible to sleep; I was awoken by the noise which only stopped when the police were called

Person responsible for the noise

If the name of the person causing the noise is known, their name should be entered.

Eg: Mr Peter Smith

Names of other witnesses

If anyone (beside the complainant/listener) heard the noise and is willing to give support to the case, their name(s) and address(es) should be recorded here. He/they must make a separate record at the time of the noise noting what he/they heard, to avoid the frequent difficulties experienced by witnesses in remembering dates and times some months after an event.

Eg: Mr J Brown, 2 Fish Hill, Thame G2 4IF; Mr F Idd, Flat 3, PCs Graham 622, Took 888

Signature

The diary sheets must be signed in order to reduce the possibility of malicious complaints.

10

NOTICE OF DANGEROUS FEATURE, FOR EXAMPLE A SWIMMING POOL

WARNING

This garden [and swimming pool *(or as the case may be)*] is private property and you use it by licence of the owner, which can be withdrawn at any time for no reason without notice, and at your own risk.

By coming into the garden [and using the pool] you accept that:

1 The owner accepts no liability for any accident of any kind or damage to or for loss of property.

2 You must not behave in a noisy, dangerous or anti-social manner and must not consume any alcoholic drink or illegal drugs.

3 You must leave the property immediately you are asked to do so by the owner or on his behalf.

(signature)

11

LICENCE FOR LIMITED ACCESS TO A GARDEN FOR NAMED INDIVIDUALS OR FOR A SOCIETY[1]

THIS LICENCE is made the .... day of .... BETWEEN:
(1) *(name of garden owner)* of *(address)* ('the Owner') and
(2) [*(names and addresses of individuals to be admitted)* *(or)* *(name of society involved)* represented by *(names and addresses of at least two committee members appointed by resolution)* as signatories] ('the Licensees' [which term is to include all persons who are now or may become members of the *(name of society)* according to its rules])

NOW IT IS AGREED as follows:

1   *Definitions*
In this agreement:
1.1 'the Plan' means the plan annexed to this licence;
1.2 'the Garden' means the garden at *(address or location)* shown edged red on the Plan, but excluding the private residence and buildings, those areas shown edged green on the Plan, and any area the Owner may from time to time specify in writing; and
1.3 'the Conditions' means the conditions and obligations set out in the schedule below, which may be varied or added to by the Owner from time to time as he considers necessary to protect the Garden or for its better management.

2   *Access agreement*
Subject to the Licensees observing and performing the Conditions, the Owner permits the Licensees to enter the Garden for the period of *(insert period)* from *(date)* [between the hours of *(state hours)*] [and thereafter from [year to year *(or as the case may be)*].

3   *Fee*[2]
In consideration of the licence granted by this agreement, the Licensees must pay to the Owner the sum of £...... [a [year *(or as the case may be)*] on *(dates for payment)* the first payment to be made] on the date of this agreement.

4   Use of the Garden

The Licensees may use the Garden for *(insert details, eg recreation or study of plants)* only, and must observe and perform the Conditions.

5   Determination

The Owner may determine this licence:

5.1 by immediate written notice in the event of wilful or unnecessary damage to the Garden or any property of the Owner;

5.2 by [7 days' *(or as required)*] written notice if the Licensee is in breach of the Conditions[; and

5.3 by not less than [2 months' *(or as required)*] written notice expiring on a date for payment of the fee under this agreement]

without prejudice to any claim of the Owner against the Licensees for breach of any provisions of this agreement. If this agreement is terminated under subclauses 5.1 or 5.2 above, the Owner is not to be obliged to refund any portion of the licence fee.

6   Owner's priority

The Owner's use and enjoyment of his property, including the Garden, and his undertakings on that property are to take precedence over use of the Garden by the Licensees, who are not to be entitled to exclusive possession or occupation of the Garden or any part of it and may not make any claim in respect of any interference with their use of it.

7   Indemnity

The Licensees must indemnify the owner against all costs, proceedings, claims, demands, losses damages or liabilities caused by or incurred as a result of the operation of this licence or the Licensees' use and enjoyment of the Garden, whether the damage is caused to the Owner, his property or persons on or connected with it, the Licensees or any other person, matter or thing, except any obligation or liability imposed on the Owner by law that cannot be borne by the Licensees.

[8   Society use

The Licensees must ensure that any member of the *(name of society)* entering the Garden accepts the Conditions before entry and complies with them, and enters on the terms of this licence.]

AS WITNESS *(see vol 12 (1994 Reissue) DEEDS, AGREEMENTS AND DECLARATIONS Form 90 [1691] et seq)*

SCHEDULE

The Conditions

(for alternative conditions see Form 85 [440] ante)

1   The Licensees must not enter the Garden except by the [gate marked 'X' on the Plan *(or as the case may be)*].

2   The Licensees must not park cars in the Garden[, except for not more than [2 *(or as required)*] cars at a time which may be parked in the area shown hatched black on the Plan [between the hours of *(state hours)*]].

3   The Licensees may not park commercial vehicles in the Garden at any time.

4   No more than *(number)* persons may use the Garden at any time.

5   The Licensees must not enter the Garden except during the hours of [daylight *(or)* *(state hours)*] [or at any time between *(date)* and *(date)*] unless the Owner has given his written consent.

6   The Licensees must not bring dogs or any other animals into the Garden.

7   The Licensees must not cause nuisance, annoyance or damage to the Owner, his property, stock, gates, fences or other property, or interfere in any way with his undertakings in the Garden, and must not disturb, damage or interfere with any flora, fauna, wildlife, game or other natural phenomena in the Garden.

8   The Licensees must not light fires in the Garden or leave any litter.

9   The Licensees must close all gates and take any reasonable steps necessary to protect the Garden.

10   The Licensees must produce any records kept by them of matters occurring in the Garden to the Owner on request and supply him with any copies he may require.

11   The Licensees enter the Garden at their own risk, and must take out such insurance as they think fit in respect of any loss or damage to [their *(or)* members'] property.

12   The Licensees must satisfy the Owner that [they *(or)* all persons permitted to enter the Garden under this agreement] are adequately insured during the period of this licence in respect of the indemnity in clause 7 above, liability for damage to the

Owner's property by fire or otherwise, and third party liability for a sum not less than £......, and must produce the policy and premium receipt to the Owner on request.

[13 The Licensees must not permit persons other than duly elected or enrolled members of the *(name of society)* to use the Garden. Members using the Garden must carry identification and a valid membership card which must be produced to the Owner or his authorised agent on demand.

14 A complete list of members' names and addresses and a copy of the rules or constitution of the *(name of society)* must be delivered to the owner on request.

15 The Licensees must not permit any member to enter the Garden if the Owner has specifically, in writing, named that member as excluded.]

(signatures of the parties)

1   As to the distinction between leases and licences see vol 22(1) (1996 Reissue) LANDLORD AND TENANT Paragraph 1 [1] et seq.

2   In fixing the fee the owner may wish to consider the effect of the licence on his insurance premiums.

12

WORDING TO GO INTO AN INVITATION TO A CHILDREN'S FIREWORK PARTY

WARNING

FIREWORKS   Date:

Note that we, *(names of parents)*, do not accept liability for injury, loss or damage occurring on our property during the party. You are welcome, but at your own risk.

13

LICENCE FOR USE OF GARDEN FOR A FÊTE OR WEDDING OR PARTY

To: *(name of licensee)*

Date

Dear *(name)*,

[1 Acacia Avenue *(or as the case may be)*]

I am writing as owner of the above property to grant you a licence to enter it and to use the garden and hold a [fête *(or)* wedding *(or)* reception *(or)* party *(or as the case may be)*] on the following conditions:

1   You may use the garden between the hours of *(hour)* and *(hour)* on *(date)* only. You may have access for your tenters or caterers by prior arrangement on [3 *(or as the case may be)*] occasions during the week prior to that date, on weekdays at reasonable hours in order to set up your arrangements.

2   You must pay me the sum of £......... ('the Deposit') and [£......... to be paid on return of a copy of this letter, and £......... to be due on the date of the function *(or as the case may be)*] ('the Agreed Payments').

3   You and your guests must use the garden only and not the house[, except the lavatories designated to you in the house for a ladies' and gentlemen's' lavatory].

4   You and your guests will have access to and from the garden via the gate and passage to the [east of the house *(or as the case may be)*] [as shown on the attached plan and marked 'gate'].

5   You and your guests may park cars [in the public highway *(or)* in the field to the [west *(or as the case may be)*] of the house *(or as the case may be)*], following the directions of the persons whom I have authorised to deal with car parking and causing as little disturbance as possible.

6   You may not sell any alcoholic beverage or allow the use of drugs or cause any loud noise, nuisance or annoyance to me or my family or my neighbours.

7   You may put up one marquee only, of not more than *(number)* square feet in area, in the position agreed between us before erection, and must put down flooring or carpeting in it and up to the entrance of it from the paths, and must not allow the lawn to be damaged by the heels of ladies shoes or otherwise.

8   [You may use, and allow your guests to use, the lavatories and the kitchen and facilities in the house agreed between us beforehand only, with access as agreed [through the kitchen only *(or as the case may be)*] *(or)* You may provide a temporary portable lavatory in the position shown on the plan, and must keep it clean and maintained and remove it after the event].

9   The function, and the use of my garden[, lavatories, the kitchen in my house] and parking as above are to be at your own risk, and I am not to be responsible for any death, injury or damage to persons or property, for lost or stolen items or in any other way to yourself or your guests or other third parties, and [you must insure, and provide written evidence that you have insured, against damage to my property and third party liability as above with a reputable insurance company for not less than [£50,000 *(or as the case may be)*] such insurance to be in place before the event *(or)* you must repay me the amount I have to pay in taking out and maintaining insurance against such risks upon my producing details to you].

10 You must indemnify me against all actions, proceedings, costs, claims and expenses howsoever arising in connection with the function or use of my garden.

11 These arrangements are personal to you and may not be assigned or the benefit passed on by you to any other person.

12 In the event of anyone coming onto my property under the arrangements in this letter taking drugs or becoming drunk or violent, I shall, or you must on my behalf, require them to leave the property immediately and their right to be there will cease.

13 Upon determination of this licence I will refund to you the Deposit less any amount which I may have to deduct in repairing damage or making good my property.

14 Following the event, or if it is cancelled, or on determination of the arrangements in this letter, you must remove the marquee, flooring and catering facilities, [clean the kitchen and lavatories,] clear all rubbish and unused stock and make good the garden to my property generally to my reasonable satisfaction.

15 The arrangements in this letter shall determine:
    (a) if the event is cancelled (of which you will give me written notice as soon as it happens);
    (b) if you fail to keep the terms of this letter;
    (c) if you fail to pay me the Agreed Payments; and
    (d) if by reason of any unforeseen circumstances within my family or events beyond my control it becomes necessary

for me to withdraw from the arrangement in which case I will use my best endeavours to give you [7 days' *(or as the case may be)*] written notice except in emergency.

You agree the above terms by signing, dating and returning the additional copy of this letter and letting me have your remittance for the amounts in paragraph 2 whereupon the arrangements will become legally binding and shall continue until you have made all the Agreed Payments and discharged your obligations in this letter notwithstanding the date of the event.

Yours sincerely,

(signature)

(on copy)

[I *(or)* We] agree to the above terms.

Signed:

Dated:

14

'BEWARE OF THE DOG' NOTICE

WARNING!

BEWARE OF THE DOG KEPT ON THIS PRIVATE PROPERTY

[Users of the public footpath must do so in a quiet and non provocative manner and ensure that the gate is always kept fastened so that the dog does not escape.]

No liability is accepted for injury to any person or damage to any property by the dog and you may be held responsible if the dog escapes to cause injury or damage outside the property by reason of your action provoking the dog or allowing it to escape.

15

OFFER OF EMPLOYMENT

OFFER OF EMPLOYMENT TO [   ]
(GARDENER)
DATE:

FROM [EMPLOYER]

Dear

Employment as Gardener

1. I am writing to confirm that I have agreed to employ you and you have agreed to work as gardener at my house 1 Acacia Avenue from the   day of   until the day of   or until your employment is terminated as provided in this letter subject to the following terms.

2. The date in which your period of continuous employment taking account of employment with a previous employer which counts towards such period is [nil].

3. Your job title is [gardener] and you are expect to do the usual work of planting, weeding, mowing lawns, trimming and lopping trees etc as required.

4. Your normal hours of work are 9.30 to 5pm on [   ] days per week for [   ] weeks in a year.

5. I will pay you £[   ] per hour payable weekly/monthly in arrears on the last [Friday] of every week/month or such other sum as is from time to time agreed between us.

6. You are entitled to [15] working days paid holiday in every year in addition to public and bank holidays.

7. The arrangements in this letter will be determinable by each of us giving to the other one month's written notice to determine at the end of the next subsequent week/month of employment.

8. 8.1 In the event of absence on account of sickness or injury you or someone on your behalf must inform me of the reason for your absence as soon as possible and must do so no later than the end of the working day on which absence first occurs.

    8.2 In respect of absence lasting [five] or fewer calendar days you are not required to produce a medical certificate unless specifically requested by me but must complete the self-certification form which I will supply on return to work from such absence.

8.3 In respect of absence lasting more than [five] days you must on the [sixth] day of absence provide me with a medical certificate stating the reason for absence and thereafter provide a like certificate each week to cover any subsequent period of absence and if reasonably required by me undergo a medical examination.

8.4 You will be paid your normal basic remuneration less the amount of any statutory sick pay or social security sickness benefit which you may be entitled to for [14] days in total in any one year which runs from the date of this letter to the next subsequent year and after that period I may determine your employment on written notice.

[9. I do not operate a pension scheme and you are not entitled to any pension in relation to the above remuneration.]

10. I may also determine this Agreement on immediate written notice in the event of your failing faithfully to perform your duties, disobeying my reasonable orders or any misconduct.

11. For the purposes of the Employment Protection (Consolidation) Act 1978, section 3 I confirm

11.1   There are [no] collective agreements which directly affect the terms and conditions of your employment.

11.2   Current practice as to disciplinary rules etc

(a) Disciplinary rules and grievance procedure.

(i) Any complaint or grievance should be referred to me in writing within [7] days of the happening of the incident or the matter arising.

(ii) I shall inform you within one month of the date of receipt of my acceptance or rejection of a complaint.

(iii) In the event of my failure to do so or not being satisfied as to my response we may either of us refer to an Employment Tribunal for the matter to be settled.

I will give you [one] written warning of any act or omission which I consider a failure to perform this contract prior to formal dismissal.

(b) Appeals procedure - [none].

(c) A contracting out certificate is [not] in force in respect of your employment.

I hope that you will take up this offer of employment which you accept by returning the spare copy of this letter having signed the form at the foot.

Yours faithfully,

[Employer]

On Copy:

I agree the above terms

[Gardener] [Date]

16

NOTICE DETERMINING EMPLOYMENT

To [Gardener]

From [Employer]

Date

Dear

Employment as Gardener

I refer to your contract of employment as gardener dates the day of   19[ ] and write to give you formal notice to determine such employment.

[On the date of expiration of the month of your employment which shall next determine after four weeks from the date of this notice pursuant to the arrangements which we have made for determination by notice in the contract]

or

immediately/on the day of   19[ ] in view of your breach of contract and misconduct in [eg failing to carry out my instructions and swearing at me *or* failing to account for monies which I gave you to purchase plants and equipment *or* having failed to attend for work without having sent me a medical certificate or given any other satisfactory explanation of your absence].

Will you please therefore remove your personal effects and equipment from my property by the date of determination of this notice.

[This notice also applies to determine the service occupancy of [   ] cottage which you occupy under the terms of your contract and you should give vacant possession of this property at the date of determination of this notice.]

Yours faithfully

[Employer]

17

LETTER CONFIRMING TERMS ON WHICH GARDENS WILL BE MANAGED

From *(name and address of management company)* ('the Managers')

To   *(name and address of owner)* ('the Owner')

Dear Sir,

Management and labour for *(details of gardens)* as shown on the attached plan ('the Gardens')

1   *Commencement*

This agreement is to commence on *(date)* and is to continue for a period of[5 years *(or as the case may be)*], subject to prior termination as provided by this agreement, and thereafter until terminated by [3 months' *(or as the case may be)*] notice in writing given by either party to the other and expiring at any time after the end of that period, and we the Managers and you the Owner agree as follows:

2   *Obligations of the Managers*

2.1 Advice and labour

During the continuance of this agreement the Managers will supply advice and labour in connection with the management , maintenance and improvement of the Gardens upon the terms set out below.

2.2 Annual management scheme

After consultation with the Owner, the Managers will prepare annually a detailed plan of operations as to how the Gardens are to be managed ('the Management Scheme').

2.3 Manpower and machinery

The Managers will provide the manpower and machinery, including fuel and other costs, necessary to implement the Management Scheme and maintain the Gardens.

2.4 Meetings

The Managers will meet with the Owner not less than twice each calendar year to report on, assess and progress the Management Scheme.

2.5 Objectionable employees

The Managers must not employ for the purposes of this agreement any person to whose employment reasonable objection is taken by or on behalf of the Owner.

2.6 Statutory provisions

The Managers must ensure that all statutory provisions and requirements affecting the work to be carried on under this agreement or the conduct of their employees or agents while on or in the vicinity of the Gardens are complied with.

2.7 Assignment

The Managers must not assign or sub-contract any of their rights or duties under this agreement without the consent in writing of the Owner.

3   Indemnity and insurance

3.1 Liability to employees

The Managers must insure all persons employed in pursuance of this agreement against accident, and agree to indemnify the Owner against all liability in that regard.

3.2 Liability to others

Without prejudice to their liability to indemnify the Owner as provided by this agreement, the Managers must at their own expense at all times maintain with reputable insurers such insurances as may be necessary to cover all liability which the Managers may incur in respect of any personal injury, death or damage to property whatsoever caused by or arising out of or in the course of the carrying out of the Managers' duties under this agreement, such insurance to be for at least [£100,000 *(or as the case may be)*] and to be approved in writing by the Owner.

4   Obligations of the Owner

4.1 Payments

In consideration of the services to be rendered by the Managers under this agreement the Owner shall pay to the Managers the following amounts:

4.1.1 management fees of £...... [per year *(or)* for each month during the subsistence of this agreement]; and

4.1.2 a sum equal to the direct labour and material cost to the Managers of providing the services set out in clause 2.3 above.

4.2 Invoicing

The Managers must deliver in respect of each calendar month a detailed computation of any sums claimed to be payable under clause 4.1 above together with copies of all relevant time sheets and vouchers and a VAT invoice.

4.3 Payment

Any sums due under clause 4.1 above are to be payable [30 days *(or as required)*] after the date of the relevant invoice.

5 *VAT*

All sums payable under this agreement, unless otherwise stated, are exclusive of VAT and other duties or taxes. Any VAT or other duties or taxes payable in respect of such sums are to be payable in addition to them.

6 *Determination*

The Owner may determine this agreement by immediate written notice in the event of the Managers:

6.1 failing to keep the terms of this agreement; or

6.2 going into liquidation, or having an administration order made against them, or suffering execution to be made on any goods in the Gardens.

Yours faithfully,

(signature on behalf of Managers)

(on the copy)

I agree the above terms.

(signature of Owner)

Date:

18

BLIGHT NOTICE[1]

TOWN AND COUNTRY PLANNING ACT 1990
Blight Notice

To.. [1]

At.. [2]

I/We..of............................[3]

HEREBY GIVE YOU NOTICE under section 150(1) [and by virtue of section 158][4] of the Town and Country Planning Act 1990 ('the Act') as follows:—

1.   I am/We are entitled to the interest described in Schedule 1[5] to this Notice in the property described in Schedule 2[6] to this Notice.

2.   The whole/Part of[7] that property is blighted land within paragraph(s) ....[8] of Schedule 13 to the Act.

3.   My/Our interest in that property qualifies for protection under Chapter II in Part VI of the Act because

[EITHER]

the property is [part of][9] a hereditament whose annual value does not exceed the amount prescribed for the purposes of section 149(3)(a) of the Act and I am an owner-occupier/we are owner-occupiers of that hereditament.

[OR]

the property is [part of][9] a hereditament and I am a resident owner-occupier/we are resident owner-occupiers of that hereditament.

[OR]

the property is [part of][9] an agricultural unit and I am an owner-occupier/we are owner-occupiers of that unit.

4.(1)   *[EITHER]* I/We have made reasonable endeavours to sell my/our interest in that property, and details of those attempts are set out in [Schedule 3 to/the letter accompanying][10] this Notice. *[OR]* The powers of compulsory acquisition relevant for the purposes of paragraph 21/22 of Schedule 13 to the Act remain exercisable[11].

(2)   In consequence of the fact that [part of][12] the hereditament / agricultural unit was, or was likely to be, comprised in blighted land, I/we have been unable to sell my/our interest except at a price substantially lower than that for which it might reasonably have been expected to sell if no part of the hereditament/unit were, or were likely to be, comprised in blighted land.

5.[13]   The [part of the][9] agricultural unit in which my/our interest subsists contains land which is not blighted land as well as land which is, and the land which is not blighted land is not reasonably capable of being farmed, either by itself or with other relevant land, as a separate agricultural unit.

6.   I/We therefore require you to purchase my/our interest in

[EITHER]

the property described in Schedule 2 to this Notice[14].

[OR]

so much of the property described in Schedule 2 to this Notice as is blighted land[15].

SCHEDULE 1

The Interest to which this Blight Notice Relates

SCHEDULE 2

The Property to which this Blight Notice Relates

SCHEDULE 3

Details of Attempts to Sell the Interest to which the Blight Notice Relates

Dated ....
Signed ....
[Solicitor/Surveyor/land agent, of ....
on behalf of ....][16]

NOTES

1.   Insert name of the appropriate authority.
2.   Insert address of the appropriate authority.
3.   Give full name(s) and address(es) of claimant(s).

4.   Delete unless this notice relates to an agricultural unit and a claim and requirement under section 158(2) of the Act are to be included.

5.   Schedule 1 should contain a description of the interest of the claimant, a list of any mortgages to which that interest is subject with the names and addresses of the mortgagees, and a list of any other incumbrances affecting the interest.

6.   The boundaries of the property should normally be clearly marked on a plan annexed to the Blight Notice.

7.   Use 'Part' instead of 'The whole' if only some of the land is blighted land.

8.   Insert relevant paragraph number(s).

9.   Delete unless the interest is in only part of the hereditament or unit.

10. Delete as appropriate.

11. The second alternative may be used only if paragraph 2 of this notice refers to paragraph 21 or 22 of Schedule 13 to the Act.

12. Delete unless only part of the property is blighted land.

13. Use this paragraph (and the reference to section 158 at the top of the notice—see Note 4 above) only to make a claim under section 158(2).

14. Use if the property is a hereditament, or is an agricultural unit and paragraph 5 has been included.

15. Use if the property is an agricultural unit but paragraph 5 has been deleted.

16. If this notice is signed by an agent, insert here full name and address of agent or firm, and name(s) of claimant(s).

---

1   This form is prescribed by the Town and Country Planning General Regulations 1992/1492, reg 16 and is Crown copyright. The form, or one substantially to the like effect must be used.

19

NOTIFICATION OF INTENTION TO LOP TREES, ROOTS AND BRANCHES

(date)

Dear *(name of neighbour)*

[3 Acacia Avenue *(or as the case may be)*]

I am writing to you concerning certain [branches] [and] [roots] from the [oak] tree[s] on your above property which are intruding over the boundary into my property [1 Acacia Avenue *(or as the case may be)*]. This intrusion is a trespass and legal nuisance and I am legally entitled to take steps to remedy the position by cutting, lopping or trimming back the [branches] [and] [roots].

Whilst I could do this without your consent, I write to inform you that it is my intention to bring in contractors to do this on *(date)* at approximately *(time)* and I would be grateful for your agreement that I [and my contractors] may enter your property temporarily to carry out this work.

I confirm that all [branches] [and] [roots] will be returned to your side of the boundary and all damage to the soil on your side and fences will be made good.

Please could you kindly confirm your agreement to access to your property on that day by returning the spare copy of this letter having signed the form at the foot. I am most grateful to you for your co-operation.

I also have to say that if there is found to be any damage resulting from the encroaching [branches] [and] [roots] notwithstanding the work described above, I must reserve my rights in respect of any legal claim. The latter point is not made in any hostile way but merely for the record.

Yours sincerely,

(signature of owner)

20

LETTER TO A LOCAL AUTHORITY SEEKING CONSENT TO FELLING, TOPPING, LOPPING OR UPROOTING TREES THE SUBJECT OF A TREE PRESERVATION ORDER OR IN A CONSERVATION AREA

To: The Chief Planning Officer
       .... Council

(date)

Dear Sir,

TOWN AND COUNTRY PLANNING ACT 1990
Tree Preservation Order No ....
Trees at [1 Acacia Avenue *(or as the case may be)*]

I am writing to you as owner of [1 Acacia Avenue *(or as the case may be)*] with regard to trees *(insert numbers on the order, eg T1, T2 etc)* [as shown on the plan annexed to the above Tree Preservation Order *(or)* in my garden] as I understand that I am prohibited from cutting down, topping, lopping or uprooting these trees [because the property is in a conservation area]. I now ask for your formal consent to the following work *(give details, eg to cut down tree T1 and lop and trim tree T2)*

My reasons for wanting to do this work are as follows: [*(give details, eg —)* to stop the branches overhanging my neighbour's property causing a nuisance *(or)* to construct a swimming pool *(or)* to construct a new access to the rear of [1 Acacia Avenue *(or as the case may be)*] *(or as the case may be)*]. I confirm that I will plant replacement [ash *(or)* oak *(or as the case may be)*] trees in another part of my garden.

Please will you kindly acknowledge receipt of this letter and let me hear from you within 7 days confirming that I may do the above work failing which I reserve the right to appeal to the Secretary of State or to take such legal steps as are open to me to pursue the matter.

Yours faithfully,

(signature of owner)

Appendix B

1

WILDLIFE AND COUNTRYSIDE ACT 1981
(EXTRACTS)

13 Protection of wild plants

(1)   Subject to the provisions of this Part, if any person—

      (a)   intentionally picks, uproots or destroys any wild plant included in Schedule 8; or

      (b)   not being an authorised person, intentionally uproots any wild plant not included in that Schedule,

he shall be guilty of an offence.

(2) Subject to the provisions of this Part, if any person—

    (a) sells, offers or exposes for sale, or has in his possession or transports for the purpose of sale, any live or dead wild plant included in Schedule 8, or any part of, or anything derived from, such a plant; or

    (b) publishes or causes to be published any advertisement likely to be understood as conveying that he buys or sells, or intends to buy or sell, any of those things,

    he shall be guilty of an offence.

(3) Notwithstanding anything in subsection (1), a person shall not be guilty of an offence by reason of any act made unlawful by that subsection if he shows that the act was an incidental result of a lawful operation and could not reasonably have been avoided.

14 Introduction of new species etc.

(1) Subject to the provisions of this Part, if any person releases or allows to escape into the wild any animal which—

    (a) is of a kind which is not ordinarily resident in and is not a regular visitor to Great Britain in a wild state; or

    (b) is included in Part I of Schedule 9,

he shall be guilty of an offence.

(2) Subject to the provisions of this Part, if any person plants or otherwise causes to grow in the wild any plant which is included in Part II of Schedule 9, he shall be guilty of an offence.

(3) Subject to subsection (4), it shall be a defence to a charge of committing an offence under subsection (1) or (2) to prove that the accused took all reasonable steps and exercised all due diligence to avoid committing the offence.

(4) Where the defence provided by subsection (3) involves an allegation that the commission of the offence was due to the act or default of another person, the person charged shall not, without leave of the court, be entitled to rely on the defence unless, within a period ending seven clear days before the hearing, he has served on the prosecutor a notice giving such information identifying or assisting in the identification of the other person as was then in his possession.

(5) Any person authorised in writing by the Secretary of State may, at any reasonable time and (if required to do so) upon producing evidence that he is authorised, enter any land for the purpose of ascertaining whether an offence under subsection (1) or (2) is being, or has been, committed on that land; but nothing in this subsection shall authorise any person to enter a dwelling.

19 Enforcement

(1) If a constable suspects with reasonable cause that any person is committing or has committed an offence under this Part, the constable may without warrant—

   (a) stop and search that person if the constable suspects with reasonable cause that evidence of the commission of the offence is to be found on that person;

   (b) search or examine any thing which that person may then be using or have in his possession if the constable suspects with reasonable cause that evidence of the commission of the offence is to be found on that thing;

   (c) < . . . >

   (d) seize and detain for the purposes of proceedings under this Part any thing which may be evidence of the commission of the offence or may be liable to be forfeited under section 21.

(2) If a constable suspects with reasonable cause that any person is committing an offence under this Part, he may, for the purpose of exercising the powers conferred by subsection (1) [or

arresting a person, in accordance with section 25 of the Police and Criminal Evidence Act 1984, for such an offence], enter any land other than a dwelling-house.

(3) If a justice of the peace is satisfied by information on oath that there are reasonable grounds for suspecting that—

    (a) an offence under section 1, 3, 5, 7 or 8 in respect of which this Part or any order made under it provides for a special penalty; or

    (b) an offence under section 6, 9, 11(1) or (2), 13 or 14,

has been committed and that evidence of the offence may be found on any premises, he may grant a warrant to any constable (with or without other persons) to enter upon and search those premises for the purpose of obtaining that evidence.

In the application of this subsection to Scotland, the reference to a justice of the peace includes a reference to the sheriff.

20 Summary prosecutions

(1) This section applies to—

    (a) any offence under section 1(1) or 3(1) involving the killing or taking of any wild bird or the taking of an egg of such a bird;

    (b) any offence under section 9(1) involving the killing or taking of any wild animal; and

    (c) any offence under section 13(1) involving the picking uprooting or destruction of any wild plant.

(2) Summary proceedings for an offence to which this section applies may be brought within a period of six months from the date on which evidence sufficient in the opinion of the prosecutor to warrant the proceedings came to his knowledge; but no such proceedings shall be brought by virtue of this section more than two years after the commission of the offence.

(3) For the purpose of this section a certificate signed by or on behalf of the prosecutor and stating the date on which such evidence as aforesaid came to his knowledge shall be conclusive evidence of that fact; and a certificate stating that matter and purporting to be so signed shall be deemed to be so signed unless the contrary is proved.

27 Interpretation of Part I

(1) In this Part, unless the context otherwise requires—

"advertisement" includes a catalogue, a circular and a price list;

"advisory body" has the meaning given by section 23;

"agriculture Minister" means the Minister of Agriculture, Fisheries and Food or the Secretary of State;

"authorised person" means—

(a) the owner or occupier, or any person authorised by the owner or occupier, of the land on which the action authorised is taken;

(b) any person authorised in writing by the local authority for the area within which the action authorised is taken;

(c) as respects anything done in relation to wild birds, any person authorised in writing by any of the following bodies, that is to say, [any of the Nature Conservancy Councils], < ... > a district board for a fishery district within the meaning of the Salmon Fisheries (Scotland) Act 1862 or a local fisheries committee constituted under the Sea Fisheries Regulation Act 1966;

[(d) any person authorised in writing by the [Environment Agency], a water undertakers or a sewerage undertaker;]

so, however, that the authorisation of any person for the purposes of this definition shall not confer any right of entry upon any land;

"automatic weapon" and "semi-automatic weapon" do not include any weapon the magazine of which is incapable of holding more than two rounds;

"aviculture" means the breeding and rearing of birds in captivity;

"destroy", in relation to an egg, includes doing anything to the egg which is calculated to prevent it from hatching, and "destruction" shall be construed accordingly;

"domestic duck" means any domestic form of duck;

"domestic goose" means any domestic form of goose;

"firearm" has the same meaning as in the Firearms Act 1968;

"game bird" means any pheasant, partridge, grouse (or moor game), black (or heath) game or ptarmigan;

["inland waters" means—

(a) inland waters within the meaning of the Water Resources Act 1991;

(b) any waters not falling within paragraph (a) above which are within the seaward limits of the territorial sea;

(c) controlled waters within the meaning of Part II of the Control of Pollution Act 1974 other than ground waters as defined in section 30A(1)(d) of that Act.]

"livestock" includes any animal which is kept—

(a) for the provision of food, wool, skins or fur;

(b) for the purpose of its use in the carrying on of any agricultural activity; or

(c) for the provision or improvement of shooting or fishing;

"local authority" means—

(a) in relation to England < . . . >, a county, district or London borough council < . . . >;

[(aa)   in relation to Wales, a county council or county borough council;]

(b) in relation to Scotland, a [council constituted under section 2 of the Local Government etc (Scotland) Act 1994];

"occupier", in relation to any land other than the foreshore, includes any person having any right of hunting, shooting, fishing or taking game or fish;

"pick", in relation to a plant, means gather or pluck any part of the plant without uprooting it;

"poultry" means domestic fowls, geese, ducks, guinea-fowls, pigeons and quails, and turkeys;

"sale" includes hire, barter and exchange and cognate expressions shall be construed accordingly;

"uproot", in relation to a plant, means dig up or otherwise remove the plant from the land on which it is growing;

"vehicle" includes aircraft, hovercraft and boat;

"water authority", in relation to Scotland, has the same meaning as in the Water (Scotland) Act 1980;

"wild animal" means any animal (other than a bird) which is or (before it was killed or taken) was living wild;

"wild bird" means any bird of a kind which is ordinarily resident in or is a visitor to Great Britain in a wild state but does not include poultry or, except in sections 5 and 16, any game bird;

"wild plant" means any plant which is or (before it was picked, uprooted or destroyed) was growing wild and is of a kind which ordinarily grows in Great Britain in a wild state.

(2) A bird shall not be treated as bred in captivity for the purposes of this Part unless its parents were lawfully in captivity when the egg was laid.

(3) Any reference in this Part to an animal of any kind includes, unless the context otherwise requires, a reference to an egg, larva, pupa, or other immature stage of an animal of that kind.

[(3A) Any reference in this Part to the Nature Conservancy Councils is a reference to the Nature Conservancy Council for England, [Scottish Natural Heritage] and the Countryside Council for Wales.]

(4) This Part shall apply to the Isles of Scilly as if the Isles were a county and as if the Council of the Isles were a county council.

(5) This Part extends to the territorial waters adjacent to Great Britain, and for the purposes of this Part any part of Great Britain which is bounded by territorial waters shall be taken to include the territorial waters adjacent to that part.

SCHEDULE 8

PLANTS WHICH ARE PROTECTED

Sections 13, 22, 24

Common name	*Scientific name*
[Adder's-tongue, Least	Ophioglossum lusitanicum]
Alison, Small	Alyssum alyssoides
[Anomodon, Long-leaved	Anomodon longifolius]
[Beech-lichen, New Forest	Enterographa elaborata]
[Blackwort	Southbya nigrella]
[Bluebell (in respect of section 13(2) only)	Hyacinthoides non-scripta]
[Bolete, Royal	Boletus regius]
Broomrape, Bedstraw	Orobanche caryophyllacea
Broomrape, Oxtongue	Orobanche loricata
Broomrape, Thistle	Orobanche reticulata
[Cabbage, Lundy	Rhynchosinapis wrightii]
Calamint, Wood	Calamintha sylvatica
[Caloplaca, Snow	Caloplaca nivalis]
[Catapyrenium, Tree	Catapyrenium psoromoides]
Catchfly, Alpine	Lychnis alpina
[Catillaria, Laurer's	Catellaria laureri]
[Centaury, Slender	Centaurium tenuiflorum]
Cinquefoil, Rock	Potentilla rupestris

[Cladonia, Convoluted	Cladonia convoluta]
[Cladonia, Upright Mountain	Cladonia stricta]
[Clary, Meadow	Salvia pratensis]
Club-rush, Triangular	Scirpus triquetrus
[Colt's-foot, Purple	Homogyne alpina]
Cotoneaster, Wild	Cotoneaster integerrimus
[Cottongrass, Slender	Eriophorum gracile]
Cow-wheat, Field	Melampyrum arvense
[Crocus, Sand	Romulea columnae]
[Crystalwort, Lizard	Riccia bifurca]
[Cudweed, Broad-leaved	Filago pyramidata]
Cudweed, Jersey	Gnaphalium luteoalbum
[Cudweed, Red-tipped	Fiago lutesoens]
[Cut-grass	Leersia oryzoides]
[Deptford Pink (in respect of England and Wales only)	Dianthus armeria]
Diapensia	Diapensia lapponica
[Dock, Shore	Rumex rupestrls]
[Earwort, Marsh	Jamesoniella undulifolia]
Eryngo, Field	Eryngium campestre
[Feather-moss, Polar	Hygrohypnum polare]
Fern, Dickie's Bladder	Cystopteris dickieana
Fern, Killarney	Trichomanes speciosum
[Flapwort, Norfolk	Leiocolea rutheana]
[Fleabane, Alpine	Erigeron borealis]
[Fleabane, Small	Pulicaria vulgaris]
[Frostwort, Pointed	Gymnomitrion apiculatum]
[Fungus, Hedgehog	Hericium erinaceum]
Galingale, Brown	Cyperus fuscus
Gentian, Alpine	Gentiana nivalis
[Gentian, Dune	Gentianella uliginosa]
[Gentian, Early	Gentianella anglica]
[Gentian, Fringed	Gentianella ciliata]
Gentian, Spring	Gentiana verna
[Germander, Cut-leaved	Tevarium botrys]
Germander, Water	Teucrium scordium
Gladiolus, Wild	Gladiolus illyricus

[Goblin Lights   Catolechia wahlenbergii]
[Goosefoot, Stinking   Chenopodium vulvaria]
[Grass-poly   Lythrum hyssopifolia]
[Grimmia, Blunt-leaved   Grimmia unicolor
[Gyalecta, Elm   Gyalecta ulmi]
Hare's-ear, Sickle-leaved   Bupleurum falcatum
Hare's-ear, Small   Bupleurum baldense
[Hawk's-bead, Stinking   Crepis foetida]
[Hawkweed, Northroe   Hieracium northroense]
[Hawkweed, Shetland   Hieracium zetlandicum]
Hawkweed, Weak-leaved   Hieracium attenuatifolium]
Heath, Blue   Phyllodoce caerulea
Helleborine, Red   Cephalanthera rubra
[Helleborine, Young's   Epipactis youngiana]
[Horsetail, Branched   Equisetum ramosissimum]
[Hound's-tongue, Green   Cynoglossum germanicum]
Knawel, Perennial   Scleranthus perennis
Knotgrass, Sea   Polygonum maritimum
Lady's-slipper   Cypripedium calceolus
     < . . . >   < . . . >
[Lecanactis, Churchyard   Lecanactis hemisphaerica]
[Lecanora, Tarn   Lecanora archariana]
[Lecidea, Copper   Lecidea inops]
Leek, Round-headed   Allium sphaerocephalon
Lettuce, Least   Lactuca saligna
[Lichen, Arctic Kidney   Nephroma arcticum]
[Lichen, Ciliate Strap   Heterodermia leucomelos]
[Lichen, Coralloid Rosette   Heterodermia propagulifera]
[Lichen, Ear-lobed Dog   Peltigera lepidophora]
[Lichen, Forked Hair   Bryoria furcellata]
[Lichen, Golden Hair   Teloschistes flavicans]
[Lichen, Orange Fruited Elm   Caloplaca luteoalba]
[Lichen, River Jelly   Collema dichotomum]
[Lichen, Scaly Breck   Squamarina lentigera]
[Lichen, Stary Breck   Buellia asterella]
Lily, Snowdon   Lloydia serotina
[Liverwort   Petallophyllum ralfsi]

[Liverwort, Lindenberg's Leafy	Adelanthus lindenbergianus]
Marsh-mallow, Rough	Althaea hirsuta
[Marshwort, Creeping	Apium repens]
[Milk-parsley, Cambridge	Selinum carvifolia]
[Moss	Drepanocladius vernicosus]
[Moss, Alpine Copper	Mielichoferia mielichoferi]
[Moss, Baltic Bog	Sphagnum balticum]
[Moss, Blue Dew	Saelania glaucescens]
[Moss, Blunt-leaved Bristle	Orthotrichum obtusifolium]
[Moss, Bright Green Cave	Cyclodictyon laetevirens]
[Moss, Cordate Beard	Barbula cordata]
[Moss, Cornish Path	Ditrichum cornubicum]
[Moss, Derbyshire Feather	Thamnobryum angustifolium]
[Moss, Dune Thread	Bryum mamillatum]
[Moss, Flamingo	Desmatodon cernuus]
[Moss, Glaucous Beard	Barbula glauca]
[Moss, Green Shield	Buxbaumia viridis]
[Moss, Hair Silk	Plagiothecium piliferum]
[Moss, Knothole	Zygodon forsteri]
[Moss, Large Yellow Feather	Scorpidium turgescens]
[Moss, Millimetre	Micromitrium tenerum]
[Moss, Multifruited River	Cryphaea lamyana]
[Moss, Nowell's Limestone	Zygodon gracilis]
[Moss, Rigid Apple	Bartramia stricta]
[Moss, Round-leaved Feather	Rhyncostegium rotundifolium]
[Moss, Schleicher's Thread	Bryum schleicheri]
[Moss, Triangular Pygmy	Acaulon triquetrum]
[Moss, Vaucher's Feather	Hypnum vaucheri]
[Mudwort, Welsh	Limosella australis]
[Naiad, Holly-leaved	Najas marina]
[Naiad, Slender	Najas flexilis]
[Orache, Stalked	Halimione pedunculata]
Orchid, Early Spider	Ophrys sphegodes
Orchid, Fen	Liparis loeselii
Orchid, Ghost	Epipogium aphyllum
[Orchid, Lapland Marsh	Dactylorhiza lapponica]
Orchid, Late Spider	Ophrys fuciflora

Orchid, Lizard	Himantoglossum hircinum
Orchid, Military	Orchis militaris
Orchid, Monkey	Orchis simia
[Pannaria, Caledonia	Pannaria ignobilis]
[Parmelia, New Forest	Parmelia minarum]
[Parmentaria, Oil Stain	Parmentaria chilensis]
Pear, Plymouth	Pyrus cordata
[Pennyroyal	Mentha pulegium]
[Penny-cress, Perfoliate	Thlaspi perfoliatum]
[Pertusaria, Alpine Moss	Pertusaria bryontha]
[Physcia, Southern Grey	Physcia tribacioides]
[Pigmyweed	Crassula aquatica]
[Pine, Ground	Ajuga chamaepitys]
Pink, Cheddar	Dianthus gratianopolitanus
Pink, Childling	Petroraghia nanteuilii
[Plantain, Floating Water	Luronium natans]
[Polypore, Oak	Buglossoporus pulvinus]
[Pseudocyphellaria, Ragged	Pseudocyphellaria lacerata]
[Psora, Rusty Alpine	Psora rubiformis]
[Puffball, Sandy Stilt	Battarraea phalloides]
[Ragwort, Fen	Senecio paludosus]
[Rampion, Spiked	Phyteuma spicatum]
[Ramping-fumitory, Martin's	Fumaria martinil]
[Restharrow, Small	Ononis reclinata]
[Rock-cress, Alpine	Arabis alpina]
[Rock-cress, Bristol	Arabis stricta]
[Rustworth, Western	Marsupella profunda]
Sandwort, Norwegian	Arenaria norvegica
Sandwort, Teesdale	Minuartia stricta
Saxifrage, Drooping	Saxifraga cernua
[Saxifrage, Marsh	Saxifrage hirulus]
Saxifrage, Tufted	Saxifraga cespitosa
[Solenopsora, Serpentine	Solenopsora lipinara]
Solomon's-seal, Whorled	Polygonatum verticillatum
Sow-thistle, Alpine	Cicerbita alpina
Spearwort, Adder's-tongue	Ranunculus ophioglossifolius
[Speedwell, Fingered	Veronica, triphyllas]

Speedwell, Spiked	Veronica spicata
[Spike-rush, Dwarf	Eleocharis parvula]
< . . . >　　< . . . >	
[Stack Fleawort, South	Tephroserisintegrifolia (ssp maritima)]
[Star-of-Bethlehem, Early	Gagea betremica]
Starfruit	Damasonium alisma
[Stonewort, Bearded	Chara canescens]
[Stonewort, Foxtail	Lamprothamnium papulosum]
[Strapwort	Carrigiola litoralis]
[Sulphur-tresses, Alpine	Alectoria ochroleuca]
[Threadmoss, Long-leaved	Bryum neodamense]
[Turpswort	Geocalyx graveolens]
[Viper's-grass	Scorzonera humilis]
Violet, Fen	Viola persicifolia
Water-plantain, Ribbon leaved	Alisma gramineum
Wood-sedge, Starved	Carex depauperata
Woodsia, Alpine	Woodsia alpina
Woodsia, Oblong	Woodsia ilvensis
Wormwood, Field	Artemisia campestris
Woundwort, Downy	Stachys germanica
Woundwort, Limestone	Stachys alpina
Yellow-rattle, Greater	Rhinanthus serotinus

Note. The common name or names given in the first column of this Schedule are included by way of guidance only; in the event of any dispute or proceedings, the common name or names shall not be taken into account.

SCHEDULE 9

ANIMALS AND PLANTS TO WHICH SECTION 14 APPLIES

Part II
Plants

Common name	*Scientific name*
Hogweed, Giant	Heracleum mantegazzianum
Kelp, Giant	Macrocystis pyrifera

[Kelp, Giant	Macrocystis angustifolia
Kelp, Giant	Macrocystis integrifolia
Kelp, Giant	Macrocystis laevis
Kelp, Japanese	Laminaria japonica]
Knotweed, Japanese	Polygonum cuspidatum
[Seafingers, Green	Codium fragile tomentosoides
Seaweed, Californian Red	Pikea californica
Seaweed, Hooked Asparagus	Asparagopsis armata]
Seaweed, Japanese	Sargassum muticum
[Seaweeds, Laver (except	
native species)	Porphyra spp except—
p. amethystea	
p. leucosticta	
p. linearis	
p.miniata	
p. purpurea	
p. umbilicalis]	
[Wakame	Undaria pinnatifida.]

Note. The common name or names given in the first column of this Schedule are included by way of guidance only; in the event of any dispute or proceedings, the common name or names shall not be taken into account.

2

PLANT VARIETIES ACT 1997
(EXTRACTS)

1 Plant breeders' rights

(1) Rights, to be known as plant breeders' rights, may be granted in accordance with this Part of this Act.

(2) Plant breeders' rights may subsist in varieties of all plant genera and species.

(3) For the purposes of this Act, "variety" means a plant grouping within a single botanical taxon of the lowest known rank, which grouping, irrespective of whether the conditions for the grant of plant breeders' rights (which are laid down in section 4 below) are met, can be—

    (a) defined by the expression of the characteristics resulting from a given genotype or combination of genotypes,

    (b) distinguished from any other plant grouping by the expression of at least one of those characteristics, and

    (c) considered as a unit with regard to its suitability for being propagated unchanged.

2 The Plant Variety Rights Office

(1) The office known as the Plant Variety Rights Office shall continue in being for the purposes of this Part of this Act under the immediate control of an officer appointed by the Ministers and known as the Controller of Plant Variety Rights ("the Controller").

(2) Schedule 1 to this Act (which makes further provision about the Plant Variety Rights Office) shall have effect.

3 Grant on application

(1) Subject to this Part of this Act, plant breeders' rights shall be granted to an applicant by the Controller on being satisfied that the conditions laid down in section 4 below are met.

(2) The Controller may by notice require an applicant for the grant of plant breeders' rights to provide him, within such time as may be specified in the notice, with such information, documents, plant or other material, facilities or test or trial results relevant to the carrying out of his function under subsection (1) above as may be so specified.

(3) If an applicant fails to comply with a notice under subsection (2) above within the period specified in the notice, the Controller may refuse the application.

4 Conditions for the grant of rights

(1) The conditions which must be met in relation to an application for the grant of plant breeders' rights are—

    (a) that the variety to which the application relates is a qualifying variety, and

    (b) that the person by whom the application is made is the person entitled to the grant of plant breeders' rights in respect of the variety to which it relates.

(2) For the purposes of subsection (1) above, a variety is a qualifying variety if it is—

    (a) distinct,

    (b) uniform,

    (c) stable, and

    (d) new;

and Part I of Schedule 2 to this Act has effect for the purpose of determining whether these criteria are met.

(3) Subject to subsections (4) and (5) below, the person entitled to the grant of plant breeders' rights in respect of a variety is the person who breeds it, or discovers and develops it, or his successor in title.

(4) If a person breeds a variety, or discovers and develops it, in the course of his employment, then, subject to agreement to the contrary, his employer, or his employer's successor in title, is the person entitled to the grant of plant breeders' rights in respect of it.

(5) Part II of Schedule 2 to this Act shall have effect as respects priorities between two or more persons who have independently bred, or discovered and developed, a variety.

(6) In this section and Schedule 2 to this Act, references to the discovery of a variety are to the discovery of a variety, whether growing in the wild or occurring as a genetic variant, whether artificially induced or not.

6 Protected variety

(1) Plant breeders' rights shall have effect to entitle the holder to prevent anyone doing any of the following acts as respects the

propagating material of the protected variety without his authority, namely—

(a) production or reproduction (multiplication),

(b) conditioning for the purpose of propagation,

(c) offering for sale,

(d) selling or other marketing,

(e) exporting,

(f) importing,

(g) stocking for any of the purposes mentioned in paragraphs (a) to (f) above, and

(h) any other act prescribed for the purposes of this provision.

(2) The holder of plant breeders' rights may give authority for the purposes of subsection (1) above with or without conditions or limitations.

(3) The rights conferred on the holder of plant breeders' rights by subsections (1) and (2) above shall also apply as respects harvested material obtained through the unauthorised use of propagating material of the protected variety, unless he has had a reasonable opportunity before the harvested material is obtained to exercise his rights in relation to the unauthorised use of the propagating material.

(4) In the case of a variety of a prescribed description, the rights conferred on the holder of plant breeders' rights by subsections (1) and (2) above shall also apply as respects any product which—

(a) is made directly from harvested material in relation to which subsection (3) above applies, and

(b) is of a prescribed description,

unless subsection (5) below applies.

(5) This subsection applies if, before the product was made, any act mentioned in subsection (1) above was done as respects the harvested material from which the product was made and either—

(a) the act was done with the authority of the holder of the plant breeders' rights, or

(b) the holder of those rights had a reasonable opportunity to exercise them in relation to the doing of the act.

(6) In this section—

(a) "prescribed" means prescribed by regulations made by the Ministers, and

(b) references to harvested material include entire plants and parts of plants.

11 Duration

(1) A grant of plant breeders' rights shall have effect—

    (a) in the case of potatoes, trees and vines, for 30 years from the date of the grant, and

    (b) in other cases, for 25 years from that date.

(2) The Ministers may by regulations provide that, in relation to varieties of a species or group specified in the regulations, subsection (1) above shall have effect with the substitution in paragraph (a) or (b), as the case may be, of such longer period, not exceeding—

    (a) in the case of paragraph (a), 35 years, and

    (b) in the case of paragraph (b), 30 years,

as may be so specified.

(3) The period for which a grant of plant breeders' rights has effect shall not be affected by the fact it becomes impossible to invoke the rights—

    (a) because of Article 92(2) of the Council Regulation (effect of subsequent grant of Community plant variety right), or

    (b) because of suspension under section 23 below.

12 Transmission

Plant breeders' rights shall be assignable like other kinds of proprietary rights, but in any case rights under section 6 above and rights under section 7 above may not be assigned separately.

13 Remedies for infringement

(1) Plant breeders' rights shall be actionable at the suit of the holder of the rights.

(2) In any proceedings for the infringement of plant breeders' rights, all such relief by way of damages, injunction, interdict, account or otherwise shall be available as is available in any corresponding proceedings in respect of infringements of other proprietary rights.

19 Duty to use registered name

(1) Where a name is registered under section 18 above in respect of a variety, a person may not use any other name in selling, offering for sale or otherwise marketing propagating material of the variety.

(2) Subsection (1) above shall have effect in relation to any variety from the date on which plant breeders' rights in respect of that variety are granted, and shall continue to apply after the period for which the grant of those rights has effect.

(3) Subsection (1) above shall not preclude the use of any trade mark or trade name (whether registered under the Trade Marks Act 1994 or not) if—

    (a) that mark or name and the registered name are juxtaposed, and

    (b) the registered name is easily recognisable.

(4) A person who contravenes subsection (1) above shall be liable on summary conviction to a fine not exceeding level 3 on the standard scale.

(5) In any proceedings for an offence under subsection (4) above, it shall be a defence to prove that the accused took all reasonable precautions against committing the offence and had not at the time of the offence any reason to suspect that he was committing an offence.

20 Improper use of registered name

(1) If any person uses the registered name of a protected variety in offering for sale, selling or otherwise marketing material of a different variety within the same class, the use of the name shall be a wrong actionable in proceedings by the holder of the rights.

(2) Subsection (1) above shall also apply to the use of a name so nearly resembling the registered name as to be likely to deceive or cause confusion.

(3) In any proceedings under this section, it shall be a defence to a claim for damages to prove that the defendant took all reasonable precautions against committing the wrong and had not, when using the name, any reason to suspect that it was wrongful.

(4) In this section—

"class" means a class prescribed for the purposes of regulations under section 18(1) above,

"registered name", in relation to a protected variety, means the name registered in respect of it under section 18 above.

3

PLANT HEALTH ACT 1967
(EXTRACTS)

1 Objects of Act, and competent authorities under it

(1) This Act shall have effect for the control < . . . > of pests and diseases injurious to agricultural or horticultural crops, or to trees or bushes, and in the following provisions of this Act—

  (a) references to pests are to be taken as references to insects, bacteria, fungi and other vegetable or animal organisms, viruses and all other agents causative of any transmissible disease of agricultural or horticultural crops or of trees or bushes, and also as including references to pests in any stage of existence;

  (b) references to a crop are to be taken as including references to trees and bushes.

(2) The competent authorities for purposes of this Act shall be—

  (a) as regards the protection of forest trees and timber from attack by pests, the Forestry Commissioners ("timber" for this purpose including all forest products); and

  (b) otherwise, for England and Wales the Minister of Agriculture, Fisheries and Food and for Scotland the Secretary of State.

2 Control of introduction of pests into Great Britain

(1) A competent authority may from time to time make such orders as the authority thinks expedient [or called for by any community obligation] for preventing the introduction of pests into Great Britain.

(2) Where it appears to the competent authority that the landing in Great Britain of articles of any description (and in particular plants, trees or bushes or any part or produce thereof) is likely to introduce a pest into Great Britain, the orders may prohibit or regulate the landing of those articles, and may direct or authorise their destruction if landed (without prejudice to provisions of [the Customs and Excise Management Act 1979] imposing penalties or liability to forfeiture).

[(3) In subsection (2) above references to the landing of any article include references to its importation through the tunnel system as defined in the Channel Tunnel Act 1987.]

3 Control of spread of pests in Great Britain

(1) A competent authority may from time to time make such orders as the authority thinks expedient [or called for by any Community obligation] for preventing the spread of pests [or the conveyance of pests by articles exported from Great Britain].

(2) The orders may direct or authorise—

(a) the removal [treatment] or destruction of any crop, or any seed, plant or part thereof [or any container wrapping or other article] or any substance, which has on it, or is infected with, a pest, or to or by means of which, a pest is in the opinion of the competent authority likely to spread;

(b) the entering on any land [or elsewhere] for the purpose of any removal [treatment] or destruction authorised by the orders, or any examination or inquiry so authorised, or for any other purpose of the orders.

(3) The orders may prohibit the selling or exposing or offering for sale, or the keeping, of living specimens of a pest, or the distribution in any manner of such specimens.

[(4) An order made by a competent authority under this section may provide that a person guilty of an offence against the order shall be liable on summary conviction to a fine of an amount not exceeding level 5 on the standard scale, < . . . > , or not exceeding a lesser amount.

(4A) An order so made for preventing the spread in Great Britain of the Colorado beetle (*Leptinotarsa decemlineata* (Say)) may provide that a person guilty of an offence against the order relating to the keeping of living specimens of the beetle (in any stage of existence), or to the distribution in any manner of such specimens, shall be liable on summary conviction to imprisonment for not more than three months, as well as, or as an alternative to, a fine under subsection (4) above.]

(5) Proceedings for an offence against an order under this section may < . . . > be instituted at any time within twelve months from the day on which the alleged offence was committed.

4 Execution of Act by government departments

(1) Orders under this Act may enable inspectors authorised by the Minister of Agriculture, Fisheries and Food or, in Scotland, the Secretary of State—

(a) in the case of any specified pest which has been introduced into Great Britain, to take the following action, that is to say—

    (i) to remove or destroy, or cause to be removed or destroyed, any crop, or any seed, plant or part thereof, which has on it or is infected with the pest, or to or by means of which, the pest is likely to spread; and

    (ii) generally to take such steps as he may think expedient in connection with any crop, or any seed, plant or part thereof, for preventing the spread of the pest;

(b) to enter on any land [or elsewhere] for the said purposes, or for the purpose of any examination or inquiry authorised by the orders, or for any other purpose of the orders;

and may impose in respect of any certificate given in pursuance of the order after an inspection such fee or other charge as, with the consent of the Treasury, may be prescribed by the Minister or Secretary of State.

(2) The Minister or Secretary of State may pay compensation in respect of any crop, or any seed, plant or part thereof, which is removed or destroyed by or under the instruction of an inspector authorised by him; and its value shall be taken to be the value which it has at the time of the removal or destruction and, if the Minister or Secretary of State so requires, shall be ascertained by his officers or by arbitration.

(3) The expenses of the Minister and Secretary of State in the execution of this Act, including any compensation under subsection (2) above, shall be paid out of moneys provided by Parliament, but shall not without the consent of the Treasury exceed two thousand pounds in any year.

5 Execution of Act by local authorities

(1) A competent authority may require a local authority to carry into effect any order under this Act, and may, with the consent of the local authority, require a local authority to pay compensation in respect of any crop, or any seed, plant or part thereof, which is removed or destroyed in pursuance of any such order; but—

    (a) the local authority may withhold compensation in respect of anything removed or destroyed if, in relation thereto, the owner or person having charge thereof has, in their judgment, done anything in contravention of, or failed to do anything in compliance with, any order under this Act; and

    (b) the value of anything removed or destroyed shall be taken to be the value which it has at the time of removal or

destruction and, if the local authority so require, shall be ascertained by their officers or by arbitration.

(2) Every local authority shall keep . . . a record relative to proceedings in pursuance of any order made under this Act by the competent authority; and the record shall state the date of any removal or destruction in pursuance of the order, and other proper particulars, and shall be admitted in evidence.

[(3) The local authorities for the purposes of this Act shall be the councils of non-metropolitan counties, metropolitan districts and London boroughs and the Common Council of the City of London [but, in relation to Wales, shall be the councils of counties and county boroughs].]

4

PLANT HEALTH (GREAT BRITAIN) ORDER 1993
(EXTRACTS)

3 Prohibition on importing into Great Britain from a third country plants, plant pests etc

(1) [There shall not be imported] into Great Britain from a third country—

    (a) any plant pest of a description specified in Part A of Schedule 1;

    (b) any plant or plant product of a description specified in the second column of Part A of Schedule 2 carrying or infected with a plant pest of a description specified in the first column of that Part opposite the reference to that description of plant or plant product;

    (c) any plant, plant product or other object of a description specified in the first column of Part A of Schedule 3 which originates in a country specified in the second column of that Part opposite the reference to that description of plant or plant product;

    (d) subject to the provisions of paragraph (2) of this article, any plant, plant product or other object which is of a description specified in the first column of section 1 of Part A of Schedule 4 unless the special requirements specified in the second column of that section opposite the reference to that description of plant, plant product or other object have been satisfied;

    (e) subject to the provisions of paragraph (2) of this article, any plant, plant product or other object which is of a description specified in section 1 of Part B of Schedule 5 unless it has been the subject of a satisfactory plant health inspection by an authorised officer in the country of origin or the consignor country and is accompanied by a valid phytosanitary certificate;

    (f) any plant pest which, although not specified in Part A of Schedule 1, Part A of Schedule 2, or section 1 of Part A of Schedule 4, is a plant pest which is not normally present in Great Britain and which is likely to be injurious to plants in Great Britain.

(2) The requirements of paragraphs (1)(d) and (e) of this article shall not apply to any plants or plant products not showing any

signs of any plant pest which are landed in Great Britain contained in the baggage of a passenger or other traveller and which:

(a) are not intended for use in the course of trade or business, and

(b) are intended for household use, and

(c) are in one of the following categories, not exceeding the stated quantities—

from all third countries,

(i) fruit and raw vegetables (other than potatoes)—together 2 kg,

(ii) cut flowers and any parts of plants together forming a single bouquet)—1 bouquet,

(iii) seeds (other than seeds of potatoes)—5 retail packets, that is to say packets in which the seed in question is normally sold to the consumer (other than for use in the course of a trade or business) or packets of similar size,

and, in addition, from non-European Community countries of the Euro-Mediterranean area,

(iv) bulbs, corms, tubers (other than potatoes) and rhizomes—together 2 kg,

(v) other plants [not being potatoes]—5 plants.

4 Prevention of the spread of plant pests within the European Community

[text of section not included]

10 Official statements in respect of plants etc moved within the European Community

[text of section not included]

SCHEDULE 1

Part A
Plant pests whose introduction into, and whose spread within, Great Britain shall be banned

Section 1
Plant pests not known to occur in any part of the Community and relevant for the entire Community

(a) INSECTS, MITES AND NEMATODES, AT ALL STAGES OF THEIR DEVELOPMENT

1　*Acleris* spp (non-European)

2　*Amauromyza maculosa* (Malloch)

3　*Anomala orientalis* Waterhouse

4　*Anoplophora chinensis* (Förster)

5　*Anoplophora malasiaca* (Thomson)

6　*Arrhenodes minutus* Drury

7　*Bemisia tabaci* Genn (non-European populations) vector of viruses such as:

    (a)　Bean golden mosaic virus

    (b)　Cowpea mild mottle virus

    (c)　Lettuce infectious yellows virus

    (d)　Pepper mild tigré virus

    (e)　Squash leaf curl virus

    (f)　Euphorbia mosaic virus

    (g)　Florida tomato virus

8　Cicadellidae (non-European) known to be vectors of Pierce's disease (caused by *Xylella fastidiosa*), such as:

    (a)　*Carneocephala fulgida* Nottingham

    (b)　*Draeculacephala minerva* Ball

    (c)　*Graphocephala atropunctata* (Signoret)

9　*Choristoneura* spp (non-European)

10　*Conotrachelus nenuphar* (Herbst)

11　*Heliothis zea* (Boddie)

12　*Liriomyza sativae* Blanchard

13　*Longidorus diadecturus* Eveleigh et Allen

14　*Monochamus* spp (non-European)

15　*Myndus crudus* Van Duzee

16　*Nacobbus aberrans* (Thorne) Thorne et Allen

17　*Premnotrypes* spp (non-European)

18　*Pseudopityophthorus minutissimus* (Zimmermann)

19　*Pseudopityophthorus pruinosus* (Eichhoff)

20　*Scaphoideus luteolus* Van Duzee

21　*Spodoptera eridania* (Cramer)

22　*Spodoptera frugiperda* (J E Smith)

23　*Spodoptera litura* (Fabricius)

24　*Thrips palmi* Karny

(a) INSECTS, MITES AND NEMATODES, AT ALL STAGES OF THEIR DEVELOPMENT
[*See Order for details*]

(d) VIRUS AND VIRUS-LIKE ORGANISMS
[*See Order for details*]

NB In Part B of this Schedule Member States are indicated by the initials in general use in the European Community and relevant regions of the Member States appear in parentheses.

SCHEDULE 2

Article 3(1)

Part A

Plant pests whose introduction into, and whose spread within, Great Britain shall be banned if they are present on certain plants or plant products

Section 1

Plant pests not known to occur in the Community and relevant for the entire Community

(a) INSECTS, MITES AND NEMATODES, AT ALL STAGES OF THEIR DEVELOPMENT
[*See Order for details*]

(b) BACTERIA
[*See Order for details*]

(c) FUNGI
[*See Order for details*]

(d) VIRUSES AND VIRUS-LIKE ORGANISMS
[*See Order for details*]

Section 2

Plant pests known to occur in the Community and relevant for the entire Community

(a)   INSECTS, MITES AND NEMATODES, AT ALL STAGES OF THEIR DEVELOPMENT
[*See Order for details*]

(b)   BACTERIA
[*See Order for details*]

(c)   FUNGI
[*See Order for details*]

(d)   VIRUSES AND VIRUS-LIKE ORGANISMS
[*See Order for details*]

Part B
Plant pests whose introduction into, and whose spread within, certain protected zones shall be banned if they are present on certain plants or plant products

(a)   INSECTS, MITES AND NEMATODES, AT ALL STAGES OF THEIR DEVELOPMENT
[*See Order for details*]

(b)   BACTERIA
[*See Order for details*]

(c)   FUNGI
[*See Order for details*]

(d)   VIRUSES AND VIRUS-LIKE ORGANISMS
[*See Order for details*]

SCHEDULE 3

Article 3(1)

Part A
Plants, plant products and other objects the introduction of which shall be prohibited in Great Britain

[*See Order for details*]

Part B
Plants, plant products and other objects the introduction of
which shall be prohibited in certain protected zones

[*See Order for details*]

*NB In Part B of this Schedule Member States are indicated by the initials
in general use in the European Community and relevant regions of the
Member States appear in parentheses.*

SCHEDULE 5

Plants, Plant Products and Other Objects Which Must be Subject
to a Plant Health Inspection—at the Place of Production if
Originating in the Community, Before Being Moved Within the
Community—in the Country of Origin or the Consignor
Country, if Originating Outside the Community—before Being
Permitted to Enter the Community

Article 3(1)

Part A
Plants, Plant Products and Other Objects Originating in the
Community

I. Plants, plant products and other objects which are potential
carriers of plant pests of relevance for the entire Community, and
which must be accompanied by a plant passport.

1 *Plants and plant products.*
[*See Order for details*]

**2 Plants, plant products and other objects produced by
producers whose production and sale is authorised to persons
professionally engaged in plant production, other than those
plants, plant products and other objects which are prepared
and ready for sale to the final consumer, and for which it is
ensured by the responsible official bodies of the Member
States, that the production thereof is clearly separate from
that of other products.**
[*See Order for details*]

**3 Bulbs and corms intended for planting produced by
producers whose production and sale is authorised to persons
professionally engaged in plant production, other than those
plants, plant products and other objects which are prepared**

and ready for sale to the final consumer and for which it is
ensured by the responsible official bodies of the Member
States, that the production thereof is clearly separate from
that of other products of:

[*See Order for details*]

1 Plants, plant products and other objects

[*See Order for details*]

**2 Plants, plant products and other objects produced by
producers whose production and sale is authorised to persons
professionally engaged in plant production, other than those
plants, plant products and other objects which are prepared
and ready for sale to the final consumer, and for which it is
ensured by the responsible official bodies of the Member
States, that the production thereof is clearly separate from
that of other products.**

Part B
Plants, Plant Products and Other Objects Originating in
Territories, Other Than Those Territories Referred to in Part A

[*See Order for details*]

SCHEDULE 6

List of Plant Pests Which Shall be Notifiable to the Responsible
Plant Protection Service and Which May Not be Kept Without
the Authority of an Inspector

Article 4(3)

1   All plant pests in Schedule 1 Part A section 1.

2   All plant pests in Schedule 1 Part A section 2, with the modification described
     in paragraph 7.

3   All plant pests in Schedule 1 Part B, with the modification described in
     paragraph 7.

4   All plant pests in Schedule 2 Part A section 1.

5   All plant pests in Schedule 2 Part A section 2 when present on, or associated
     with, host material specified therein with the modification described in
     paragraph 7.

6   All plant pests in Schedule 2 Part B when present on, or associated with, host
     material specified therein with the modification described in paragraph 7.

7 The following plant pests, insofar as they may be a subspecies or strain normally present in Great Britain shall only be notifiable when they are found at registered premises. In the case of plant pests listed in Schedule 2 they shall only be notifiable if they are also on or in association with the relevant specified hosts.

A. LIVE ORGANISMS OF THE ANIMAL KINGDOM AT ALL STAGES OF THEIR EXISTENCE

[*See Order for details*]

B. BACTERIA

[*See Order for details*]

C. CRYPTOGAMS

[*See Order for details*]

D. VIRUSES AND VIRUS-LIKE PATHOGENS

[*See Order for details*]

SCHEDULE 9

Information That Shall Appear on a Plant Passport

[*See Order for details*]

5

AGRICULTURAL HOLDINGS ACT 1986

79 Additional rights with respect to improvements for tenants of market gardens

(1) Subsections (2) to (5) below apply in the case of an agricultural holding in respect of which it is agreed by an agreement in writing that the holding shall be let or treated as a market garden; and where the land to which such agreement relates consists of part of an agricultural holding only, those subsections shall apply as if that part were a separate holding.

(2) The provisions of this Act shall apply as if improvements of a kind specified in Schedule 10 to this Act begun on or after 1st March 1948 were included amongst the improvements specified in Part I of Schedule 8 to this Act and as if improvements begun before that day consisting of the erection or enlargement of buildings for the purpose of the trade or business of a market gardener were included amongst the improvements specified in Part II of Schedule 9 to this Act.

(3) In section 10 above—

   (a) subsection (2)(c) shall not exclude that section from applying to any building erected by the tenant on the holding or acquired by him for the purposes of his trade or business as a market gardener, and

   (b) subsection (2)(d) shall not exclude that section from applying to any building acquired by him for those purposes (whenever erected).

(4) It shall be lawful for the tenant to remove all fruit trees and fruit bushes planted by him on the holding and not permanently set out, but if the tenant does not remove them before the termination of his tenancy they shall remain the property of the landlord and the tenant shall not be entitled to any compensation in respect of them.

(5) The right of an incoming tenant to claim compensation in respect of the whole or part of an improvement which he has purchased may be exercised although his landlord has not consented in writing to the purchase.

6

ENDANGERED SPECIES (IMPORT AND EXPORT) ACT 1976
(EXTRACTS)

1 Restriction of importation and exportation of certain animals and plants

(1) Subject to subsection (2) below, the importation and the exportation of the following things are hereby prohibited, namely—

    (a) a live or dead animal of any of the kinds to which Schedule 1 of this Act for the time being applies;

    (b) a live or dead plant of any of the kinds to which Schedule 2 to this Act for the time being applies;

    (c) an item to which Schedule 3 to this Act for the time being applies.

(2) Subsection (1) above does not apply to the importation or exportation of anything under and in accordance with the terms of a licence issued by the Secretary of State.

(3) The Secretary of State shall submit any application for a licence, under subsection (2) above to whichever one of the scientific authorities (as defined in section 2 below) he considers is the best able to advise him as to whether a licence should be issued in pursuance of the application and, if so, its terms; and, before he issues or declines to issue a licence in pursuance of the application, he shall allow the authority a reasonable time so to advise him.

[(3A) Subsection (3) above shall not apply in relation to an application of any description if the scientific authority concerned has advised the Secretary of State as to whether licences should be issued in pursuance of applications of that description and, if so, their terms.

(3B) Where the Secretary of State is satisfied that the issue of a licence authorising the importation or exportation of any item which—

    (a) is part of or derives from or is made wholly or partly from an animal of any of the kinds to which Schedule 1 or a plant of any of the kinds to which Schedule 2 to this Act for the time being applies; but

    (b) is not an item to which Schedule 3 to this Act for the time being applies,

would facilitate the importation or exportation of that item, he may, if he considers it expedient to do so, issue such a licence.]

(4) A licence issued under subsection (2) [or (3B)] above—

- (a) may be, to any degree, general or specific,
- [(aa) may be issued either to all persons, to persons of a class or to a particular person;
- (ab) may be subject to compliance with any specified conditions, ;]
- (b) may be modified or revoked at any time by the Secretary of State, and
- (c) subject to paragraph (b) above, shall be valid for [such] period as is stated in the licence.

(5) The Secretary of State may charge for the issue of a licence under subsection (2) [or (3B)] above such sum (if any) as is for the time being prescribed by order of the Secretary of State.

(6) A person who, for the purpose of obtaining, whether for himself or another, the issue of a licence under subsection (2) [or (3B)] above,—

- (a) makes a statement or representation which he knows to be false in a material particular,
- (b) furnishes a document or information which he knows to be false in a material particular,
- (c) recklessly makes a statement or representation which is false in a material particular, or
- (d) recklessly furnishes a document or information which is false in a material particular,

shall be liable on summary conviction to a fine not exceeding [the prescribed sum] or on conviction on indictment to imprisonment for a term not exceeding two years or a fine, or both.

(7) Where a licence is issued under subsection (2) [or (3B)] above and, for the purpose of obtaining its issue, a person commits an offence under subsection (6) above, the licence shall be void.

(8) Where—

- (a) any live or dead animal or plant, or
- (b) an item to which Schedule 3 to this Act for the time being applies,

is being imported or exported or has been imported or brought to any place for the purpose of being exported, a person commissioned by the Commissioners of Customs and Excise or a person authorised by them may require any person

possessing or having control of the animal, plant or item to furnish proof that its importation or exportation is or was not unlawful by virtue of this section; and if such proof is not furnished to the satisfaction of the said Commissioners the animal, plant or item shall be liable to forfeiture under [the Customs and Excise Management Act 1979].

[(9) Where, in the case of a live animal or plant of any kind which is condemned or deemed to be condemned as forfeited, the Commissioners of Customs and Excise incur any expenses in connection with, or with a view to—

(a) its return to the wild; or

(b) its being kept at premises (whether within or outside the United Kingdom) which are suitable for the keeping of animals or plants of that kind,

those expenses may be recovered, as a debt due to the Crown, from the importer or intending exporter of the animal or plant or any person possessing or having control of it at the time of its seizure.

In this subsection expressions which are also used in the Customs and Excise Management Act 1979 have the same meanings as in that Act.

(10)   Any person duly authorised in writing by the Secretary of State may, at any reasonable time and (if required to do so) upon producing evidence that he is so authorised, enter any premises where animals of any of the kinds to which Schedule 1 or plants of any of the kinds to which Schedule 2 to this Act for the time being applies are kept (whether temporarily or permanently) in order to ascertain whether any of the animals or plants kept there have been imported contrary to this section.

(11)   Any person who wilfully obstructs a person acting under subsection (10) above shall be liable on summary conviction to a fine not exceeding [level 3 on the standard scale.]

SCHEDULE 5

Plants the Sale etc of which is Restricted

Section 4

Family	Kind
Araceae	Alocasia sanderana
Caryocaraceae	Caryocar costaricense
Caryophyllaceae	Gymnocarpus prewalskii

	Melandrium mongolicus
	Silene mongolica
	Stellaria palvinata
Gentianaceae	Prepusa hookeriana
Humiriaceae	Vantanea barbourii
Juglandaceae	Engelhardtia pterocarpa
Leguminosae	Ammopiptanthus mongolicum
	Cynometra hemitomophylla
	Platymiscium pleiostachyum
	Tachilgalia versicolor
Melastomataceae	Lavoisiera itambana
Meliaceae	Guarea longipetiola
Moraceae	Batocarpus costaricensis
Pinaceae	Abies nebrodensis
Podocarpaceae	Podocarpus costalis
Saxifragaceae (otherwise known as Grossulariaceae)	Ribes sardoum
Ulmaceae	Celtis aetnensis
Welwitschiaceae	Welwitschia bainesii
Zingiberaceae	Hedychium philippinense]

7

STATUTORY INSTRUMENTS RELATING TO SPECIFIC SPECIES OR GROUPS

Species or group	*SI*
Cherries and cherry rootstocks	1977/143
Clover, red and white	1977/142
Cocksfoot. *See* Timothy, etc	
Compositae	1985/1093
Conifers and taxads	1969/1025
Cymbidiums	1971/1092
Damsons. See Plums and damsons	
Delphiniums, perennial	1966/643
Elatior begonias	1982/1096
Fenugreek	1978/301
Festulolium	1990/1593
Field beans. *See* Vegetables	
Field peas. *See* Vegetables	
Fodder kale and swedes	1982/1097
Freesias. *See* Narcissi, etc	
Gladioli. *See* Narcissi, etc	
Herbaceous perennials	1995/526
Hops	1977/144
Lilies	1977/145
Lucerne	1968/257
Lupins	1978/302
Meadow fescue. *See* Timothy, etc	
Meadow grass: rough, smooth-stalked, swamp and wood	1978/308
Miscellaneous ornamental plants	1995/527
Narcissi, freesias and gladioli	1969/1026
Nerine	1985/1097
Oil and fibre plants	1980/318 (as amended)
Ornamental plants. *See* Miscellaneous ornamental plants	
Pears. *See* Apples and pears	
Pelargoniums	1972/85

Plums and damsons	1968/620
Poinsettias	1985/1094
Potatoes	1965/724 (as amended)
Quince rootstocks	1993/2781
Red fescue (including Chewings fescue)	1978/305
Rhododendrons	1968/623
Rhubarb	1966/644
Roses	1965/725
Ryegrass	1968/258 (as amended)
Sainfoin and birdsfoot trefoil	1993/2779
Saintpaulia	1982/1100
Shrubs. *See* Trees, etc	
Soft fruits	1980/331 (as amended)
Streptocarpus	1972/86
Sweet peas	1995/529
Tall fescue. *See* Timothy, etc	
Taxads. *See* Conifers and taxads	
Timothy, cocksfoot, tall fescue and meadow fescue	1977/147
Tomatoes	1993/2777
Trees, shrubs and woody climbers	1993/2776 (as amended)
Vegetables (including field beans and field peas)	1980/319 (as amended)
Velvet bent, red top, creeping bent and brown top	1978/307

Index